GUINNESS BOOK OF
PET RECORDS

GOLDFISH
41 YEARS
'Fred'
Died: Sussex 1980

CAT
34 YEARS
Tabby 'Ma'
Died: Devon 1957

DOG
29 YEARS 5 MONTHS
Queensland 'Heeler' 'Blue
Died: Australia 1939

BUDGERIGAR
29 YEARS 2 MONTHS
'Charlie'
Died: London 1977

GUINEA PIG
14 YEARS 10½ MONTH
'Snowball'
Died: Nottinghamshire 19

RABBIT
18 YEARS★
European
Died: 1977

RAT
5 YEARS 8 MONTHS
Died: USA 1924

GERBIL
8+ YEARS
'Squirt'
Died: USA 1977

MOUSE
6 YEARS 6 MONTHS
'Hercules'
Died: Surrey 1976

PET LONGEVITY
The greatest recorded ages for commonly kept pets

★ 18 Years also reported for a doe still living in 1947.

Note: A report of 10 years 2 months for a hamster has been published but details are lacking.

Pat Gibbon © Guinness Superlatives Limited

GUINNESS BOOK OF
PET RECORDS

Gerald L. Wood

Animals are such agreeable friends—
they ask no questions, they pass no criticisms.

Scenes of Clerical Life.
Mr Gilfil's Love Story.
George Eliot (1819–1880)

Guinness Books

TO JAKE
Who missed many long walks
while this book was being written.

ACKNOWLEDGEMENTS

Many hundreds of pet-owners and breeders have very kindly
supplied me with information and source material for this book,
but as a list of their names would be much too long to reproduce
here, I hope I will be forgiven if I express my gratitude to them
with one big collective 'thank you'.

However, special mention must be made of Beatrice Frei and
David Roberts of Guinness Superlatives Ltd, and the designer Ian
Wileman, as I owe them a special debt of gratitude for all their help
in preparing the book for publication.

I am particularly grateful to my wife Susan who, apart from
undertaking all the typing and indexing, made many valuable
suggestions and criticisms, and was a continual source of
encouragement and support throughout.

Editor: Beatrice Frei
Design and Layout: Ian Wileman

© Gerald L. Wood and Guinness Superlatives Ltd 1984

Published in Great Britain by Guinness Superlatives Ltd., 2 Cecil
Court, London Road, Enfield, Middlesex

Typeset in 10/11 pt Bembo
Typeset, printed and bound in Great Britain by
Redwood Burn Limited, Trowbridge, Wiltshire.

'Guinness' is a registered trade mark of Guinness Superlatives Ltd

British Library Cataloguing in Publication Data

Wood, Gerald
  The Guinness book of pet records.
  1. Pets
  I. Title
  636.08'87   SF413

ISBN 0–85112–275–2

ILLUSTRATION CREDITS

Winnie Acheson
Ernest Albright
The American Museum of
  Natural History
Lyall M Anderson
Associated Press
Howard Baron
Doug Beghtel and Dale
  Swanson/Oregonian
J V Bodenheimer
Ron Boeger
Josep Borreu
British Museum
Sylvia Britt
California League for the
  Handicapped
Mike Coltman
Colin Crawford
Marjorie Cummerfield
F Curran
Daily Press-Times Herald
Dann and Co. Reading
P Davies
Reginald L Dean
Edison Photography
Joan Egerton
Jerry K Gerbracht
The Gravesend and Dartford
  Reporter Ltd
P J Havlin
Pat Hillman
John Holmes
Illustrated Black Star
Imperial War Museum
Thomas Irwin
KPLC TV
Lynne Kirkman
Carmen J Koper

Darren Kreit
Lincolnshire Standard
Dorothy Magallon
Manchester 'Evening News'
Manchester Museum
Mike McLaren
Mexican National Museum
G Morton
National Enquirer
Naturhistorisches Museum,
  Berne
Novosti Press
Nugget
Adrian Nyoka
Obi Productions
Photo Researchers
Nicol Plummer
E Reed
Erno Rossi
Smithsonian Institution
Mindy Saunders/Southfield
  Eccentric
Mrs St George Moore
Lady Averil Swinfen
Andrew G Taylor
Roar Torsteinsen
UPI
US Army Photograph
Thomas Vyse
Frederick Wackett
Maureen Willis
Tony Tunbridge/Witham
  Times
Barbara C Wolman
G L Wood
Sylvia D Wyse
The Zoological Society of
  London

CONTENTS

LARGEST PET LITTERS

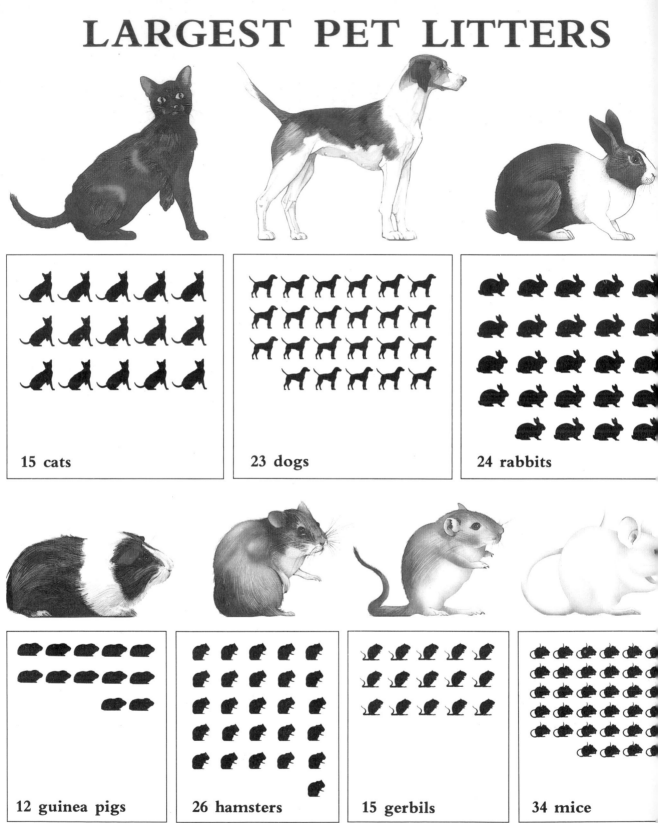

15 cats

23 dogs

24 rabbits

12 guinea pigs

26 hamsters

15 gerbils

34 mice

Not drawn to scale

INTRODUCTION

The seeds of this book were sown in 1972 when I devoted a few pages to pet achievements in the first edition of my compilation *The Guinness Book of Animal Facts and Feats*. Since then pet-keeping has become one of the most popular pastimes in the civilised world and, in order to meet the ever-growing demand from the public for information on record-breaking pets, I have put together the present volume in the hope that it might shed some light on this fascinating subject—and also settle some arguments at the same time!

As it would be impossible to do justice to the many hundreds of different kinds of animals that are kept as pets today in a book of less than encyclopaedic proportions, I have concentrated this first effort mainly on the domesticated creatures which serve not only as companions but also have a mutually beneficial relationship with their owners. This means that cold-blooded animals such as reptiles, amphibians, fishes etcetera only get a brief mention in the Miscellany section, but I would hope to redress the balance in a future—and enlarged—edition provided enough superlative data can be obtained. I would therefore be pleased to hear from any readers who have information on superlative pets which might merit inclusion in a future edition of *The Guinness Book of Pet Records*.

Gerald L. Wood, June 1984

DOGS

Although the evolution of the true dog, *Canis familiaris*, can be traced back to the tree-climbing Miacis, a small weasel-like carnivore which lived about 50 million years ago, the recognised patriarch of all true canids was the now extinct *Tomarctus*, which did not appear on the scene until 35 million years later. This stealthy predator with its short prick ears and long tail reached its culminating phase in *Canis*, and by the middle of the Pleistocene period (1 million years BP*) the longer-limbed and more active wolves and jackals were already well-established.

The common ancestry of the domestic dog has still to be determined by cynologists, and it is doubtful whether there was a single origin. The strongest contender among existing species, however, is the highly social wolf (*Canis lupus*), which has similar dental characteristics, and behaviourists are quick to point out that when a domesticated dog reverts to the wild state it always adopts the habits of wolves. It is also interesting to note that when the 400 000-year-old tooth of Peking man (*Pithecanthropus pekinensis*) was discovered in a cave at Choukoutien, China, in 1927 the bones of a *non-domesticated* small wolf (*Canis l. variabilis*) were also found at the same site. According to some theorists the wolf was domesticated by various early tribes in different areas and the subsequent wolf-dog later backcrossed with the wolf, but unfortunately the skeleton that could confirm this progression from wolf to dog has yet to be found. Along the way, however, there must also have been an admixture of jackal blood and that of various wild dogs (such as the dingo and the pariah) to account for the enormous variety of shapes and sizes found in modern dog breeds.

*BP: Before Present

The oldest dog fossil on record has been radio-carbon dated at 14 000 years. The jaw fragment, with some teeth, was found in a cave at Palegawra, northern Iraq, in 1955. Previous to that another dog fossil from Jaguar Cave in eastern Idaho, USA had been dated at 10 450 years, and in 1979 Israeli archaeologists digging in the Levant discovered the remains of a man and a puppy in close proximity—the man's hand was actually resting on the dog—among the remains of a 10 000-year-old Natufian settlement.

Britain's oldest dog fossil has been dated at 9700 years. It was found in 1947 amongst the remains of a Middle Stone Age settlement occupied by hunting people at Star Carr, North Yorkshire.

All above mentioned four animals were probably examples of the Spitz type, the oldest and most primitive family of dogs.

The earliest known occurrence of an identifiable pure-bred dog is that of the Saluki, which derives its name from the now vanished town of Saluk in the Yemen, Southern Arabia. This 'sight' hound was already an old breed in the days of the Pharaohs, and recent excavations of the Sumerian Empire dated at 7000 BC have produced rock carvings of dogs which bear a striking resemblance to the Saluki. Its original ancestor was probably the small-skulled desert wolf (*Canis l. arabs*). The ancient Egyptians were also using a Saluki-type dog (Sloughi?) for coursing before 4000 BC, as well as two other hunting dogs similar to the modern Pharaoh hound and the closely-related Ibizan hound, and the latter breed has been dated back to 4770 BC from skeletal remains. Another dog practically identical to the Italian greyhound was found in a tomb built in *c* 4000 BC; the Maltese, another dog with a low body like a dachshund, and a large hound reminiscent of the modern harlequin Great Dane can also be traced back to early Egyptian times.

The Afghan hound is first mentioned about 3500 BC by an Egyptian recorder who described it as a 'cyncephalus' ('monkey-faced hound'), and representations on green slate tablets of the same period also suggest that prototypes of the greyhound, the basenji and the pointer had already made their appearance. Much further north, in Norway, remains of a definite elkhound type dated at between 4000 and 5000 BC have been found in the Vista Cave at Jaeren, along with various stone implements, whilst on the other side of the world in China various 'mastiff' strains existed long before her history began in *c* 3000 BC. (The chow chow appeared about 2000 BC.)

The oldest British pure-bred dog is probably the Cardigan Welsh corgi, which can be traced back to dogs brought to Wales by the Celts from the shores of the Black Sea about 1200 BC. The Celtic swifthound arrived in *c* 400 BC, but there is some evidence that Phoenician traders may have brought these greyhound types to Cornwall even earlier and exchanged them for local minerals. The original Celtic population may also have had dogs of the mastiff type which later spread to the rest of Europe. These exceptionally large war-dogs ('canis pugnaces'), descendants of the Tibetan mastiff, were already here when Julius Caesar's legions first invaded these shores in 55 BC, and they may have been introduced by the Phoenicians from the eastern parts of the Mediterranean (where it was known as the Assyrian mastiff) in the last centuries BC. The bearded collie was also well established in Scotland before the Roman invasion.

The origins of the Irish wolfhound (Wolf Dog) are lost in the mists of antiquity and, like so many dogs from the Emerald Isle, it is difficult to separate fact from fantasy. It is believed to have been used initially to hunt wolves, boar and the giant deer (or Irish elk)—although the latter became extinct about 8000 BC!—but the fact that it is a wire-haired sighthound, and thus a natural inhabitant of the steppes or plains, would seem to rule out the British Isles as being its ancestral home.

The oldest record of the Irish wolfhound dates back to 391 BC when Flavianus, brother of the Roman Consul Quintus Aurelius Symmachus, sent home seven of these gigantic dogs to fight in the Circus Maximus—'all Rome viewed them with wonder'—but the progenitors of this race were probably brought to Ireland from Greece or Albania by the Celts in *c* 600 BC. The Irish wolfhound of today, however, is a comparatively recent breed (see page 16).

Mention should also be made of the mysterious skeleton of a young dog found in a flint mine gallery at Grimes Graves near Weeting, West Norfolk, which has been dated at 2450–2280 BC. According to one report it had a short, wide head reminiscent of a rudimentary bulldog, and might well have been the forerunner of a mastiff-type dog.

Although domestication of the dog in North America occurred about AD 500, more than another thousand years were to pass before the first pure-bred dog arrived in the New World.

The oldest American breed is the American foxhound which dates back to 1650 when the Englishman Robert Brooke settled in Maryland with his pack of foxhounds—later crossed with

'Benedictine Schwarzwald Hof', the 305 lb, 138 kg St Bernard, with a young relative.

other strains imported from England, Ireland and France. The harrier has also been known in America since colonial times, and when the *Mayflower* sailed from Plymouth a mastiff and a 'spannel' were included on the ship's manifesto.

The classification of dogs varies from country to country, but in Britain the Kennel Club has divided the recognised breeds into six groups: hound, gundog, terrier, utility, working and toy. The American Kennel Club also has six groupings (sporting, hound, working, terrier, toy and non-sporting), but these are based primarily on behavioural traits rather than racial evolution.

Largest

Of the 350 recognised breeds of dog living today (up to 800 have been described!), only seven have been reliably credited with weights in excess of 200 lb, 91 kg. They are the St Bernard, the English and Neapolitan mastiffs, the Irish wolfhound, the Great Dane, the Anatolian Karabash (Anatolian sheepdog) and the Newfoundland.

The heaviest breed of domestic dog is the St Bernard, a descendant of the Molossian dogs of ancient Greece and Rome. This canine giant was brought to the monastery of St Bernard de Menthon, whence came its name, in the Swiss Alps between 1660 and 1670, and was originally used as a

The St Bernard 'Jason', the heaviest dog ever recorded in Britain.

guard dog and guide. In 1856 the Hospice kennels were almost wiped out by the dual calamity of an avalanche and a distemper epidemic, and the monks were forced to introduce an admixture of Great Pyrenees, Newfoundland and Great Dane blood in order to save the remaining stock from extinction and restore the line to its former strength and vigour. The monks kept only smooth-coated dogs because they found a heavy coat quickly clogged up with snow and hampered the dog's movements. The rest were passed on to Swiss fanciers in the lower valleys, and it is from this line that the heavier rough-coated version with which the public is now familiar was evolved.

During the 1870s the Americans developed a sudden craze for St Bernards of exceptional weight and stature, and high prices were paid to British breeders for specimens meeting these requirements. One of the largest St Bernards exported to the USA was a champion dog named 'Sir Bedivere', who tipped the scales at 212 lb, 96 kg (shoulder height 33.5 in, 85 cm). He was sold by his owner, Mr T H Green, for £1300, which was an awful lot of money in those days. Another British export, 'Princess Florence', was even bulkier, weighing 223 lb, 101 kg, and up to 1958 this enormous animal was the heaviest dog on record.

The heaviest St Bernard ever recorded is 'Benedictine Schwarzwald Hof', owned by Thomas and Ann Irwin who run the famous Schwarzwald Hof Kennels in Grand Rapids, Michigan, USA. He was whelped on 17 December 1970 and tipped the scales at an awesome 305 lb, 138.34 kg in May 1978. He has not been weighed since, but his owners believe he has put on some additional poundage in the interim period.

The previous title-holder was another dog from the same kennel, 'Schwarzwald Hof Duke', owned by Dr A M Bruner of Oconomowoc, Wisconsin, USA. He was whelped on 8 October 1964 and weighed 183 lb, 83 kg at 12 months and 295 lb, 133.8 kg on 2 May 1969, dying three months later from a massive heart attack. This dog measured 32.5 in, 82.5 cm at the shoulder (40.5 in, 102.8 cm to the crown of the head), and 55 in, 139 cm around the chest.

In February 1983 Schwarzwald Hof Kennels announced that 'Benedictine Jr', the son of the current record-holder, was expected to weigh 310 lb, 140.6 kg by the spring, but this poundage has not yet been confirmed.

The greatest weight ever recorded for a St Bernard in Britain was the 298¼ lb, 135.5 kg reached by 'Heidan Dark Blue' (whelped 23 April 1978), also called 'Jason', in September 1981. By January 1983, however, he had reduced to 210 lb, 95.25 kg after his owner, Mr Nicol Plummer of Skeffington, Leicestershire, had put him on a crash diet, and shortly before his death on 4 November 1983 he scaled 208 lb, 94.3 kg.

Another over-sized example named 'Burton Black Magician' (1969–76) owned by Mrs Sheila Bangs of Mitcham, Surrey, recorded a peak weight of 266 lb, 120.8 kg in October 1973, and a third dog called 'Brandy' belonging to Miss Gwendoline L White of Chinnor, Oxfordshire, scaled 259 lb, 117.4 kg shortly before his death on 5 March 1966 aged 6½ years.

At one time the word 'mastiff' was used indiscriminately by writers to describe any dog of unusual size and strength, irrespective of breed, but today it is restricted to the seven races of heavily-built dog that are known by this name. The true mastiff stock originated in Tibet, and probably owed its lineage to the woolly Tibetan wolf (*Canis l. chanco*).

According to some of the early historians, the mastiffs kept by the Kings of Assyria and Babylon over 2000 years ago regularly weighed between 200 and 300 lb, 91–136 kg, and it is certainly a known fact that on festive occasions the most powerful dogs in the royal household were sent into the pits to do battle with lions! A clay tablet in the British Museum showing a mastiff with an Assyrian soldier holding it by a short leash would also tend to support this claim, because the huge-headed dog with pendulous ears depicted in the picture is built on tremendously bulky lines. This would also explain why the Roman invaders, who already had their own large Molossian fighting dogs, were somewhat taken aback by the size and power of the war-dogs that 'greeted' them when they landed on British soil.

The heaviest mastiff on record of which there is definite information, however, was a dog named 'Montmorency of Hollesley', also known as Monty, owned by Mr Randolph Simon of Wilmington, Sussex. He was whelped on 1 May 1962 and tipped the scales at 259 lb, 117.4 kg (neck 33 in, 83.8 cm, chest 56 in, 142 cm) in July 1969. Shortly before he died in April 1971 aged 8 years 11 months he recorded a weight of 270 lb, 112.4 kg.

Although the Great Dane and the Irish wolfhound are less ponderous animals than the two dogs already mentioned, and have lighter leg bones, certain individuals have also attained some very impressive poundages. In January 1971 a weight of 225 lb, 102 kg was reported for a dog named 'Zazon of Clarendon' owned by Mr Ernest Booth of Romiley, Cheshire, while another heavyweight called 'Moderator of Merrowlea' belonging to Mr Terry Hoggarth of North Wingfield near Chesterfield, Derbyshire, recorded a weight of 230 lb, 104.3 kg on 14 October 1971 when aged four years.

A clay tablet depicting the huge bulk of the Assyrian mastiff.

'Shamgret Danzas' (see page 18), the tallest dog of all time, tipped the scales at 225 lb, 102 kg on 4 November 1982. At that time, however, he was on a diet and his owner thinks he probably weighed at least 240 lb, 108.8 kg at his heaviest.

The winner of the 'Biggest Dog' competition organised by the American newspaper *The National Enquirer* in 1982 was a harlequin Great Dane called 'Beau Brutus' owned by Mrs Betty Lulewicz of Azusa, California, who weighed in at 226 lb, 102.5 kg.

Miss Sheelagh Seale, owner of the famous Bally-kelly Irish wolfhounds in Arklow, Co Wicklow, Ireland, once bred two dogs which both scaled over 224 lb, 101.6 kg, but the Irish wolfhound is generally not quite so heavy or massive as the Great Dane.

In 1967 Dr Daan Marais, a noted South African geneticist, announced to the world that after 13 years of selective breeding he had finally produced a new strain of giant dog at his farm at Muldersdrift near Johannesburg. The prototype, a 200 lb, 91 kg dog named 'Pony', resembled a giant boxer with a huge chest, tapering quarters and a big square forehead. Eventually, said Dr Marais, he hoped to develop 250 lb, 113 kg examples bearing strains of St Bernard, mastiff and Great Dane with a touch of European wolf that would not flinch from tackling a leopard or baboon, the scourge of cattle farmers in southern Africa. Despite intensive enquiries by the author, however, it has not been possible to ascertain if he achieved his ambition.

Tallest

The tallest breeds of dog in the world are the Great Dane, the Irish wolfhound, the St Bernard, the English mastiff, the borzoi and the Anatolian Karabash, all of which can reach or exceed 36 in, 91.4 cm at the shoulder. They are followed by the deerhound and the Tatra mountain sheepdog (up to 34 in, 83.8 cm), the Komondor and the Newfoundland (up to 33 in, 83.8 cm), the Russian Owtcharka,

---

Table 1. The eight heaviest breeds of dog

Breed	Average weight (adult male)*		Maximum weight recorded	
St Bernard	155 lb+,	70 kg+	305 lb,	138 kg
English mastiff	170 lb,	77 kg	270 lb,	122 kg
Great Dane	130 lb,	59 kg	240 lb†,	109 kg
Irish wolfhound	120 lb,	54.5 kg	224 lb,	101 kg
Tibetan mastiff	130 lb,	59 kg	220 lb‡,	100 kg
Newfoundland	150 lb,	68 kg	210 lb,	95 kg
Neapolitan mastiff	150 lb,	68 kg	210 lb,	95 kg
Anatolian Karabash	145 lb,	65.8 kg	203 lb,	92 kg

* American dogs tend to be heavier than their British counter-. terparts
† Weight estimated
‡ Rarely exceeds 160 lb, 72.5 kg

© *Gerald L Wood 1984*

The enormous old English mastiff 'Monty', who attained a weight of 270 lb, 112 kg shortly before his death.

the Pyrenean mountain dog, the Sloughi, the Great Pyrenees, the Ibizan hound and the Fila brasileiro (up to 32 in, 81.2 cm) and the Rafeiro do Alentejo, the Leonberger, the Pyrenees mastiff, the Tibetan mastiff and the greyhound (up to 31 in, 78.7 cm).

The modern height standard for the Kuvasz is 28–29½ in, 71–75 cm, but at one time this breed was larger and often exceeded 32 in, 81.2 cm. Another dog that has 'shrunk' over the years is the Pyrenean mountain dog (see above), which originally stood as high as 35½ in, 90 cm, and was said to be even bigger and stronger than the St Bernard.

The tallest breed of dog in the world is the Irish wolfhound. The minimum height standard for dogs is 31 in, 87.5 cm, but most show exhibits average 32 to 34 in, 81–86 cm. The tallest specimen to win a Challenge Certificate was probably Mrs Jean Taylor's 'Ch. Eaglecrag Kyle'. He was measured officially at 37⅞ in, 96.1 cm at the Irish Wolfhound Club Show, and won the Height Cup for four years in succession.

The modern Irish wolfhound would not be here today but for the splendid efforts of Captain George Graham of Dursley, Gloucestershire, who reconstructed the breed in the mid-19th century. Capt Graham started his rescue operation in c 1863 when the Irish wolfhound was near extinction, and by carefully outcrossing the few surviving dogs with deerhounds and Great Danes, and later the borzoi, he revitalised the breed to such an extent that by 1905 dogs of excellent size and substance were being produced. (The largest specimen bred by Capt Graham stood 33 in, 83.8 cm at the shoulder.)

At one time it was firmly believed that the early forerunners of this gentle giant were as big as donkeys, and even William Youatt, the noted 19th-century writer on dogs, said he had seen some specimens which were four feet high! If anything, however, the Irish Wolf Dog of yesteryear was somewhat smaller than its modern counterpart, and this is confirmed by a series of fossil skulls found at Dunshaughlin, Co Meath, during the last century. Interpretations of their size indicate that the owners of these skulls must have measured between 31 in, 81 cm and 33 in, 83.8 cm at the shoulder in life.

The tallest Irish wolfhound on record was a dog named 'Broadbridge Michael' (whelped in 1920) owned by Mrs Mary Beynon of Sutton-at-Hone, Kent, who measured 39½ in, 100.3 cm at the age of two years and was still alive in December 1929. This dog was abnormally large even by Irish wolfhound standards, and although heights up to 41 in, 104 cm have since been claimed for other outstanding examples of this breed, none of these measurements have been confirmed. In every single case the dog was either measured incorrectly or its height was exaggerated by the over-zealous owner.

'Broadbridge Michael', the tallest Irish wolfhound on record, shown here with his owner, Mrs Mary Beynon.

Today an Irish wolfhound standing more than 38 in, 96.5 cm would be adjudged a giant among giants if measured correctly. Such a dog is 'Paddy', owned by Mrs Helen Reid of Balnakeilly, Perthshire, Scotland, who recorded a height of 38.3 in, 97.3 cm in 1976. Another outsized individual bred in the USA was credited with a shoulder height of 38¼ in, 97 cm (weight 190 lb, 86 kg) in 1973.

Although great size is desirable in the Irish wolfhound, the height has to be proportional to the length, otherwise the gait and the structure would not be correct. The same principle also applies to the Great Dane, or Deutsche Dogge (German Hound) as it is more correctly known, which has a minimum height standard of 30 in, 76 cm; however, some breeders have recently started specialising in exceptionally tall—but not always symmetrical—dogs of very rangy build to meet the popular demand for outsized individuals. Unfortunately, if this worrying trend continues, there is a real danger that the Great Dane will eventually become so big (c 44 in, 111.7 cm) that it will have to pay the price, not only in terms of quality and temperament, but also controllability, which would then rule it out completely as a pet.

In 1857 a Great Dane owned by Mr Francis Butler of Wyoming, USA, was measured at 37 in, 94 cm, and this remained a height record for the breed until 1934 when another dog measuring 39 in, 99 cm was

'Shamgret Danzas', the tallest dog ever recorded, with his owner.

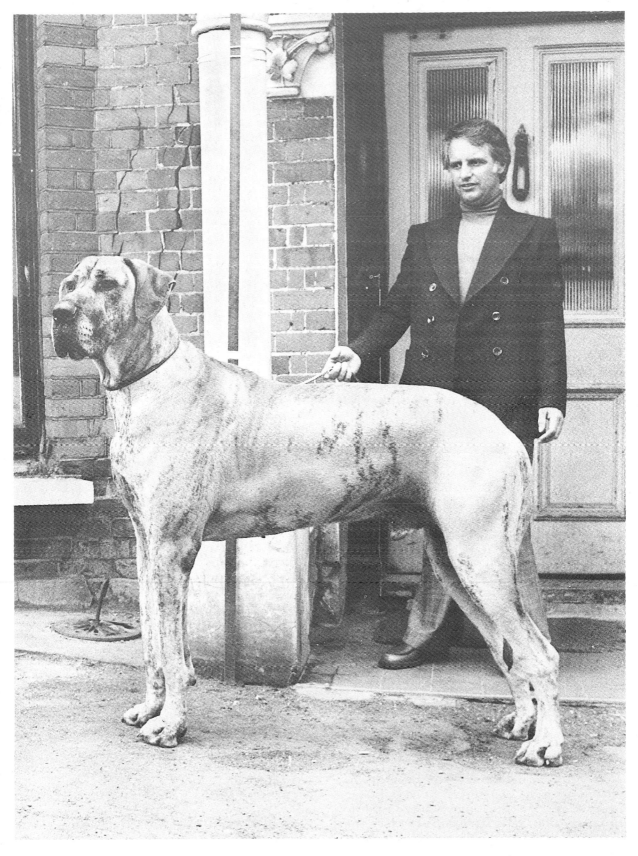

exhibited in Berlin, Germany. Nearly another 40 years were to pass, however, before this latter measurement was finally eclipsed by 'Brynbank Apollo' (1970–78), owned by Mrs Iris Bates of Harlow, Essex, who recorded a height of 39¾ in, 100.8 cm. On 23 July 1979 a two-year-old Great Dane called 'Patrick of Potters' belonging to Mrs Sara Stevenson of Bryanston in the Transvaal, South Africa, was officially measured at 40 in, 101.3 cm, and in 1982 the same height was recorded for 'Beau Brutus' (see page 14).

According to one writer, the largest of the Great Dane strains is the harlequin, and most adult examples (males) seen at shows do appear to be at least 36 in, 91.4 cm tall.

The tallest dog ever recorded is a Great Dane called 'Shamgret Danzas' owned by Mr and Mrs Peter Comley of Milton Keynes, Buckinghamshire. This well-proportioned colossus, who was whelped in 1975, measures an incredible 41½ in, 105.4 cm at the shoulder (42 in, 106.6 cm when he sees a cat and his hackles go up!), and stands 6 ft 9 in, 205.7 cm tall on his hind legs. Other statistics include a chest girth of 46 in, 117 cm, a front paw circumference of 14½ in, 36.8 cm and a nose to tail length of 7 ft 10½ in, 2.4 m.

The tallest Great Dane ever to win a Challenge Certificate was probably 'Ch. Dicarl the Prizefighter' (1973–82) owned by Mrs D Johnson of Loughborough, Leicestershire. He measured 37½ in, 92.5 cm.

In 1887 a German boarhound standing 40¼ in, 102.8 cm was reportedly a winner at the International Dog Show held in Hamburg, but this measurement was to the crown of the head (shoulder height c 34 in, 86.3 cm). The dog was a cross between the mastiff of southern Germany and the Great Dane.

There are very few authentic records of the St Bernard reaching or exceeding 36 in, 91.4 cm at the shoulder. The extreme recorded example is 'Benedictine Schwarzwald Hof', currently the world's heaviest dog (see page 13), who stands 39 in, 99 cm. 'Heidan Dark Blue', formerly his nearest rival in the weight stakes, measured a more modest 34 in, 86.3 cm, while 'Schwarzwald Hof Duke' was (surprisingly) only 32½ in, 82.5 cm.

The tallest show champion on record was the famous 'Ch. Lorenz von Liebiwal', owned by Dr Antonio Morsiani of the Del Soccorso Kennels at Ravenna, Italy, who measured 36½ in, 92.7 cm in the early 1970s.

The tallest borzoi on record was a specimen reported from the USA in 1972 which measured 36¼ in, 92 cm, but this height was exceeded by a freakishly large Anatolian Karabash which stood 38½ in, 97.8 cm (usual height 28–30 in, 71–76 cm).

In 1121 the people of Liu, a province in West China, sent a huge 'Ngao', a mastiff of the Tibetan type, to the Emperor Wun-Wang as a gift. The dog, which had been specially trained for man-hunting, was reported to have stood four feet tall. The explorer Marco Polo (1254–1324) also saw dogs in Tibet which he said were 'as large as donkeys'; they were used for hunting wild animals, especially the yak. A height of four feet was also reported for a Suliot dog (another name for the German boarhound), captured by the Austrians during one of their wars with the Turks, and later presented to the King of Naples. In extreme examples like this, however, the measurement must have been taken from the ground to the top of the head instead of to the shoulder, and it is interesting to note that 'Shamgret Danzas', the world's tallest dog, measures 50 in, 127 cm to his crown.

In the 1960s the skull of a giant canid dating from the Miocene era some 12–15 million years ago was found on a ranch at Piney Creek near State Bridge, Colorado, USA. The lower jaw measured 14 in, 35.5 cm in length, and it was estimated that the owner of this skull must have measured at least 9 ft, 2.74 m in total length when alive. In 1970 the fossil was handed over to Dr G E Lewis of the US geological Survey in Denver, who positively identified it as belonging to the species *Amphicyon major*, which was a kind of 'bear-dog' with wolf-like proportions.

Smallest

The smallest breed of dog in the world is the Chihuahua of Mexico. Most show dogs go under 4 lb, 1.81 kg, but these mighty midgets tend to vary considerably in size, and the normal weight range is given as 2–6 lb, 0.9–2.72 kg. A mature bitch preserved in the Peabody Museum of Natural History at Yale University, New Haven, Connecticut, USA, scaled only 24 oz, 679 kg when it was alive, and the same weight was also recorded for a 22-month-old dog called 'Tiny Tim' (whelped July 1976) owned by Mrs M E Highland of Cleveland, Yorkshire. In March 1972 a weight of only 10 oz or 283 g was reported for a diminutive bitch living in Clemson, South Carolina, USA, but it is not known whether this individual was fully adult at the time (cf. 12 oz, 339 g for a *small* puppy at the age of nine weeks). Mention should also be made of the skeleton of a fully-grown Chihuahua in the Museo de Historia Natural in Mexico City, Mexico, which measures only 7 in, 17.7 cm in total length. No weight was quoted for this dog, which was presented in 1910, but it must have been less than 1 lb, 453 g if the size of its bones is anything to go by.

The smallest dog ever to win a Challenge

Certificate was probably the famous 'Ch. Peaster's Little Pedro', owned by Mrs Bertha Peaster of Philadelphia, Pennsylvania, USA, in the 1920s. He was credited with a weight of 'about a pound and a half'.

The Yorkshire terrier is another breed which has no fixed size. The modern standard states that this dog should not exceed 7 lb, 3.17 kg, but some of the early Yorkies in the latter half of the 19th century scaled as much as 15 lb, 6.8 kg. The great majority today weigh 6–7 lb, 2.72–3.17 kg, but some excellent specimens have weighed as little as 3 lb, 1.36 kg or even less. According to Mrs Mona Huxham, a leading authority on the breed, her tiny Yorkie 'Emmrill Christmas Fudge' never exceeded 1 lb, 0.45 kg.

The smallest adult Yorkie on record was a bitch called 'Dollar' owned by Mr Dennis Lowther of Dipton, Durham. She weighed only 12 oz, 339 g at the age of three years. Another bitch named 'Sylvia' belonging to Mrs Connie Hutchins of Walthamstow, Greater London (who later emigrated to Australia), weighed only 10 oz, 283 g in April 1971, but this dog was only 14 months old at the time (maturity is reached at 18 months).

During the Second World War a small number of Yorkies were trained in Britain to carry communication lines through narrow pipes, and the system apparently worked extremely well.

The Pomeranian, which is basically a 'miniature sled dog', was originally medium-sized (ie 30–40 lb, 13.6–18.14 kg), but in the second half of the 19th century British breeders decided to miniaturise this German sheepdog because there was a popular demand for the 'runts' weighing about 16 lb, 7.25 kg that cropped up in large litters. In some cases they managed to reduce the size to only 24 oz, 679 g, but this dwarf strain proved a disaster in terms of breeding. Today the average dog weighs 4–4½ lb, 1.81–2 kg (bitches are slightly larger), although a weight of under 16 oz, 453 g was reliably reported for a fully-grown specimen in 1937.

The English toy terrier, also called the toy Manchester or Black and Tan (standard weight 6–8 lb, 2.72–3.62 kg), was another dog which was miniaturised at one time, but the dramatic reduction in size robbed the breed of its stamina. During the Victorian era there was a tremendous demand for miniature dogs in glass cases, and there was always a ready market for these novelties. Among the many examples in the British Museum (Natural History) there is a 'Toy Manchester Dog' which measures only 4 in, 10 cm in total length, but this record is invalid because the exhibit was only 13 weeks old at the time of its death. Three other 'black and tan' dogs of comparable size and age can be found in the Horniman Museum, South London, and among the curiosities of taxidermy shown at the Great Exhi-

bition of 1851 was an English terrier bitch named 'Tiny' belonging to Lady Archibald Maclaine, who reportedly measured just over 3 in, 7.62 cm in length. In 1971 zoologist Peter Dance was shown a glass case containing a pair of miniature dogs which measured 3–4 in, 8–10 cm in length and had decorative paper collars round their necks. The owner, who lived in West Wales, told him they were 'Roman dogs' and as such were the last of a miniature race which lived in the ancient ruins of the Eternal City [sic], but photographic evidence suggests they were Chinese dwarf dogs, which were built on the lines of the Chihuahua. (The Mexicans have always called their hairless dogs 'Perros Chinos' or Chinese dogs.) Two other dwarf dogs from China were exhibited in Mexico City in 1780, and a glass-case mounted trio fitting this description can currently be seen in a pub in Orford, Suffolk.

Not all of the toy dogs set up by taxidermists of the 19th century, however, were immature specimens. In February 1981 a Mr P J Havlin (who unfortunately omitted his address) supplied the author with details of another English toy terrier in his possession which measures 2½ in, 6.3 cm at the shoulder and 5 in, 12.6 cm to the root of the tail in the mounted position. According to Mr Havlin this dog, which was fully-grown at the time of its death, was bred in the 1880s by his wife's great-grandfather, a noted English toy terrier fancier, whose speciality was pygmisation of this breed. If this statement is correct then 'Gleam', as he was called, probably weighed no more than 6 oz, 170 g in the flesh!

In January 1971 a weight of 13 oz, 368 g (shoulder height 4 in, 10 cm) was recorded for a fully-grown toy poodle named 'Giles' bred by Mrs Sylvia Wyse of Bucknall, Staffordshire, who later exported the dog to Canada. His sire 'Samson' was also very diminutive, tipping the scales at 16 oz, 453 g. The standard weight for this breed is 8–10 lb, 3.63–4.53 kg.

The Maltese has also been credited with exceptionally low weights. In the USA the standard for this breed is 4–6 lb, 1.81–2.72 kg, but in June 1982 Miss Stephanie Gundermann of Philadelphia, Pennsylvania, reported that she had bred two specimens called 'Stefany's Villa Malta Otto' and 'Stefany's Villa Malta Olga' who scaled only 9 oz, 255 g and 10 oz, 282 g respectively at the age of 12 months.

Although the modern Pekingese (standard 7–12 lb, 3.17–5.14 kg) is no longer in contention, the original 'sleeve dogs' of China were much smaller and some Pen-Lo versions ranged down to 2½ lb, 1.13 kg (shoulder height 3½ in, 8.9 cm). Unlike the other breeds already mentioned, however, which owe their small size to selective breeding, these dogs

The toy poodles 'Samson' and 'Giles' who together weighed 29 oz, 821 g.

were mainly the result of artificial dwarfing; this meant they were placed in closely-fitting wire cages as puppies and kept there until they were mature. It was a barbarously cruel practice, and was only stopped when the voluminous sleeves of the members of the Imperial Household—where these tinies were concealed—went out of fashion in *c* 1900. Recently an English breeder has successfully produced a 'toy Pekingese' by selective breeding which is even smaller than the sleeve dogs. This remarkable creation stands 3 in, 7.6 cm at the shoulder and weighs only 24 oz, 679 g.

The smallest Pekingese to win a Challenge Certificate is the bitch 'Ch. Weipas Sunni Dawn' (whelped November 1973) owned by Mr and Mrs Ray Alcock of Orono, Ontario, Canada. Her best show weight was 2 lb, 905 g exactly.

The smallest fully-grown dog on record was a matchbox-size specimen owned by Mr Arthur F Marples of Blackburn, Lancashire, a former Editor of the magazine *Our Dogs*. This tiny atom, which died in *c* 1945 aged nearly two years, has a mounted height of 2½ in, 6.3 cm at the shoulder and measures 3¾ in, 9.5 cm from the tip of its nose to the

This toy Pekingese, bred in England, weighed only 24 oz, 679 g when it was fully grown.

Mr Arthur F Marples' 4 oz, 113 g 'Yorkie' standing alongside a cigarette for comparison of size.

root of its tail. Its weight when alive was an incredible 4 oz, 113 g! This micro-dog was described as a Yorkshire terrier but, although it has the head of a Yorkie, it is short-coated and may have been a cross between this breed and the English toy terrier.

Dwarfism also occurs in other breeds of dog outside of the Toy Group. One classic example was a German shepherd (Alsatian) called 'Bruiser', who weighed only 6½ lb, 2.94 kg (shoulder height 7½ in, 19 cm) in January 1975 when aged two years. The ideal weight for this breed is 77–85 lb, 35–38 kg (height 24–26 in, 61–66 cm). Despite his extraordinarily small size his owner, Miss Deborah Culler of Albuquerque, New Mexico, USA, said Bruiser had a very deep bark and was quite ferocious. 'I think he believes that he is a big dog, or he wouldn't attempt some of the things he does', she commented wryly.

Oldest

Most dogs live between 8 and 15 years, and small breeds tend to live longer than large ones because they have a much lower level of tumour incidence. The upper limit for all breeds lies somewhere in the region of 30 years, but ages over 18 years are very uncommon. In one lengthy kennel book series of 189 Irish wolfhounds born between 1927 and 1945 the mean ages at death for both sexes were only 4.95 years and 6.59 years respectively, whereas the mean expectation of life in a shorter series of cocker spaniels (males) was 9.5 years. Since then, however, the potential life span of most breeds has been increased considerably thanks to better nutrition and veterinary treatment, and today some of the longest-lived dogs are found in the Toy Group, despite the fact that most of them usually lose their teeth in the middle years. Abnormally long-lived dogs can also be produced by crossing pedigree dogs of different breeds, especially if the parents come

from long-lived strains as we known as 'hybrid vigour'.

The greatest reliable dog is 29 years 5 months cattle-dog named 'Bluey Rochester, Victoria, Australia. 18 kg herder was obtained as a puppy New South Wales, and was worked regularly two owners—his first master, William Hall, died in 1922—among cattle and sheep for nearly 20 years. In November 1936 Bluey was presented with a special commemorative collar for being the oldest dog (26 years) in Victoria, and he died three years later on 14 November 1939.

On 8 March 1984 the death was reported of an Australian cattle-dog/labrador cross named 'Chilla' aged 32 years 3 days, but this claim has not yet been fully authenticated. According to the dog's owner, 38-year-old David Gordon of Broadbeach, Queensland, Australia, he was given Chilla as a present by his parents when he had polio as a child, and they grew up together. On his 31st birthday this canine Methuselah received the 'Bone to the City' from the Mayor of the Gold Coast, and the Queen Mother also sent him a congratulatory letter.

The oldest dog ever recorded in Britain was probably a Welsh collie named 'Taffy' owned by Mrs Evelyn Brown of Forge Farm, West

The cattledog 'Bluey', the oldest dog on record, wearing his over-large commemorative collar.

ch, West Midlands. He was whelped on 2 ~1952 and died on 9 February 1980, aged 27 ~ 10 months 9 days. This longevity record may ~e been fractionally eclipsed by a Welsh collie ~ross named 'Toots' belonging to Mr Barry Tuckey of Glebe Farm, Stockton, Warwickshire, but unfortunately this case is not quite so well documented. Toots reportedly arrived at the farm as a 12-week-old puppy in about April 1948 and died on 4 November 1975, aged an estimated 27 years 11 months. The only other dog in Britain known to have passed the 27-year mark was a black labrador gun-dog named 'Adjutant', who was whelped on 14 August 1936 and died on 20 November 1963, aged 27 years 3 months in the care of his lifetime owner, James Hawkes, a gamekeeper at the Revesby Estate, near Boston, Lincolnshire.

The oldest American dog on record was probably a black and brown beagle named 'Ginger Baby' owned by Mrs Margaret J Leos of Verona Beach, NY. This dog was whelped on 12 July 1949 and died on 27 June 1976, aged 26 years 11½ months. In 1974 the death was reported of an American cocker spaniel bitch allegedly aged 29 years 2½ months in Graytown (?), Ohio, but as the greatest

The black Labrador gun-dog 'Adjutant' who lived 27 years 3 months, shown here with his life-time owner James Hawkes.

Table 2. Age comparisons between dog and man*

Dog Years	Man Years
1	5
2	15
3	24
4	32
5	36
6	40
7	44
8	48
9	52
10	56
12	64
15	76
18	85
21	94
24	103
27	109
28	111
29†	113
30	115
31	117
32	119

* This can only be an approximation, because certain breeds age at a faster rate than others.
† Oldest dog on record.

© *Gerald L Wood 1984*

age accepted for this breed up until then was a more modest 14 years, this claim can be discounted. On 25 October 1977, a collie cross named 'Sugar' celebrated her 25th birthday at the Lewis-Clark Animal Shelter in Lewiston, Idaho, but more up-to-date information is lacking. She arrived at the shelter in 1955 when her age was estimated to be three years.

The longest-lived twin dogs on record were 'Sandy' and 'Squirt', a pair of cross-bred terriers whelped in Bedford, Pennsylvania, USA, on 14 May 1954. They were raised to hunt fox by going into brush and flushing them out, and Mrs Joseph B Arnold, the owner of Squirt, said both dogs 'looked death square in the eye' on several occasions. Her dog was shot once by a rifle, and was also knocked down by a car. The bullet went clear through Squirt's body, but the car accident cost him his left eye. Sandy, owned by Mrs Bernard Arnold, was also blinded in one eye. On another occasion he was hit by a motor-cycle, and was also poisoned. Squirt died on 14 May 1975, one day short of his 19th birthday, while Sandy lived until 5 January 1976.

The shortest-lived dogs are found among the breeds which have a strong inherited tendency towards acromegaly, which is a condition caused by excess production of growth hormone. In these animals the bone structure is much heavier than usual, particularly in the region of the head and feet, and there is general abnormal gigantism. Dogs in this group include the St Bernard, the English mastiff and the bloodhound, all of which have an average life-span of seven to eight years. (In some cases 'true senility' is evident as early as the fifth year.) Another strong contender is the strange Mexican hairless dog or Xoloitzcuintli (see page 63), which many people confuse with the Chihuahua. This breed is reported to live only six to seven years, although one specimen reached the age of 13.

The length of the gestation period in dogs is generally about 63 days. Some bitches, however, have whelped as early as the 55th day (particularly giant breeds), while others have retained the young for up to 76 days.

Largest Litters

Most dog litters average between four and seven, with the larger breeds having 12 or more, and the toy breeds often only two or three.

The largest litter of puppies ever recorded was one of 23 thrown on 19 June 1944 by 'Lena', an American foxhound bitch owned by Commander W N Ely of Ambler, Pennsylvania, USA. Remarkably all of them survived and reached maturity. On 6–7 February 1976 'Careless Ann', a St Bernard bitch owned by Robert and Alice Rodden of Benanon, Missouri, USA, also threw a litter of 23, but on this occasion only 14 of the puppies survived. The previous year (June 1975) another St Bernard bitch belonging to Mr Jimmy Griffin of Fink (?), Texas, USA, had thrown a litter of 21 puppies, 14 of which also survived.

The largest litter of puppies ever recorded in Britain was one of 22 (15 survived) thrown on 10 January 1974 by a red setter bitch named 'Settina Baroness Medina' belonging to Mgr M J Buckley, Director of the Wood Hall Centre in Wetherby, West Yorkshire. On 9 February 1895 a St Bernard bitch named 'Lady Millard', owned by Mr Robert Thorpe of Northwold, Norfolk, threw a litter of 21, but it is not known how many survived.

On 11 November 1981 a five-year-old Welsh springer spaniel called 'Lucy' gave birth to 15

The record litter of 23 puppies thrown by the foxhound bitch 'Lena' in 1944.

puppies, making a total of 74 puppies in five litters. According to her owner, Mrs J Baxter of Exeter, Devon, she had put in a full day's work as a gun-dog the day before the litter arrived. This average of 14.9 puppies was later bettered by a Great Dane bitch named 'Kara of Kilcrony' belonging to Mrs D E Coyne of Melton Mowbray, Leicestershire, who produced 48 puppies in three litters (13,19,16), and there is also a record of an English mastiff bitch throwing 50 puppies in three litters (19,18,13) to give an average of 16.6 puppies per litter!

Another very impressive achievement considering her small size was that of a Yorkshire terrier bitch owned by Mrs Mary Beech of Sheffield. She had 29 puppies in four litters (6,8,7,8) and reared them all.

A yellow labrador which had been mated with a black labrador threw eight puppies—four yellows and four blacks—on 30 December 1977. Her owner, Mrs Sharyn Brewer of Parker, Arizona, USA, said the bitch first threw two yellows, followed by two blacks, two more yellows and finally two blacks. The yellows consisted of two males and two females, and so did the blacks. This is probably the only record of a dog going 'half and half' all the way!

The largest litter of puppies reported of the same sex is one of 14 in the case of a Dobermann pinscher called 'Katy' owned by Mrs Betty G Maerker of Summerville, South Carolina, USA. She threw 14 males (one stillborn) on 26 November 1979.

Although matings between such strongly contrasting breeds as the Chihuahua (dog) and the Great Dane (bitch) have not been reported, such a coupling would be possible if the conditions were right!

Perhaps the most improbable litter of puppies on record was one thrown by a Great Dane called 'Bella' in December 1972 after an illicit love-affair with a dachshund! No one quite knows for certain how 11-year-old 'Fritz', an old-age pensioner in breeding terms, managed this seemingly impossible feat, but Mrs Paddy Homer of Llandovery, South Wales, owner of the two dogs, believes the little sausage dog sneaked up on the object of his affections when she was sleeping on the lawn. The 13 'Little Danes' or 'Great Dachshunds' were all short in the leg like their father, but some had the characteristic Great Dane head and ears.

Another illicit liaison between a Great Dane and a dachshund took place at New Radnor, Powys, North Wales, in August 1980, which suggests there must be something in the Welsh air that triggers off these canine 'David and Goliath' encounters! The five puppies in the litter were later secretly found homes to protect the reputation of the mother.

A mismating between a Great Dane and a cocker spaniel has also been reported in the Basingstoke, Hampshire area. This time, however, only two puppies were born, and the sole survivor is said to look like a Great Dane-sized cocker spaniel!

Most Prolific

The greatest sire of all time was the champion racing greyhound 'Low Pressure' owned by Mrs Bruna Amhurst of Regent's Park, London. From December 1961 until his death on 27 November 1969, aged 12 years, he fathered 2404 registered puppies, with at least 600 others unregistered.

A champion basset hound named 'Hamlet' (whelped in 1967) belonging to Mr Keith Keen of Kilburn, London, is also worthy of mention. He sired 1973 puppies, including a record sized litter of 18 (17 females and one male), before a romp in the local park put paid to his sexual activities. It appears Hamlet was playing with two small rubber balls, and one went missing. The following day he went off his food, and his worried owner took him to the local vet to be examined. An X-ray revealed that the missing ball was lodged in the area of his groin. An operation to remove the offending object was carried out successfully, and at first all seemed well, but then Hamlet was put to stud with seven more bitches—and each time he failed to deliver the goods. The 77 lb, 35 kg dog, whose fame had earlier spread to the USA where he was hailed as 'the sexiest hound dawg of them all', died soon afterwards from the sheer shame of it all.

In 1977 a champion German shepherd named 'Lex' died at a police training centre near Lincoln aged ten years after siring 1706 puppies, many of which are now used by police forces all over the world, and in February 1984 it was reported that a labrador named 'Boss' had sired 567 puppies in ten years for use as guide-dogs for the blind.

Over a period of seven years the progeny of one bitch can range from 72 puppies under controlled conditions to a few hundred if there is no restraint.

A labrador/border collie cross owned by Mrs Marie Bartlett of West Ewell, Surrey, threw 225 puppies in 14 years. Whelped in July 1960, she had her first litter at the age of one year and produced her last litter (a healthy male) in 1974. She was still alive in July 1977, aged 17 years.

Youngest and oldest mothers

Although bitches have been known to reach sexual maturity as early as six months of age, breeders prefer to wait until they are 14 to 16 months old and in their second heat period before they are mated. Sometimes, however, accidents do occur.

The youngest bitch on record to produce a live litter was probably an eight-month-old cocker spaniel owned by Mr Marnie Walsh of Burnaby, British Columbia, Canada. This innocent victim was seduced by a boisterous labrador and threw a litter of ten pups on 14 December 1978. The offspring had to be hand-reared because the mother was too young to feed them properly.

The oldest recorded bitch to have puppies was a crossbred collie owned by Mr and Mrs A Leeming of Kirkby Malzeard, Yorkshire. In 1949, at the remarkable age of 20 years, she threw a litter of three puppies, all of which survived. She died six years later, aged 26.

On 30 December 1975 a 19-year-old Chihuahua bitch belonging to a woman living in Chicago, Illinois, USA, threw a litter of two, but neither of the puppies survived. Just over four years later, on 11 January 1980, a Pekingese/poodle cross called 'Tutu' owned by Mrs Rhoda Cofield of Biloxi, Mississippi, USA, had a single puppy when aged 15 years 11 months, but this one also died shortly after birth. The father was a 'fast-talking' Chihuahua who came a-courting via a tunnel it had dug under the garden fence. In August 1982 a mongrel bitch called 'Blackie' threw three puppies (one died later) at the age of 17. Her owner, Mr Stephen Conley of Keighley, Yorkshire, said the litter was the result of an amorous encounter with a dog which clambered over the garden fence.

The veterinary profession, incidentally, frowns on bitches having litters after the age of seven years.

The normal whelping period for a bitch is 6–24 hours, but with a large litter it can be relatively quick, ie one to two hours, while some protracted whelpings can take up to two days.

The longest whelping period recorded for a bitch is an incredible 5 days 5 hours 32 minutes for a German shepherd dog owned by Mrs Pamela Wood of Broadstairs, Kent, in 1980. The period between arrivals went as follows: 5 July, 8.30 pm, dog (born dead); 8 July, 6.30 pm, bitch; 9 July, 8.10 am, bitch (born dead); 9.40 am, bitch; 4.45 pm, bitch; 6.45 pm, dog; 10 July, 11.20 am, bitch; 12.02 pm, bitch; 4.50 pm, dog; 8.33 pm, dog; 11 July, 2.02 am, dog. All nine live-born puppies survived.

The lowest birthweights are recorded, not surprisingly, in the toy breeds where the average puppy weighs about 4 oz, 113 g at birth. Many owners, however, are apt to understate the size of their newborn puppies, particularly in the case of Chihuahuas and toy poodles, and weights ranging down to an extreme 0.5 oz, 14 g have been claimed for some 'runts'. It should also be noted that the weights of puppies at birth seldom indicate the size they will eventually reach.

Table 3. Ages and litter sizes in 133 breeds of dog

Breed	Age		Litter	
	Average	Maximum	Average	Maximum
Afghan hound	10	17	6–8	17
Airedale terrier	12	17	8	14
Alaskan Malamute	10–12	—	5–6	12
Australian terrier	12	15	5–6	7
Basenji	16	20	5–6	7
Basset hound	12	15	9	19
Beagle	10–12	26	6–8	11[i]
Bedlington terrier	13	20	5	9
Belgian shepherd dog	10–11	13	9–10	12
Bernese mountain dog	10	12	7	15
Bichon Frise	13	13	5	9
Bloodhound	7–8	14	6–7	17
Border terrier	12	20	5	11
Borzoi	10	15	8	18
Boston terrier	10–12	17[a]	4	9
Bouvier	10	—	8–9	10
Boxer	10–11	17[a]	7–8	15
Briard	10–12	13	8–10	21
Bulldog	7–8	16	5–6	13
Bull mastiff	10	12	8	17
Bull terrier	10–11	18	6–8	12
Bull terrier (miniature)	10	16	4	8

Breed	Age		Litter	
	Average	Maximum	Average	Maximum
Cairn terrier	15	18	3–4	6
Cavalier King Charles spaniel	9–12	19	4	15
Chihuahua (smooth & long)	11–12	27	2–3	11
Chinese crested dog	—	14[a]	4	8
Chow chow	10–11	16	5	11
Collie (bearded)	10	17	6	11
Collie (border)	9	15	7	14
Collie (rough)	12–13	16	7–9	13
Collie (smooth)	10	16	6–8	12
Dachshund miniature (long)	12–15	19[a]	3–4	7
Dachshund miniature (smooth)	12–15	17	3–4	7
Dachshund miniature (wire-haired)	11	15	4	9
Dachshund standard (long)	11–13	17	5–7	8
Dachshund standard (smooth)	11–13	17	5–7	10
Dachshund standard (wire-haired)	11–13	16	5–7	10
Dachshund standard	13–14	19[a]	5–7	12
Dalmatian	13	26	10	19
Dandie Dinmont	12	21	4	10
Deerhound	9–10	14	8–9	17
Dobermann pinscher	10	15	8	17
Elkhound	12	17	6–8	13
English toy terrier	12–14	19	3–4	6
Eskimo dog	10–12	14	4–5	9
Finnish Spitz	10	—	4–5	9
Fox terrier (smooth)	12	21	4	8
Fox terrier (wire-haired)	12	15[a]	4	8
French bulldog	10	14	4	9
German shepherd dog (Alsatian)	10	15	8	19[p]
Great Dane	8–9	14	10	19[b]
Greyhound	10–12	15	8	17
Griffon Bruxellois	11–12	17	3–4	7
Hungarian Puli	12	13[j]	4–5	8
Hungarian Vizslas	12	15	5–6	10
Ibizan hound	14	17[m]	8	21
Irish terrier	12–14	17[c]	7–8	13
Irish wolfhound	8–9[n]	14	6	19
Italian greyhound	10–12	17	2–3	7
Jack Russell[o]	14	21	5–6	11
Japanese Spitz	—	—	3–4	5
Keeshond	13	19[a]	5–7	13
Kerry Blue	12–15	18	6–8	10
Lakeland terrier	15	20	4	10
Leonberger	8	14	10–12	16
Lhasa Apso	12	17	5	—
Löwchen	13	—	3–5	7
Maltese	15	19	2	8
Manchester terrier	10	21[l]	4	7
Maremma	10–11	13	8–9	16

Breed	Age		Litter	
	Average	Maximum	Average	Maximum
Mastiff (English)	9	14	8	19
Miniature Pinscher	10–12	20	4–6	11
Newfoundland	9	·14·	9	19
Norfolk terrier	10–12	17[a]	2–4	7
Norwegian Behund	10	13	4–6	—
Norwich terrier	14	19	3	9
Old English sheepdog	10	17	6–8	15
Papillon	15	20	6–8	15
Pekingese	12	27	3	9
Pharaoh hound	12	14	7–8	13
Pointer	11	15	7–8	17
Pomeranian	8–10	25[d]	2	10
Poodle (miniature)	14	19[a]	6–8	12
Poodle (standard)	14	20	8	21
Poodle (toy)	12	26	4	9
Portuguese water dog	—	—	7	15
Pug	10	22[a]	4	7
Pyrenean mountain dog	8	15	8	15
Retriever (curly-coated)	12	20[k]	10	15
Retriever (flat-coated)	10	15	8–9	16
Retriever (golden)	12	16	8	16
Retriever (labrador)	11–12	15[a]	8–9	14
Rhodesian ridgeback	12	15	9	13
Rottweiler	8–9	13	8	14
St Bernard	8	16	8	23
Saluki	12	18	6–8	18
Samoyed	12–15	16	6	14
Schipperkes	14–16	24	4	8
Schnauzer (giant)	10	14	10	18[g]
Schnauzer (miniature)	14	16	5	11
Schnauzer (standard)	14	16	6	13
Scottish terrier	10–12	24[a]	4–5	12
Sealyham	12	21	5	9
Setter (English)	11–12	17	7	22
Setter (Gordon)	11–12	16[a]	8–9	16
Setter (Irish)	9–12	20	8–9	18
Shar-pei	10	14	5	9
Shetland sheepdog	12–15	24	4	13
Shi Tzu	12–15	23	4–5	10
Siberian husky	11	15	5	9
Skye terrier	12–13	15	7	13
Sloughi	11	20[h]	8–9	13
Soft-coated wheaten terrier	10–12	18	4–5	6
Spaniel (American cocker)	11–12	14[e]	5	10
Spaniel (Clumber)	10	13	6	8
Spaniel (English cocker)	12	18[f]	7	12
Spaniel (English springer)	10–12	14[a]	6–8	14
Spaniel (Field)	12–14	16	6–8	14
Spaniel (Irish water)	12	18	8	14
Spaniel (Sussex)	10–11	15	6–8	14
Spaniel (Welsh springer)	12	17	6	9
Staffordshire bull terrier	8–10	19	6	11

Breed	Age			Litter	
	Average	Maximum		Average	Maximum
Tibetan terrier	12–13	18		4	12
Tibetan spaniel	12	18		4–5	10
Weimaraner	10	14		8	14
Welsh corgi (Cardigan)	12–14	15		8	11
Welsh corgi (Pembroke)	10–12	17		5–6	7
Welsh terrier	12–13	18		5	12
West Highland white terrier	12	20		5	12
Whippet	14	16		4–6	9
Xoloitzcuintli	6–7	13		—	—
Yorkshire terrier	10–12	17[a]		3–4	9

NOTES:

a. Still alive
b. Unconfirmed litter of 21 from USA
c. Unconfirmed age of 28 years
d. Lost all coat two years before death except for one tuft of hair on tail
e. Unconfirmed age of 29 years 2 months
f. Unconfirmed age of 27 years
g. Litter of 22 claimed
h. Morocco

i. Unconfirmed litter of 18
j. Britain
k. Not fully authenticated
l. Adult when received
m. Put down after breaking two legs
n. Six years in the USA
o. Not recognised as a breed by Kennel Club
p. Litter of 24 claimed

GENERAL NOTE:

American dogs generally live longer than their British counterparts. One explanation is better nutrition and less exercise.

© Gerald L Wood 1984

Guide dogs

The first guide dogs for the blind were trained in Germany to lead and protect veterans who had lost their sight in the First World War. By 1923 the Organisation of Guide Dogs for the Civilian Blind had been established in Germany and, five years later, Mrs Dorothy Harrison Eustis, a wealthy American then training German shepherds in Switzerland for the army and police, started up her own guide dog centre at Vevey after her husband had paid a visit to Potsdam to watch some of these dogs being put through their paces. Her first success was a German shepherd called 'Buddy I', who was later to become the eyes of Mr Morris Frank, the first American to have a guide dog. In 1929 Mrs Eustis opened the first guide dog organisation in the USA—The Seeing Eye, Inc—at Nashville, Tennessee (later transferred to Morristown, New Jersey), and in Britain this was followed in 1934 by the Guide Dogs for the Blind Association. Ninety per cent of guide dogs in Britain are labrador retrievers.

Guide dogs are usually accepted for training at the age of *c* 12 months, and are passed on to their new owners three to four months later. The average *working* life of a guide dog is eight to nine years.

The longest period of active service recorded for a guide dog is 13 years 2 months in the case of a labrador retriever bitch named 'Polly' (whelped 10 October 1956) belonging to Miss Rose Resnick, Director of the California League for the Handi-capped, San Francisco. Polly was handed over to her mistress at the age of 18 months, and was retired when she was 14 years 8 months. She was put to sleep on 15 December 1971, aged 15 years.

The longest-serving British guide dog was probably the famous black labrador 'Emma', belonging to Mrs Sheila Hocken of Stapleford, Nottinghamshire, who later wrote a best-selling book about her pet. Emma faithfully performed her duties for 11 years, and her story took a remarkable twist in 1978 when her owner, who was born blind, had her sight restored after an operation. Soon afterwards Emma developed cataracts and, when her sight started to fail, Mrs Hocken swopped roles with her companion and guided her around instead. Emma died in November 1981 aged 17, thus making her **the oldest guide dog on record.**

Strange as it may seem, the dogs most suited to be guide dogs, ie labradors, golden retrievers and German shepherds, are also the ones most likely to go blind, although the reasons for this paradox are not known. In 1983 veterinary scientists at the Animal Health Trust at Newmarket, Suffolk, examined about 2000 guide dogs and found that 900 of them had eye problems! Fortunately most of these animals can be helped with the aid of improved diagnosis and treatment, which in turn means an extension of their working life.

Although guide dogs do a marvellous job, they are not infallible. On one occasion a Kent man instructed his four-legged companion to lead him to the public toilet at a main-line railway station. Unfortunately the dog guided him into the 'ladies' where his presence was not exactly appreciated, and the embarrassed man had to make a hurried retreat!

Another guide dog given his marching orders was a specimen owned by a surgeon living in Ogdensburg, NY, USA, who somehow managed to perform eight operations after he went blind in 1980! Eventually the doctor was reported and disciplined by the New York State Board of Regents for practising medicine with his ability impaired, and they also barred him from taking his guide dog with him on hospital rounds in future.

On the other side of the coin, there have also been some remarkable blind dogs. One of the most outstanding examples is a German shepherd called 'Radar', who was bred from an old Australian line renowned for its excellent workers. Born perfectly normal, Radar was doing extremely well at puppy training classes, and had a bright future ahead of him when disaster struck. In June 1976, when he was only six months old, he was hit by a car and the accident left him totally blind. Fortunately his owners Peter and Julie Rallings of North Shore near Parrammatta, New South Wales, stood by their pet and, when he had recovered sufficiently from his injuries, they decided to take him back to training

classes again to see how he would fare. Radar responded with complete trust in his human friends and, although he made some errors in the early stages and sometimes ran into a tree when exercising, he was soon coping well with the situation, thanks to his extremely sharp nose and ears. By the time he had reached 15 months he had progressed so well that the Rallings entered him in trials at three local shows. He passed with two scores of 179 and one of 183, and gained a third place despite his handicap. Since then Radar, who oddly enough was given this name before the tragic accident, has learned to jump over a low hurdle with complete confidence and also retrieve, and today he is a familiar sight in North Shore where he often collects for Guide Dogs for the Blind.

In China, where guide dogs are banned 'for public health reasons', scientists have recently developed sonar 'eye-glasses' that enable the blind person to detect objects through sound waves.

Hearing dogs

In 1976 the Americans started training dogs for the deaf, and the idea worked so well that today more than 200 dogs have been placed successfully with people suffering from this affliction. In 1982 the Royal National Institute for the Deaf sent a former police dog handler to the USA to learn the training techniques, and a few months later a training centre was set up at Chinnor, Oxfordshire. In April 1983 the first of four British-trained hearing dogs went into service. Dogs are chosen for their ability to respond to sounds such as a doorbell, telephone, alarm clock, whistling kettle ... or even a baby crying, and are trained to alert their owners with visual signals or physical contact. They must also respond to voice and hand signals, because many profoundly deaf people pronounce their words in a different way to their trainers.

Ratting

The finest ratters among dogs are the small and medium sized terriers, and some of the bulldog and old English terrier crosses ('bull and terriers') which dominated the rat pits in Victorian England set up records in time contests which will never be beaten.

These specialist dogs were incredibly fast and methodical, and the moment one of them entered a pit it would start killing rats at a phenomenal rate. The little canine executioner (many of the dogs weighed less than 20 lb, 9.07 kg) would give each rat a hard bite and a quick toss and then move on to its next victim, and it was not unknown for a seasoned campaigner to have two dead rats in the air at the same time!

Long-serving guide-dog 'Polly' with her owner Miss Rose Resnick.

The most celebrated ratter of them all was a 26 lb, 11.8 kg dog named 'Billy', owned by Mr Charles Dew, who put up some really astonishing performances. Between 1820 and 1823 he is stated to have won ten matches with ease, and by 1825 this vermin destroyer *par excellence* had reportedly killed 4000 rats in 17 hours, a remarkable feat considering that the dog was blind in one eye (an 'inimical rat' had turned on him in some previous engagement). His most notable achievement was the killing of 100 rats in 5 minutes 30 seconds in his ninth match at the Cockpit in Tufton Street, Westminster, London, on 23 April 1825, but this contest was not bound by the later rules whereby the handler could not touch either the dog or the rats. In a much larger match Billy allegedly killed 1000 rats in only 54 minutes [sic], but the dog hasn't been born yet that could despatch rats at the rate of one every 3.25 seconds and keep it up for nearly an hour! (In those days five seconds a rat was considered very good going.) Even when he was ten years old Billy was still able to give a good account of himself, and in one match staged in June 1826 he managed to kill a hundred rats in 8 minutes 30 seconds, while 'a good young dog' took 12 minutes. He died on 23 February 1829, aged 13 years.

James Searle's famous bitch 'Jenny Lind', an ancestor of the modern Staffordshire bull terrier, was another great ratter. On 12 July 1853 she was backed to kill 500 rats in under three hours at 'The Beehive' in Old Crosshall Street, Liverpool, and completed the job in 1 hour 36 minutes. After her death Jenny Lind was mounted in a glass case, and this relic of the rat pits is now in the possession of Mr D Metcalfe of Stow, Galashiels and Selkirkshire, Scotland, Searle's great-great-grandson.

When good-quality farm rats became scarce (disease-carrying sewer rats often infected the dogs they were fighting) various handicaps were brought in and dogs often had to kill as many rats as there were pounds in their own bodyweight, the quickest being the winner. This meant that the smaller varieties had a distinct advantage over their heavier counterparts, and breeders were quick to develop this type of dog specially for the sport. One of the most successful ratters in this category was the miniature Black and Tan but, although these dogs could kill rats with great speed, they were generally too small to stand up to the bloody punishment that was dished out in the really big matches. One notable exception was 'Tiny—the Wonder', a 5½ lb, 2.5 kg dog owned by Mr Jemmy Shaw, a publican prize-fighter who ran a well-known 'raticide' at the 'Queen's Tavern' in the Haymarket, London. In 1848 he matched this dog, which wore a lady's bracelet as a collar, to kill 300 rats in three hours, and won the wager when the tiny gladiator accomplished the feat in an unprecedented time of 54

The celebrated 'Billy' despatching 100 rats in 5 minutes 30 seconds at the Cockpit in Tufton Street, Westminster, London, on 23 April 1825.

minutes 50 seconds. In 1861 another of his famous Black and Tans called 'Jacko', who tipped the scales at 13 lb, 5.9 kg, killed 25 rats in 1 minute 28 seconds, and a few months later accounted for 60 rats in two minutes! The following year he despatched 1000 rats in 1 hour 40 minutes, but this extraordinary feat was performed over a period of ten weeks in batches of one hundred at a time. The first hundred were accounted for in 10 minutes 55 seconds, and the last hundred (1 May) in a record 5 minutes 28 seconds. In 1863 he killed 200 rats in 14 minutes 37 seconds.

Finally, mention should also be made of the Jack Russell terrier, another notorious rat-killer. One intrepid dog owned by Brian Plummer, a leading authority on the terrier breeds and writer on the subject, once accounted for 1126 rats in a single day, and in 1977 his famous stud dog 'Vampire' killed over a ton (2240 lb, 1016 kg) of rats.

Tracking

Because the dog's world is primarily one of scents, its olfactory ability far exceeds that of man. In an adult human nose the smelling membrane covers an area of only 3 cm^2, 0.5 in^2; in the average canine nose, however, the area is almost 130 cm^2, 20 in^2 which means man's best friend has a much finer discrimination for the scent messages that reach the enlarged olfactory centre in its brain. But not all dogs have the same sense of smell and the acuity differs from breed to breed, as well as amongst individuals of the same breed. The dachshund, for instance, has 125 million sensory cells in its nose, compared to 147 million for the fox terrier and 220 million for the German shepherd. Man, on the other hand, has only five million but, although one might conclude from this evidence that the latter dog's sense of smell is 44 times better than its human equivalent, scientific research has revealed that its nose works a million times more efficiently! Investigators have also found that a dog's nose is so sensitive it can detect the odour of meat through seven layers of thick paper (15 layers after being injected with the pep-drug amphetamine), and can also recognise sulphuric acid in a dilution of one part in ten million. Dogs have also been known to find a cache of drugs tightly wrapped in mothballs, which must take a lot of beating in terms of olfactory camouflage!

But tracking dogs are not always infallible: they can be put off the scent by adverse weather conditions and competing odours—and can also be confused by trails made by identical twins! In one interesting experiment a small number of dogs were trained to select a handkerchief which had been handled for only two seconds by a person from a group of seven, but they failed miserably when two handkerchiefs handled by identical twins were introduced.

The finest tracking dog in the world is the bloodhound, which is estimated to have an olfactory ability three million times as powerful as the human sense of smell. This breed is in a class of its own when it comes to following 'cold' trails, and one of the most famous examples was a dog called 'Nick Carter' (whelped in 1899), who was owned and trained by Captain Volney G Mullikin, head of the police force in Lexington, Kentucky, USA. This dog, named after the fictional detective, was credited with a record 650 finds resulting in criminal conviction. He also set a record for sniffing a cold trail that was to stand for more than 25 years by tracking down an arsonist when the scent was 105 hours old. In this case a hen-house had been burnt down and the trail led to a house a mile away. On another occasion the same bloodhound set up yet another record for the shortest trail! A mentally-ill Kentucky woman had tied up her three children and put them in a chicken coop while she sharpened an axe preparatory to killing them. Fortunately a neighbour found them just in time, but the youngsters were too frightened to accuse their mother. Nick Carter sniffed the ropes which had bound the terrified children and led the police *ten feet* to the mother, who then confessed and was later committed to a mental asylum.

In October 1954 a sad-faced trio of bloodhounds named 'Doc Holiday', 'Queen Guinivere of Laureloak' and 'Big Nose Kate' set up a new world record when they tracked down a man, his wife and their 13-year-old son 14 days after they had gone missing while hunting for deer in the dense forests of western Oregon, USA. The dogs were brought in by Norman W Wilson of Los Gatos, California, after he had heard about the search on the radio. When he arrived at the search scene the trail had already been cold for 322 hours but, with the help of a woman's stocking found in the abandoned family car, he quickly started up his hounds, and 14 hours later they led the search party to the bodies of the missing people who had all died of exposure. This record was equalled in November 1967 when a 7½-month-old puppy named 'Landrover Lancelot' owned by Dr and Mrs Walter Megahan of Boise, Idaho, USA, tracked down a valuable racing greyhound which had been lost in the area. Fourteen days later, on 12 November, the eager hound found the trail of the greyhound and led his master to the spot where the dog had been shot and hidden in the undergrowth.

Although Hollywood has got a lot of mileage out of the story of the runaway convict pursued by hounds wading through miles of swamp in order to throw them off the scent, there is no truth whatso-ever in this claim. This is because scent emanates from the entire body, and not just the feet as many people suppose. Apart from getting his feet wet, the fugitive from justice would also leave billions of sweat molecules hanging in the air behind him like a fine mist as he waded through the morass and, by the time he stepped back on firmer ground again, there would probably be a canine audience waiting to greet him!

In March 1969 two bloodhounds owned by Jerome J Yelk of Wausau, Wisconsin, USA, set up a new world record for trailing through water when they located the body of a Coast Guardsman six days after he had suffered a fatal heart attack and fallen overboard while alone in a boat on the Mani-towoc River. The dogs, 'King' and 'Tony', were taken separately by boat to the area where the man was last seen alive and, about half a mile from the starting point, both animals in turn had to be re-strained from jumping into the water at the same spot. Divers searched the river in the area without success but, 14 days later, the body floated to the surface 50 ft, 15 m from the place indicated by the hounds.

In May 1983 'Hamish', the first bloodhound ever trained by police in England, started work with the West Yorkshire Police. They were the first police force in Britain to employ this breed of dog.

The greatest tracking feat on record in terms of distance covered was performed by a Dober-mann pinscher named 'Sauer', trained by Detective-Sergeant Herbert Kruger. In 1925 he followed a stock thief 100 miles, 160 km across the Great Karroo, South Africa, by scent alone.

On 19 January 1974 the body of an unidentified white female was discovered in an isolated wooded area of the Kennedy Space Centre near Titusville, Florida, USA. Over the years many different leads and suspects were investigated without success, but on 22 July 1982 some fresh information came to light. As a result a special tracking German shepherd named 'Harrass II', owned by Mr John Preston of Galton, Pennsylvania, was brought in and put on a known scent article belonging to the man now sus-pected of the murder. Approximately half a mile from the scene the dog began to track and led police to the place where the crime occurred. Later they obtained a full confession from the new suspect.

The time lapse between the murder and the track itself was an incredible 8 years 6 months and 3 days, which made the previous cold trail record of 14 days look rather pathetic by comparison. And to add insult to injury the new record-holder wasn't even a bloodhound!

The American Rescue Dog Association in Seattle, Washington, USA, has also been alerted to the fact that the German shepherd has exceptional smelling ability, and some of these dogs are now being trained to act as 'air scenters' in conjunction with helicopter and boat search teams. The dogs can pick up airborne scents as far away as 2 miles, 3.2 km.

Dogs can also be trained to sniff out illegal drugs, explosives, gas leaks ... and even iron-ore deposits!

In 1965 a highly successful iron-ore sniffing Finnish hound (Suomenajokoira) by the name of 'Lari' was presented with the equivalent of £800 worth of sausages by his country as a mark of ap-preciation for his expertise over the years. A cheque for that amount was handed over to the dog's handler in Helsinki by the Chief of the Mining Department of the Finnish Ministry of Trade, who made it abundantly clear that the money was to be spent solely on the dog's favourite food—the handler was given £170! In one competition, arranged between the hound and an ore prospector, the dog turned up 1330 pieces of iron-grained rock against the man's 270 in the same area.

Some dogs are also expert at locating narcotics because the resins in marijuana, cocaine and heroin have an unforgettable smell. Another bonus is that they show no signs of addiction, despite the steady inhalation of drugs, although a recent report claims that dogs trained to sniff out smuggled heroin at Philippine airports rapidly become addicted and have to be given regular injections of the drug.

In 1972 a German shepherd called 'Jai', who had been trained to sniff out sulphide-bearing rocks that are needed for zinc, was signed up with a New York minerals corporation, and another dog of the same breed has been trained to sniff out nests of the elusive gypsy moth for the US Department of Agri-culture. Mention should also be made of a beagle called 'Timmy', who works as a termite detector for an extermination company in Atlanta, Georgia, USA. His fee is £85 a call, and the accuracy of his nose has been underwritten by an insurance company which guarantees up to a limit of $500 000 (£330 000) if the dog falls down on his job.

The greatest drug-sniffing dog on record was a golden retriever named 'Trep' (short for 'Intrepid') who could detect 16 different drugs as well as 11 kinds of explosives. Trep was turned over to Dade County Sheriff's Department in Miami, Florida, USA, in 1973 when he was four years old, and dis-covered more than a ton of hashish worth $2 million on his very first assignment. The dog was being led to a suspect boat at Fort Lauderdale when he suddenly stopped and began responding to a racing sloop that had already been searched four times by human agents. He boarded the vessel and the hashish was found inside a double wall wrapped in heavy plastic bags. Trep also made legal history in

March 1976 when a circuit judge issued the first search warrant ever made out in a dog's name so that he could investigate a house where drugs had earlier been detected. The police subsequently found enough marijuana in the building to make a criminal arrest. Sometimes Trep got carried away by his own enthusiasm, and there were some embarrassing moments. One day he was taken by his owner and handler, Tom Kazo, to a police academy to demonstrate his sniffing ability. Cadets were given ten packets of marijuana to hide around the building . . . and Trep located eleven! On another occasion the retriever accompanied his master on a visit to a high school where he was due to give a lecture on the dangers of drug abuse—and caused pandemonium when he started clawing at lockers in the school hallway!

In 1976 Trep and his owner left the Dade County police force to work together as an independent team and, by 1978, 'Agent K9-3' had sniffed out $63 million worth of narcotics. Kazo said he would retire his wonder dog when he reached the magic $100 million mark, but it is not known whether Trep achieved this target before his retirement.

The only drug-sniffing dog with a 100 per cent arrest record was a German shepherd of the US Army called 'General'. During the period April 1974 to March 1976 this canine detective and his handler, SP4 Michael R Harris of the 591st Military Police Company in Fort Bliss, Texas, carried out 220 searches for narcotics, arrested 220 people for possession and uncovered 330 caches of drugs in areas as diverse as Fort Bliss, William Beaumont

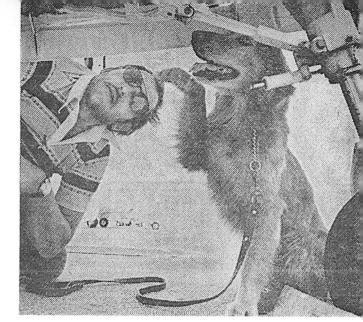

The golden retriever 'Intrepid', accompanied by his owner Tom Kazo, sniffs out marijuana hidden under a plane's cargo area.

Medical Centre, White Sands Missile Range and Holloman Air Force Base.

In December 1981 another American police dog of the same breed called 'Misty' found herself on an underworld hit list after she sniffed out $250 000 worth of drugs and led investigators to 30 major arrests. Since then the dog stays at a different place every night in the Pennsylvania township of Carroll-Franklin, and her handler always prepares her meals personally to guard against would-be assassins.

Britain's champion drug-sniffing dog was a golden retriever/labrador cross named 'Brandy' who was picked up as a stray on the streets of Southport, Lancashire, in 1973. During an eight-year career at Heathrow Airport spent nosing around aircraft and diving under cars he uncovered 160 drug caches worth more than £4 million on the black market. When he was honourably discharged from active service with Customs and Excise officers in May 1982 Brandy was presented with a National Canine Defence League Certificate in recognition of his long and successful fight against crime. Today he lives happily in retirement with his former handler in Cambridgeshire.

In November 1982 it was reported that a black labrador named 'Brumy', also working with Customs and Excise, had sniffed out drugs worth nearly £4 million in six years.

The dog with the poorest sense of smell is said to be the Great Dane, which can't even recognise its owner in the dark!

'General' the US Army drug-sniffer dog who apprehended 220 narcotics offenders.

Homing

The ability of dogs (and cats) to turn up at their old home after they have been lost on holiday, or their family has moved to a new address several hundred miles away, is well-known. How they manage to achieve such incredible journeys, without recognisable landmarks or knowledge of the terrain, however, remains something of a mystery, although modern research would seem to suggest that the animals use some form of celestial navigation for long-distance journeys of this nature.

In 1923 a rough collie named 'Bobbie', lost by his owners while they were on holiday in Walcott, Indiana, USA, turned up at the family home in Silverton, Oregon, six months later after covering more than 2000 miles, 3200 km. The dog, later identified by householders who had looked after him along the route, had apparently travelled back through the States of Illinois, Iowa, Nebraska and Colorado before crossing the Rocky Mountains in the depths of winter, and then continuing through Wyoming and Idaho.

Since then two German shepherds have also made journeys of a similar length across the USA.

One of them was a bitch named 'Nick', who was apparently 'dognapped' when she and her owner, Doug Simpson, were camping together in southern Arizona. After 14 days of frantic searching, heartbroken Doug was forced to return to his home in Pennsylvania, by which time winter was fast approaching, and deep snow already blocked the mountain passes. Unbeknown to him, however, Nick had already made good her escape from her captors and was making her way back home across the barren Arizona desert, and through the deep chasms of the Grand Canyon. Even icy rivers and snow-covered peaks failed to stop her progress and, on 5 February 1979, almost four months after her disappearance, the five-year-old German shepherd staggered up to her master's old car parked in his parents' driveway in Selah, Washington, and collapsed in an exhausted heap. She was torn and bleeding, and almost unrecognisable—but she had made it. Doug's excited mother immediately 'phoned her son in Pennsylvania, and the pair were joyfully reunited shortly afterwards.

The other dog, 'Jessie', trekked 2200 miles, 3520 km back across the USA to his old home in 1980 when his master, Dexter Gardiner, moved from East Greenwich, Rhode Island, to Aspen, Colorado. Apparently he missed the rest of the Gardiner family and the friendly dog next door, and one day he just decided to take off. When he finally reached East Greenwich six months later, however, his troubles weren't yet over. The Gardiners were on holiday and had locked up their house for the

The German shepherd bitch 'Nick' reunited with her master Doug Simpson after her incredible journey.

summer. To add insult to injury, Jessie was then picked up as a stray and put in kennels, from where he was adopted by Mrs Linda Babcock. It wasn't long, however, before he went missing again! The intelligent dog had returned to the Gardiner home and found the family back from holiday. After a few tears were shed Jessie led the Gardiners to the Babcock house and later, after a lengthy family conference, it was decided that he could live there permanently—with his original owners getting visiting rights!

On the other side of the world an eight-year-old miniature fox terrier named 'Whisky' wobbled into Mambrey Creek Station, 150 miles, 240 km north of Adelaide, South Australia, on 13 June 1974 after travelling approximately 1700 miles, 2720 km across the country's vast central wilderness in nine months. The dog had been lost by his owner, Adelaide truck-driver Geoff Hancock, at Hayes Creek, 120 miles, 192 km south of Darwin, Northern Territory, in October 1973.

This record was eclipsed in May 1979 when 'Jimpa', a labrador/boxer cross, turned up at his old home in Pimpinio, Victoria, after walking 2000 miles, 3200 km across Australia. His owner, Warren Dumesney, had taken the dog with him 14 months previously when he went to work on a farm at Nyabing, south of Perth, Western Australia. One day a neighbour took a sudden dislike to Jimpa and, when he started throwing stones at him, the dog decided Western Australia wasn't for him and headed back in the direction from which he had come! During his marathon trek Jimpa successfully negotiated the vast and almost waterless Nullarbor Plain, although how he managed this seemingly impossible feat of endurance remains something of a mystery.

The British canine 'homing' record is held by a red setter named 'Bede', who went missing on holiday in Cornwall with his owner, Father Louis Heston, in August 1976. Nearly six months later the dog arrived footsore at his master's home in Braintree, Essex, after a journey of 300 miles, 480 km. Bede was later named the Bravest Dog of 1976 by the Kennel Club, and collected his award at Cruft's Dog Show on 12 February 1977.

On 23 March 1983 an eight-month-old cross-bred collie decided he wanted to see the bright lights of London and boarded a National Express coach at Cardiff bus station, bound for the big city. He resisted all efforts to tempt him to leave and, in the end, the driver set off with his non-paying passenger curled up on a front seat. When he arrived at London's Victoria Coach Station the dog—called 'Spot' by the amused passengers—jumped off and disappeared. Several hours later, however, he returned—and jumped on the same coach just as it was about to start the 150 mile, 240 km return journey! Back in Cardiff, Spot was looked after by RSPCA staff until he was claimed by his owners.

Travel

The most travelled dog on record (excluding space flights) was a shaggy mongrel named 'Owney', who notched up more than 200 000 miles, 300 km by land and sea during his well-publicised life.

Owney's amazing story began in 1888 when he wandered into the post office in Albany, NY, USA, and was befriended by the employees. The dog was soon at home among the mail bags, and it was this unusual attraction which started him off on his career as a traveller. Soon he was riding atop the mail sacks as they were transferred by wagon to the local railroad depot, and one day he followed the pouches on board a train bound for New York City. From then onwards Owney was hooked on travel, and he started to accompany mail trains across the country. Realising that Owney's trips would take him to some places quite remote from his home, his friends at Albany post office attached a note to the identification tag on his collar asking clerks along the mail route to fix metal baggage tags to the dog's neck band so that they might keep a record of his travels. The collar was soon weighed down with souvenirs and, during a visit to Washington, DC, the Postmaster General presented Owney with a jacket on which the tags could be more evenly distributed. The dog was very proud of this accoutrement, and growled if anyone tried to tamper with the tokens, which included a tag fastened by the railway postal clerks of Rock Island, Illinois, requesting that everyone 'Be Good to Owney'. During the next few years the mongrel travelled extensively around the United States and Canada, and he also visited Mexico, but the biggest highlight of all was his trip around the world, which was arranged for him by the postal employees of Tacoma, Washington. Starting from that city on 19 August 1895 Owney visited Yokohama, Shanghai, Woosung, Foochow, Hong Kong, Singapore, Suez, Algiers and Sao Miguel in the Azores before returning to New York City. From there the postal clerks despatched the dog via the familiar railway mail cars to Tacoma, where he returned on 29 December 1895.

Many rail clerks regarded him as a 'lucky' companion to have on a trip because none of the trains he travelled on was ever involved in an accident, and he generated publicity and goodwill for the postal service wherever he went.

By 1897 Owney was beginning to show signs of old age and, when it was reported that he could eat nothing but 'milk and soft food', a post office official ordered the clerks to keep the dog in Albany. Shortly afterwards, however, he managed to ride the mail cars to Toledo, Ohio, and while he was being shown to a newspaper reporter by one of the clerks he suddenly became 'ill tempered'. What happened next will never be known for certain, but the much-loved dog died of a bullet wound on 11 June 1897.

After his death Owney's body was preserved by a Toledo taxidermist, and this exhibit is now on display in the Museum of History and Technology at the Smithsonian Institution, Washington, DC, along with the 1017 tags, tokens and medals he accumulated during his travels.

The world's most travelled dog is currently a mongrel named 'Pudding' who, up to May 1984, had notched up 218 622 miles, 349 795 km by air alone. She was born on 1 April 1970 in Martinique, French West Indies, and was adopted as a puppy by Mr Mike Coltman of Cheltenham, Gloucestershire, who is a holiday village manager for the Club Mediterranée. Since then this intrepid bitch has set paws in 25 different countries, crossed 154 frontiers and made 80 different flights with 20 different airlines.

She has also undergone 85 veterinary medicals, incorporating 41 vaccinations and injections, but she has never visited Britain because of the quarantine regulations.

The only dog to have visited both the North and South Poles and left his mark at the exact coordinates is a Jack Russell named 'Bothy' (whelped August 1977), who accompanied his owners, Sir Ranulph and Lady Fiennes on their three-year Transglobe Expedition which ended on 19 August 1982. Bothy arrived at the South Pole on 16 December 1980 after being flown in from Ryvingen (Borga Massif), South African Antarctic Territories. During his six-week stay he took part in the first cricket match ever played at the South Pole, and it was his lively fielding on the treacherous surface that helped to clinch the Expedition's victory against a team of American scientists. The North Pole was reached on 11 April 1982 after the perky little dog had been flown in from Alert (Elles-

'Owney', exhibited with his tags and medals in the Arts and Industries Building, Smithsonian Institution.

'Bothy', the only dog to have travelled to both North and South Poles, shown here with a tin of his favourite dog food.

mere Island) Northwest Territories, Canada, and he remained there for two weeks. As a counter against the extreme cold, this morale-raiser on four legs grew an extra long coat during the polar crossings, and he also put on an additional 6 lb, 2.72 kg of 'padding' thanks to a generous supply of his favourite foods—Pedigree 'Chum' and chocolate. Altogether Bothy covered 38 000 miles, 60 800 km of the 52 000 mile, 83 200 km circumpolar journey, and when he was released from the statutory six months quarantine on his return home to England he was awarded the Pro-Dogs Gold Medal as 'Pet of the Year, 1982' for his 'comforting companionship in extreme conditions.'

The only dog to have walked round Britain's entire coastline is a little border collie named 'Jack'. He set off with his master, George Williams, on 1 March 1982, and the pair arrived back in Topsham, Devon, 292 days later after a journey of 6800 miles, 10 880 km. Mr Williams undertook the walk to raise money for the Animal Rescue Centre at Sidmouth where he found Jack, who was rewarded with a 'golden bone' for his endeavours from a dog food company.

Climbing

Because their non-retractable claws are normally blunt, and therefore unsuitable for gripping hard surfaces, dogs are not renowned for their tree-climbing ability. One notable exception, however, is a bitch called 'Jenny' (whelped December 1973), a sure-footed creamy German shepherd/Siberian husky cross, who is **the only dog in the world to have been granted a 'Tree Climbing Permit'**.

The story started in 1974 when Jerry Gerbracht was browsing through a market in Sausalito, near San Francisco, California, USA and saw Jenny for sale. She was one of a litter of six, and Gerbracht said he fell in love with her when she fluttered her eyelashes at him. Although Jenny was a playful youngster, and full of nervous energy, her natural talent for climbing trees did not emerge until 20 April 1975 when she accompanied her owner on a trip to Golden Gate Park. During her romp Jenny encountered a frisky little squirrel that wanted to play. It ran and she chased it around the bushes and trees, until finally it scampered up a tree and out on a limb, from where it looked down at the dog and chattered as if to invite her up. Jenny didn't hesitate. As her amazed owner looked on, she took a running jump at the trunk and somehow scrambled up, following her new-found friend from branch to branch with uncanny skill, until she was 40 ft, 12 m off the ground. Having done it once, Jenny was well and truly hooked, and from then onwards every time she went to the park she always climbed a tree, regardless of whether there were squirrels there or not. Then one day, when she was happily engaged in this uncanine-like sport, a park patrolman happened by and caught her in the act. Being a stickler for the rulebook he informed Gerbracht that trees were strictly for tree-dwellers and that he would be taken to court if Jenny did any more climbing in his park. Not wanting his dog to be deprived of this particular form of activity, Gerbracht went to the San Francisco Park and Recreation Department to plead his case. Fortunately the Assistant Superintendent was a dog lover himself and, after listening to the story, he issued Jenny with the world's first known Tree Climbing Permit on 23 June 1975. Eight months later Jenny beat her previous record when she climbed another tree in the park to a height of 50 ft, 15 m, but, although she has never slipped or fallen while in the trees, today she is only allowed to climb between 25 and 30 ft, 7–9 m, and only under the safest possible

The canine celebrity 'Jenny', the only dog in the world to be issued with a 'Tree-climbing Permit'.

conditions. In 1977 Gerbracht packed up his few belongings and headed for Hollywood in search of a film or television role for his canine celebrity who, apart from climbing trees, can leap, walk, sit or lie on any elevated object even as narrow as 3 in, 76 mm and also jump 4–6 ft, 1.2–1.8 m over cars. The following year Jenny produced a litter of eight puppies sired by another German shepherd/Siberian husky cross Gerbracht had rescued from a Los Angeles animal shelter, and they have all been quick to follow the family tradition—right up a tree!

The greatest canine mountaineer of all time was a beagle bitch named 'Tschingel', born in a small village in the Bernese Oberland, Switzerland, in 1865. Between 1868 and 1876 this incredible dog made 53 heavy ascents, 11 of them virgin summits, as well as hundreds of lesser peaks or partial ascents in the Alps. Like all good Alpinists she started her climbing career at a tender age, and her first important expedition was the crossing of the Tschingel Pass, after which she was named. In 1868 her owner Christian Almer, one of the greatest of all Swiss guides, presented the canine mountaineer to one of his best clients, the Anglo-American climber the Rev William Coolidge. During the next eight years the dog followed her new master up nearly every peak worth climbing in the Alps, including the Jungfrau (13 668 ft, 4165 m) and the Eiger (13 040 ft, 3974 m)—and one of her greatest delights was to scramble ahead to be the first to the summit! In between times she even managed to give birth to 34 puppies, but it is not known if any of them inherited their mother's love of heights.

Tschingel was apparently able to 'scent' crevasses hidden by a thin covering of snow by sensing the cool air rising up from the depths of the glacier, and was always able to find the best route to cross them. Eventually she became so experienced in snow conditions that she could tell by merely looking at a snow bridge if it was safe to cross, and when she drew back at any point her two-legged climbing companions knew this to be a warning of danger. On one memorable occasion she even showed an expert local guide the way down some difficult rocks. On dangerous slopes Tschingel was roped through the collar for safety to the human members of the party. Occasional bleeding feet did not seem to bother her, and when some leather bootlets were specially ordered by Coolidge to save her paws, she quickly kicked them off!

Her proudest moment came in 1875 when Tschingel, by then an honorary member of the famous Alpine Club, accompanied Coolidge up Mont Blanc (15 668 ft, 4810 m), Europe's highest mountain; when she returned to Chamonix she was given a cannon salute! Tschingel died in 1881 and was buried at Dorking, Surrey.

In 1911 a British bulldog named 'Bobby' made an ascent of the Jungfrau with his owners, the Marquis and Marquise de Charette, and their two guides—a remarkable feat for a breed which suffers from respiratory problems at altitude.

Much more recently, in December 1980, a pointer bitch was found on the top of Mount Fujiyama (12 388 ft, 3775 m), Japan's highest peak, 17 days after she had disappeared from her home near the base of the mountain.

The Afghan hound is another excellent climber,

and in Lower Tibet it is said to be quite happy at an altitude of 17 000 ft, 5180 m.

Space flights

Between 1949 and 1961 more than 40 dogs were fired into space aboard rockets. The altitude record is held by a Russian Samoyed Laika bitch called 'Kudryavka', also known as 'Limonchik', the first animal ever put into orbit around the Earth. On 3 November 1957 she reached a height of 1050 miles, 1690 km as a passenger aboard the satellite 'Sputnik II'. At that time the 're-entry problems' had not yet been solved, and sadly no provisions were made to return the dog safely to Earth. She died after ten days when her oxygen ran out.

Falling

The greatest height from which a dog has fallen in a sheer drop and survived is 350 ft, 106 m in the case of a young spaniel belonging to a Dover man. In 1909 the dog was gambolling on the famous Shakespeare Cliff, 1½ miles, 2.4 km south-west of the Kentish town and port, when it slipped and fell from the highest point to the rocks below. An instantaneous death was anticipated and, as bad weather was approaching, a search for the body was not carried out until two days later; to everybody's amazement the dog was found alive, and to all appearances uninjured, in a hole in the rock at sea-level.

On 19 April 1975 a four-year-old mongrel named 'Sue' survived a fall of just over 300 ft, 91 m when she went over the cliff edge on the same coast at Leathercote Point 1 mile, 1.6 km south of St Margaret's. Sue had been walking along the cliffs with her owner, Mrs Gloria Spaul of Deal, and was happily sniffing in the long grass when she suddenly vanished. As luck would have it, Mr Norman Dixey of Dover was at the base of the cliff searching for fossils and, when he suddenly heard a terrible screaming noise above him, he looked up and saw Sue in the air. The next moment her body hit a mound of chalk which had resulted from a recent cliff fall, and it was this which broke Sue's fall and saved her life. Mr Dixey gently picked up the whimpering dog, who amazingly had suffered nothing worse than slight concussion and two bloodshot eyes, and carried her back to St Margaret's Bay. There he identified Sue by her collar name tag and drove her back to her relieved owner's home.

Just under a year later (13 March 1976) an Irish setter named 'Charley', owned by Mr and Mrs Griffiths of Santa Fe Springs, California, USA, set up an American record when he jumped 300 ft, 100 m into the Grand Canyon! The Griffiths were out walking their dog off the leash in the vicinity of Thunderbolt Lodge in Grand Canyon National Park, NW Arizona, when Charley suddenly decided

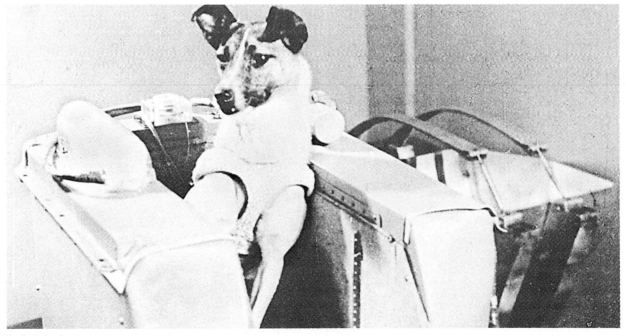

'Laika', the first animal to go into orbit round the Earth.

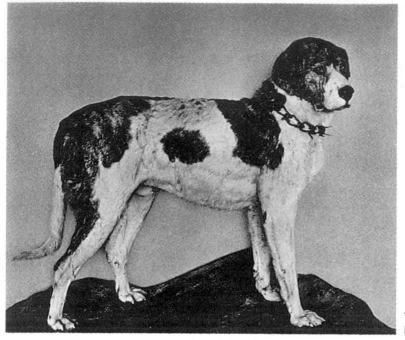

The famous rescue dog 'Barry', who saved the lives of 40 travellers.

he wanted to be the canine equivalent of Evel Knievel and leapt majestically into space. His plunge took him through a series of vertical walls and wallfall courses, until he finally ended up on a snow-covered scree slope. When rescuers reached Charley they found his left eye had been damaged beyond repair but, apart from that, there were no other serious injuries and he made a full recovery.

A seven-year-old standard poodle also thought he was doing the right thing when he took a 140 ft, 42 m leap into a pile of mud on 8 May 1978. 'Danny' was on the roof of a 14-storey building under construction in San Francisco, California, USA, when his owner, Herman Dean of New Carollton, whistled to him from the ground floor. Without hesitation Danny took the shortest possible route, and ended up with a sore leg, his only injury. Dean, a building inspector, said afterwards he thought Danny was on the ground floor when he whistled to him, but the dog apparently had climbed a staircase to the roof where bricklayers were working.

Rescue

The most celebrated mountain rescue dogs in the world are the St Bernards of the Hospice du Grand St Bernard in Switzerland (see page 12), which have been credited with saving over 2500 lives since 1750.

Today most of their Alpine rescue work has been taken over by the German shepherd, but half a dozen or so St Bernards kept at the Hospice during the winter months (the rest are sent down to a farm in the sheltered Valais valley) still work as mountain guides, and are sometimes called out to seek a lost skier or smugglers carrying contraband across the pass that links Switzerland and Italy.

Not only has the St Bernard an uncanny sense of direction, and an ability to locate bodies buried up to 10 ft, 3.05 m under the snow, but it can also anticipate avalanches seconds before the snow starts to slide—and even dangerous blizzards up to 20 minutes before they occur!

The most famous of these great pathfinders was a dog named 'Barry' (the first of many of that name), who worked at the Hospice from 1800 to 1812 and reputedly saved at least 40 lives. One of his most remarkable exploits was the rescue of a small boy, who was found unconscious on an icy ledge after his mother had been swept away by an avalanche. Barry licked the boy's face to revive him, and then carried the child on his back to the safety of the Hospice. According to one graphic report Barry was killed by the 41st person he found in the snow, a freezing and befuddled soldier, who mistook his would-be rescuer for a huge wolf and ran him through with his sword; another said the dog was killed by an avalanche whilst escorting a man to the village of St Pierre where his wife and children lived.

Fortunately for the heroic dog there was a much happier ending. When his strength began to fail, the Prior of the Hospice arranged for him to be sent to Berne, where he could spend the rest of his days in comfort and, when he died in 1814, his body was stuffed and put on display in the Berne Natural History Museum, where it can still be seen today.

Not all St Bernard mountain rescue dogs live up to their reputation, however. In 1981 a dog named 'Bruno' was banned from helping to answer emergency calls because the hapless animal kept getting lost himself and had to be rescued! His owner, Isodoro Tarriza, of Aosta, northern Italy, said things came to a head when Bruno set off with a team to locate two missing mountaineers and left the rescue party behind. Two hours later there was no sign of Bruno and, in the end, the men had to find the lost climbers without the dog's help. When they returned to base the St Bernard was still missing, and his embarrassed owner had to call for volunteers to find the dog. It took them three hours. It was the eighth time in two years that the canine 'rescuer' had lost himself and, after this débâcle, the mountain rescue unit told Bruno's owner that on no account would they ever take his dog out again on a life-saving mission.

Luckily, another St Bernard named 'George' more than made up for this besmirchment of his breed's reputation. In December of the same year he scented out 83 lambs which had been buried under 8 ft, 2.44 m of snow on his owner's hill farm near Lampeter, Dyfed, South Wales. Mr Gareth Davies was able to dig out the lambs and take them to lower pastures after George had demonstrated that, in a blizzard, a St Bernard has a much better nose than a Welsh collie.

Recently Swedish researchers have discovered a series of complex sensory receptors in the canine nose which respond to small variations of temperature and infra-red rays. This means a dog can smell out warm objects and would account for the fact that, while a St Bernard can detect a live sheep buried under several feet of snow, it cannot locate a dead one.

The British Search and Rescue Dog Association (SARDA), which was founded in 1965, has over 60 canine members, including German shepherds, border and bearded collies and labradors, and this corps of rescue animals has been trained to operate in the most ferocious winter conditions found in Scotland, North Wales and the Lake District.

Strength

The strongest breeds of dog are found in the draught group, all of which have heavy bones and cobbly bodies, which denote power. They include the Newfoundland, the St Bernard, the Pyrenean and Bernese mountain dogs and the rottweiler, as well as the Alaskan malamute, the Siberian husky and the Samoyed.

Weight-hauling contests are extremely popular in North America where competing dogs test their strength and endurance by pulling increasingly heavy loads, over measured distances, within a specified time limit. The World Championship Weight Hauling Contest is held at Bothell, Washington, as part of the annual Northwest Newfoundland Club Working Dog Trials, and there are five weight categories: under 100 lb, 45 kg; 100–130 lb, 45–59 kg; 130–165 lb, 59–75 kg; 165–190 lb, 75–86 kg, and over 190 lb, 86 kg. Each entrant (minimum age 12 months) must pull a weight equal to at least 15 lb, 6.8 kg, per 1 lb, 0.45 kg of body weight over a cement surface for a distance of 15 ft, 4.5 m within 90 seconds. Contestants are only allowed one pull in this showcase for the working breeds, and the handler must not touch or assist the dog during its haul. When the dog strains forward in his harness he is verbally rewarded at each pull. Since the first weight-pulling contest was staged on 10 October 1970, all the records have gone to Newfoundlands and St Bernards, both of which have massive bone development throughout and were originally bred for haulage purposes. The first winner was a 168 lb, 76 kg Newfoundland named 'Newfield's Nelson' owned by Mrs Barbara E Wolman, President of the NWNC. He pulled an iron-wheeled freight carrier, laden down with lead ingots weighing together 3260 lb, 1478 kg, over the concrete surface in nine seconds. In 1975 the contest was divided into two classes: the most weight moved by a dog under the official International Sled Dog Racing Association's conditions, and the most proportionate weight moved by a dog.

The greatest load ever shifted by a dog was 6400½ lb, 2905 kg pulled by a 176 lb, 80 kg St Bernard named 'Ryettes Brandy Bear' at Bothell on 21 July 1978. All of the other dogs entered in this particular contest (three Newfoundlands, two Alaskan malamutes and one St Bernard) also pulled 25 times their own body-weight on their first haul. Ten days earlier this four-year-old dog, owned by Mr Douglas Alexander of Monroe, Washington, had moved 6600 lb, 2993 kg but was 5 in, 12.7 cm short of the 15 ft, 4.5 m minimum distance when the 90 seconds were up. Sadly 'Brandy Bear', a superb working dog of outstanding temperament and disposition, died suddenly from gastric torsion the following winter.

The previous record of 6000 lb, 2721 kg had been established by another St Bernard named 'Worldtop's Kashwitna V Thor' on 9 August 1974, but the owners of this dog, Francis and Arloa B Good of Palmer, Alaska, said he had pulled over 10 000 lb, 4535 kg in exhibitions in Alaska. These latter hauls, however, involved the use of mining carts on rails, and by using steel to steel contact, with fine ball bearings and superior lubrication, it is possible to move an almost infinite amount of weight.

The strongest dog in the world in terms of most proportionate weight hauled is a Newfoundland named 'Barbara-Allen's Dark Hans' who, at only 12 months and 97 lb, 44 kg, pulled an incredible 5045½ lb, 2289 kg (= 52 lb, 23.5 kg per 1 lb, 0.45 kg of bodyweight) at Bothell on 20 July 1979. After this tremendous effort his owner, Miss Terri Dickinson of Kenmore, Washington, said: 'I still can't believe it! I knew that he was willing to work, but I was not prepared for this accomplishment. It's not often you get such dedication at such a young age.' The former record of 3120 lb, 1415 kg (= 34.8 lb, 15.7 kg) had been set by an 89 lb, 40 kg yearling Newfoundland bitch named 'Barbara-Allen's Sea Duchess', owned by Mr and Mrs David Clutter of San Ramon, California, on 28 July 1975.

Most of the giant working breeds, which are slow to mature, reach their peak pulling power at about five years of age. Instinct and sound breeding are critical, and the offspring of strong males and females usually turn into premier competitors as well.

It is interesting to note that in the 1978 contest a 29 lb, 13 kg Pembroke Welsh corgi called 'Schulhaus Billy the Kid' owned by Miss Margaret Malseed of Olympia, Washington, pulled 600 lb, 272 kg or 20.6 times his own body weight in *three seconds*!

In 1982 a 72 lb, 32.6 kg American Staffordshire terrier named 'Redbolt', owned by Tom Shimak of Chicago, Illinois, reportedly pulled 3000 lb, 1360 kg, but further details are lacking. This dog had earlier beaten larger dogs such as the Alaskan malamute in weight-pulling competitions.

The only other method comparable to pulling an iron-wheeled carrier across concrete is a freight sled hauled across pitted ice or hard-packed snow on level ground, but conditions affect the performance to a tremendous degree.

On 11 February 1961 a 70 lb, 31.7 kg Siberian husky named 'Charlie' pulled a loaded freight sled weighing 3142 lb, 1425 kg (= 44.8 lb per lb, 0.45 kg of body weight) for a distance of 50 ft, 15 m in under one minute in a test at Anchor Point, Alaska. This record stood until February 1974 when a 167 lb, 76 kg St Bernard named 'Susitna', owned by Mr and Mrs Francis Good of Palmer, Alaska, pulled 3800 lb, 1723 kg (= 22.5 lb per lb, 0.45 kg body weight) for a distance of 25 ft, 7.62 m in 38 seconds at the Anchorage Fur Rendezvous. ('Kashwitna' was placed second with a pull of 3500 lb, 1587 kg in 68 seconds.) A record field of 46 dogs competed in this contest.

The Alaskan malamute is another formidable contender in the strength stakes, and a dog named 'Naki' pulled 2200 lb, 998 kg at Fairbanks, Alaska, in 1970. The following year a bitch by the name of 'Taaralaste Naki Neiu' (whelped in 1966) reportedly pulled 1400 lb, 635 kg uphill, although the angle of elevation must have been very slight. Later the same year, at the Anchorage Fur Rendezvous, she pulled 1525 lb, 692 kg defeating 37 other dogs including St Bernards and Newfoundlands.

A huge 165 lb, 74.8 kg Alaskan malamute called 'Lobo', winner of many weight-hauling competitions, once pulled a truck and trailer with a combined weight of 10 000 lb, 4535 kg for a distance

Table 4. Progression of dog weight hauling records

Year	Weight	Time	Name of Dog and Weight	Breed	Owner
1970	3260 lb 1478 kg	9 s	Newfield's Nelson (168 lb, 76 kg)	N	Barbara E Wolman
1971	3720 lb 1687 kg	9.5 s	Barbara-Allen's Great Khan (141 lb, 64 kg)	N	Barbara E Wolman
1972	3822 lb 1733 kg	12 s	Barbara-Allen's Bonzo Bear (162 lb, 73 kg)	N	Elizabeth Stackhouse
1973	4300 lb★ 1950 kg	?	Barbara-Allen's Great Khan (141 lb, 64 kg)	N	Barbara E Wolman
1974	6000 lb 2721 kg	?	Worldtop's Kashwitna V Thor (177½ lb, 80 kg)	SB	Francis and Arloa Good
1978	6043 lb 2740 kg	33 s	Ryette's Brandy Bear (176½ lb, 80 kg)	SB	Douglas Alexander
1978	6400½ lb 2905 kg	?	Ryette's Brandy Bear (176½ lb, 80 kg)	SB	Douglas Alexander

N = Newfoundland   SB = St Bernard

★ Barbara-Allen's Bonzo Bear pulled 4400 lb, 1995 kg in a non-competitive haul at the same meeting in 12 seconds

© Gerald L Wood 1984

The huge Alaskan Malemute 'Lobo' pulling 10 000 lb, 4535 kg for a distance of 20 ft, 6 m.

of 20 ft, 6 m along a level road, but no other dogs were invited to participate in this trial of strength, and the weight was moved on highly-inflated pneumatic tyres. In other words, it was an impressive stunt but invalid for record purposes. At a weight-pulling contest held at the Lake of the Woods, Oregon, in 1973, Lobo, owned by Howard Baron of Big Bear City, California, pulled 1830 lb, 830 kg for 20 ft, 6 m over the lake ice before his footing disappeared in several inches of slush and water.

According to the 1911 Animal Protection Act, dogs cannot be used to draw carriages on a public highway, but there is nothing to stop potential British enthusiasts from staging weight-hauling competitions on private land; in fact, events like this, if properly monitored as they are in North America, would do wonders for future breeding programmes by sorting out the dogs with physical defects.

As a result of shoddy breeding practices over the past 100 years, at least 90 per cent of all giant 'working' dogs suffer from some form of hip-dysplasia and other orthopaedic problems, and the situation isn't getting any better.

If weight-hauling competitions were staged in this country no doubt the animal protection societies would protest strongly on the grounds that such events would be 'cruel and degrading' for the participants, and yet no objections have ever been raised in the past when British polar expeditions employed dogs to haul heavy loads across some of the most inhospitable terrain in the world.

Speed

The speed of a running dog depends on the length and quickness of the stride, and the gait can best be described as a series of extended bounds.

Most domestic dogs are capable of reaching or exceeding a speed of 20 miles/h, 32 km/h when running flat out, but the sprinters *par excellence* are the so-called sighthounds (gazehounds), all of which are characterised by a narrow, streamlined head, a long arched back and a long tail which acts as a very efficient rudder. Included in this group are the greyhounds (several races), the Saluki, the Sloughi, the borzoi, the whippet and the Afghan hound.

The finest racing machines in the canine world are the greyhound and the Saluki, both of which are long-limbed and deep-chested and have exceptionally well-developed hearts and lungs. They have a long springing stride which enables them to cover a long distance (c 18 ft, 5.48 m) with every bound, and no other breeds of dog are more beautifully balanced or more symmetrical than these two speedsters.

The highest speed ever recorded for a dog is 41.72 miles/h, 67.4 km/h by a greyhound named 'The Shoe', who covered the 410 yd, 374 m straightaway track at Richmond, New South Wales, Australia, in 20.1 seconds on 25 April 1968. It is estimated that the dog covered the last 100 yd, 91 m in 4.5 seconds or 45.45 miles/h, 73.14 km/h.

The British speed record is held by the famous greyhound 'Beef Cutlet', who was clocked at 39.13 miles/h, 62.9 km/h when he ran over a specially-constructed 500 yd, 457 m straight course at Blackpool, Lancashire, on 13 May 1933, but it is more than certain that some of the top-class greyhounds produced in this country since the Second World War could have surpassed the 40 miles/h, 64 km/h mark if a straight course had been available.

In September 1937 eight cheetahs—the world's fastest land mammal—were imported into England from Kenya and matched singly against a small number of greyhounds in a series of races involving a mechanical hare on the oval dog-track at Harringay, north London. The fastest times were put up by a female cheetah called 'Helen' who, despite the fact that she had difficulty negotiating the bends, recorded an average speed of 43.3 miles/h, 69.8 km/h over the three 345 yd, 315 m runs, compared to 36.9 miles/h, 59 km/h for the fastest greyhound.

The Saluki has been credited with speeds of up to 43 miles/h, 68.8 km/h, 45 miles/h, 72 km/h, and even 50 miles/h, 80 km/h; however, a series of tests carried out in the Netherlands revealed that this dog wasn't quite as fast as the greyhound, and that the 'smooth' version of the breed could outrun the 'feathered' kind. All the same, the Saluki never really gives the impression of extending itself like the greyhound under domestic conditions, and in its natural habitat of the desert this dog, which glides so effortlessly, could probably beat its chief rival for speed in a straight race if both animals were evenly matched. It has been calculated that in a 900 m, 984 yd three-lap race between a Saluki and a greyhound, the Saluki would be 2 m, 6 ft behind at the end of the first lap, 8 m, 26 ft ahead after the second lap, and would have a winning margin of 16 m, 52 ft when it crossed the finishing line.

The only other dog credited with speeds in excess of 40 miles/h, 64 km/h is the Ibizan hound, which is not a sighthound as such because it hunts primarily by scent. If we are to believe a claim by an American writer who has studied this breed, a well-trained male Ibizan hound 'can run at 65 mph, over a great distance', but this figure is much too extreme to be acceptable. The maximum velocity reached by this dog, which is not quite so graceful as the greyhound

or the Saluki, is probably in the region of 40 miles/h, 64 km/h, although the owner of an Ibizan hound told the author she had once seen her dog out-sprint a Saluki over reasonably level ground.

Unlike the dogs already mentioned, the heavier-boned Afghan hound (maximum velocity c 30 miles/h, 48 km/h) is not designed for blazing speed; but although it is less streamlined than its sprint rivals of comparable size, it is much more adept at making twists, turnabouts and rapid stops while travelling at speed, thanks to its unique 'pivotal hip joints'. The Afghan has much higher and wider-spaced hip bones than other dogs and this anomaly, plus large padded feet, makes it especially fast over hilly and rugged terrain, and it can also hurdle formidable obstacles without slackening speed. Its ability to stop in a very short space was nicely demonstrated in a race between Afghans and borzois on the 440 yd, 402 m straight track at the Pancheco Hunt Club in California, USA, which holds regular meetings for all sighthounds during the summer months. The Afghans were easily outrun by the Russian wolfhounds, but when the winners crossed the line in pursuit of the mechanical lure, they carried straight on and crashed into a fence. The Afghans, on the other hand, stopped within feet of the sandy track's end.

The American Sighthound Field Association was founded in 1972, and races are staged between greyhounds, Salukis, Afghan hounds, borzois, Irish wolfhounds, deerhounds and whippets. Three dogs compete in each event, and they are awarded points based on their enthusiasm and agility, as well as speed. This means the winner is not always necessarily the fastest dog in the race.

The fastest dog in the world over very short distances (up to 250 yd, 228 m) is the whippet, which is intermediate between the greyhound and the Italian greyhound in size. It has been timed at 8.4 seconds over a standard 150 yd, 137 m straight course (= 36.52 miles/h, 58.4 km/h), which is extraordinary for a dog of this size (18–28 lb, 8–12 kg). This greyhound in miniature differs from other sighthounds inasmuch as it does not have an ancient history, but is a 'constructed' breed dating back to the 19th century. Its ancestors include the greyhound and various terriers.

On 26 September 1930 a whippet, a racehorse, a motor cycle and a motor car took part in a race over 300 yd, 274 m at the Hooton Polo Ground, Liverpool. When the starting flag dropped the whippet flashed into an early lead, which it maintained until the three-quarter mark, before it was over-hauled by the motor cycle which won in 14 seconds. The whippet finished in 18 seconds, the horse 20 seconds and the car 22 seconds. An aeroplane was prevented from competing by a cross-wind, but later it went over the course twice, once in 18 seconds and on the second occasion in 12 seconds.

The fastest dog in the world over long distances is the foxhound, which can maintain a rapid rate of speed for hours on end. During a long day's hunting a good hound may travel upwards of 100 miles, 160 km and there is one record of a foxhound running an amazing 280 miles, 448 km from Newcastle to London before it collapsed; another covered 160 miles, 256 km in 1½ days in France. Not surprisingly, the useful life of the average foxhound is short, and there are not many fifth season hunters.

At the end of the 18th century a number of race-horses and foxhounds were raced against each other over the Beacon Course on Newmarket Heath. The course was 4 miles 1 furlong 132 yd, 6.72 km in length. The winning hound took eight minutes and a few seconds and, of the 60 horses that started, only 12 were able to run in with the hounds. The speed of the winning canine, a dog called 'Bluecap', was worked out at 31 miles/h, 49.6 km/h. Another

foxhound called 'Merkin' is said to have run the same course in 7 minutes 0.5 seconds (= 36 miles/h, 57.6 km/h), but as this rapidity would put it on a par with the fastest whippet this claim must be considered suspect.

Some of the sighthounds like the Afghan hound, and Saluki, the borzoi and the deerhound, as well as the Ibizan hound and the closely-related Pharaoh hound, are also stayers and can course for long distances, but even they can't compete with the foxhound in terms of stamina.

On 17 February 1980 a three-year-old Irish wolf-hound owned by John J Reardon of Washington, DC, USA, ran the entire distance of Washington's Birthday Marathon (26 miles 385 yd, 42.195 km) in 3 hours 29 minutes.

The dalmatian, which has a close affinity with the horse, has also been bred for stamina, and this breed became fashionable as a carriage dog during the 18th and early- to mid-19th centuries. It would often run between the wheels of the vehicles close to the feet of the horses for long distances, and in 1851 a news-

Table 5. Dog running speeds (Limited to breeds capable of reaching 30 miles/h, 48 km/h or more)*

Breed	Maximum speed		Remarks
Greyhound	41.72 miles/h	67.14 km/h	Over 410 yd, 374 m. Covered last 100 yd, 91.44 m in an estimated 4.5 s or 45.45 miles/h, 73.14 km/h
Saluki	40 miles/h+	64 km/h+	Not really suitable for track racing because it finds short distances frustrating
Ibizan hound	38–40 miles/h[1]	60.8–64 km/h	Faster than closely-related Pharaoh hound
Whippet	36.52 miles/h	58.42 km/h	Over 150 yds, 137 m. Unconfirmed report whippet covering 100 yd, 91.44 m in 4.9 s (= 41.7 miles/h, 66.72 km/h!)
Sloughi	36 miles/h[1]	57.6 km/h	Also known as the Moroccan greyhound. Exceptionally strong hindquarters
Pharaoh hound	35 miles/h	56 km/h	Not as fast as the Ibizan hound but may have more stamina
Borzoi	34 miles/h	54.4 km/h	Over 600 yd, 548 m
Dobermann pinscher	34 miles/h	54.4 km/h	The world's fastest tracking dog at a steady 10 miles/h, 16 km/h
Irish wolfhound	32 miles/h	51.2 km/h	Much faster than generally supposed
Foxhound	31 miles/h	49.6 km/h	Average speed over 4.2 miles, 6.72 km
Hungarian greyhound (Magyar agar)	30 miles/h+	48 km/h+	
Podengo Portugues	30 miles/h+	48 km/h+	Related to the Pharaoh hound. Now extremely rare
Russian greyhound (Tasy)	30 miles/h+	48 km/h+	
Sicilian hound (Cirneco dell'etat)	30 miles/h+	48 km/h+	
Spanish greyhound (Galgo Espanol)	30 miles/h+	48 km/h+	
Afghan hound	30 miles/h	48 km/h	Peak velocity reached in hurdle racing when its effortless leaping comes to the fore
Anatolian Karabash	30 miles/h	48 km/h	This dog, owned by George Burns of Aberford, Leeds, weighs 154 lb, 70 kg
Deerhound	30 miles/h[1]	48 km/h	Stayer rather than sprinter
Harrier	30 miles/h	48 km/h	Not quite as swift as the foxhound
Russian steppe hound	30 miles/h	48 km/h	

* At least two dozen other breeds of hunting dog including pointers, coonhounds and setters are probably also capable of burst speeds up to 30 miles/h, 48 km/h
1. Estimated

paper published an account of a dalmatian which used to run with a coach between London and Brighton, via Dorking, Horsham and Henfield—a distance of 72 miles, 115 km. The dog is said to have done the journey on eight successive days before it accidentally met its end under the wheels.

Identifying the **slowest breed of dog in the world** is not so easy, but one of the strongest contenders must be the achondroplastic basset hound, that well-known nose-to-the ground plodder. In 'full flight', which can best be described as a lolloping amble, some of the heavier types (ie up to 75 lb, 34 kg) which do duty as household pets or show dogs, probably never get much above 6 miles/h, 9.6 km/h—even in an emergency! The primary cause of this truncated bloodhound's lack of speed is not so much the extreme shortness and crookedness of its forelegs, as many people suppose, but the excessive depth of its chest and heavy loaded shoulders which considerably restrict the movements of the dog.

Jumping—high and long

Although the sighthounds are the athletes of the canine world, and most of them can clear a 7 ft, 2.13 m fence from a sitting position with consummate ease, they have limited learning ability and are extremely difficult to train. That is why the 'high jump' record for a leap and climb over a scramble board is held by a working dog rather than a member of the greyhound family, although the former is not in the same class when it comes to agility.

A proper scramble board consists of a number of *flat* boards which are slotted into the framework in order that the overall height of the barrier can be heightened or lowered as necessary. Narrow wooden slats or ribs running along each of the boards are not permitted because they give the dog leverage on the way up.

There is no specified distance for the run-up, but most trainers find their dogs (average weight 65 lb, 29.5 kg) do best if they start their attempt some 15–20 ft, 4.5–6 m out from the obstacle.

On 18 March 1980 a German shepherd named 'Max of Pangoula' scaled an 11 ft 5⅛ in, 3.48 m high *smooth* wooden wall (without any ribs or other aids) at Chikurubi Prison's dog training school near Salisbury (now Harare), Zimbabwe. The previous record had been set by another German shepherd named 'Crumstone Danko', owned by the De Beers Mining Company, who scaled an 11 ft 3 in, 3.43 m scramble board at a demonstration in Pretoria, Cape Province, South Africa, in May 1942. The same dog was also credited with a 16 ft 6 in, 5.0 m leap and scramble off a springboard.

On 17 July 1981 a German shepherd called 'Young Sabre', handled by Cpl David Smith, mastered an 11 ft 8 in, 3.55 m scramble board at the 24th Annual RAF Police (UK) Working Dog Trials held at RAF Newton, Nottinghamshire, but on this occasion the boards were ribbed with slats which assisted the dog in the climb.

John Holmes, a leading British dog trainer, once managed to coax two Salukis into scaling barriers measuring 10 ft 3 in, 3.12 m and 10 ft 9 in, 3.27 m in height respectively, and an Ibizan hound has been credited with a jump of 3 m, 9 ft 10 in from a standing position, but these performances were completely out of character for two breeds with a big reputation for intractability.

In December 1976 a 72 lb, 32.6 kg old English sheepdog cross called 'Wolf', owned by Craig Stahel of St Paul, Minnesota, USA, scaled an 11 ft 4 in, 3.45 m barrier which led on to the roof of a one-storey building, but this attempt was later declared invalid because the obstacle had a protective rubber covering which gave the dog a gripping surface. Since then Wolf has done 10 ft 8 in, 3.25 m using a proper scramble board.

On another occasion Brian Plummer photographed his famous lurcher 'Merle', the subject of

'Max of Pangoula', trained by Chief Prison Officer Alec Mann, setting the canine high-jump record with 11 ft 5⅛ in, 3.48 m.

A Saluki easily clears a distance of 15 ft, 4.57 m over some doggie friends.

one of his books, clearing an 8 ft 9 in, 2.66 m high wire fence with one almighty leap!

Even more impressive, relatively speaking, was a little Yorkshire terrier owned by Mr Philip McCarter of Bangor, Co Down, Northern Ireland, which regularly cleared the highest hedge (5 ft 8 in, 1.72 m) in its owner's garden. This canine rocket stood 13 in, 33 cm at the shoulder and measured 24 in, 61 cm in total length.

The basenji, also called the Congo dog, is another incredible jumper for its size (weight 22–24 lb, 9.9–10.8 kg), and it is not known as the 'up and down dog' for nothing. It has a fantastic cat-like spring and is agile enough to catch birds in mid-air!

The finest long-jumpers in the dog world are the sighthounds, which run in a series of extended bounds, and most of the breeds in this group can jump at least 18 ft, 5.5 m horizontally.

The longest canine jump on record was one made by a greyhound named 'Bang' whilst coursing a hare at Brecon Lodge, Gloucestershire, in 1849. During the chase this dog cleared a five-barred gate (height *c* 4 ft 6 in, 1.4 m) and landed on a hard road 30 ft, 9 m from where he had taken off. Despite a damaged pastern bone he still managed to kill the hare. The graceful Saluki is also a tremendous long-jumper, and a dog named 'Mazuri Fahmi' (see page 47) belonging to John Holmes once cleared 24 ft, 7.3 m of very low hurdles which had been spaced out to form a long jump. The German shepherd 'Crumstone Danko' (see page 46) was also credited with a horizontal leap of 24 ft, 7.3 m over a series of obstacles. The whippet is another very impressive performer, despite its small size, and a good dog can clear 15 ft, 4.57 m.

The top long-jumping exponent among the terriers appears to be the Staffordshire bull terrier, and one canine gladiator named 'Pedgebury Chieftain' (died 1954) is on record as having cleared 14 ft, 4.25 m of low hurdles in a demonstration event at Canterbury, Kent.

Swimming

Although all dogs can swim, they differ greatly in their ability, and the top water exponents are found amongst the sporting dogs. They include the Chesapeake Bay, curly-coated, flat-coated and labrador retrievers, the Irish water spaniel, the otterhound and the Portuguese water dog (Cao d'Agua), all of which have been specially bred for work in this medium. The only notable exception is the semi-aquatic Newfoundland which, thanks to its large webbed feet, remarkable stamina and dense water-resistant double-coat, is able to swim for long distances in the coldest and roughest waters using a 'breast stroke' rather than a dog paddle.

There is one authentic record of a male Newfoundland covering a distance of 15 miles, 24 km in the open sea, and a swim across the English Channel (shortest distance 21 miles, 33.6 km) is probably within the realms of possibility for a well-trained dog.

Mention should also be made of an incredible marathon swim completed by another Newfoundland called 'Neptune' at the turn of the century. This dog belonged to a ship's Captain, and was one of hundreds carried by ocean-going vessels in those days as a four-legged life-saver. One day the ship was being towed up the Mississippi River bound for New Orleans when she suddenly rolled. Neptune, who was walking the taffrail at the time, lost his balance and fell overboard. As it was impossible to stop the ship without disarranging the two vessels, the tearful Captain had no alternative but to leave his faithful companion to his fate. For a while Neptune was seen to be swimming powerfully after the ship,

but soon he started to fall behind, and eventually disappeared from view. Three days later, while the ship was taking on new cargo, Neptune suddenly reappeared on deck, much to everybody's amazement. To reach the ship the determined dog had swum 50 miles, 80 km *up-river* against the current to New Orleans and then negotiated the two supply vessels berthed alongside his master's ship.

The Newfoundland's main claim to fame, however, rests on its life-saving prowess, and there are numerous stories of this dog rescuing drowning children and adults. One earned a medal as late as 1919 when the coastal steamer 'Ethie' ran on to rocks during a fierce storm in Bonne Bay on the coast of Nova Scotia. The ship was listing heavily and the lifeboats had all been washed away. Raging surf prevented rescue parties from launching their boats, and one man had already been drowned in a vain attempt to swim ashore with a line. The last hope was the ship's powerful Newfoundland 'Tang' who, carrying a light line, plunged without hesitation into the boiling sea and fought his way to the shore, where willing hands pulled him to safety. The line was taken from his mouth, a hawser drawn

The Portuguese water-dog, one of the world's greatest canine swimmers.

from ship to shore, and a breeches buoy rigged up. All 92 passengers and crew were brought to safety, including a small baby who was brought ashore in a mail bag. Tang was later presented with a medal for Meritorious Service from Lloyd's of London, which he wore on his collar until he died of old age in St John's.

The prompt action of a Newfoundland may also have altered the course of world history. As Napoleon Bonaparte was secretly leaving his exile on Elba to return to France in 1815 he slipped on a rock in the darkness and fell into the sea. Unable to swim, he thrashed about in the black water as his panic-stricken followers tried to locate him. Fortunately one of the boatmen waiting to row him to the rescue ship had a Newfoundland with him and, at his command, the dog leapt into the water, caught the sinking Emperor by his collar, and towed him to the boat. If the Newfoundland had not been present there would have been no return to power for Napoleon . . . and no Waterloo!

Today teams of specially-trained Newfoundlands are kept at a number of French and Italian holiday beaches where there are treacherous tides. The dogs, wearing a harness with a rubber handle to which swimmers in trouble can cling, dive in from outboard motor dinghies steered by lifeguards, but they can also rescue unconscious or injured swimmers as well by gently clamping on to their arm. When their services are not required they are

'Gunner', seen here with his owner, demonstrates his long-jumping ability over water.

kept out of sight of bathers, otherwise they are liable to plunge into the sea and 'rescue' people who are not drowning at all! One young woman swimmer dragged struggling to the shore by an over-zealous Newfoundland found to her embarrassment that most of her flimsy costume had been ripped off during the encounter, while another victim had to be taken to a local hospital for treatment for painful lacerations. Needless to say neither person went swimming again off beaches frequented by Newfoundland life-guards!

The explorer and naturalist Paul Fountain once owned a Russian retriever which preferred salt water to fresh, and this dog often swam so far out to sea that several times it was given up for lost. The retriever, however, always came straight back to the spot on shore from whence it had started. On one occasion it followed its master's canoe for 9 miles, 14.4 km, but it was completely exhausted at the end of this marathon swim.

Another dog that loves to go swimming on its own is the Chesapeake Bay retriever. Even the coldest weather will not deter this hardy animal from taking its daily swim, and one man reports that his dog used to break through ice in order to get at the water!

A labrador retriever named 'King Tut Gunner', owned by Mr Erno Rossi of Port Colborne, Ontario, Canada, swims 2 miles, 3.2 km daily alongside his master in a rowing boat, and on 30 August 1981 he completed a 3 mile, 4.8 km swim over a marked aquatic course at the annual Canadian National Exhibition dog swim held at Peterborough, Ontario. The 45 lb, 20.4 kg dog's time was 1 hour 48 minutes 50 seconds or 1.65 miles/h, 2.64 km/h and, although the Newfoundland is the fastest swimming dog over long distances, the retriever can outpace it over shorter journeys up to half a mile, 0.8 km.

Gunner is also an excellent long jumper across water. His best jump to date from a 20 in, 51 cm high dock is 27 ft 3 in, 8.3 m measured from the take-off point to the spot where his nose entered the water, and this required a running distance of 16 ft, 4.87 m.

Mrs Barbara Wolman's Newfoundland 'Ch. Newfield's Nelson' (see page 41) also made several similar leaps during his lifetime. On one occasion he cleared 23 ft, 7 m from a dock 27 in, 68.5 cm above water level in an effort to pounce on some mallard ducks, and another time he jumped off a dock 10 ft, 3 m high from a standing crouch start and cleared over 28 ft, 8.53 m.

The dogs in the terrier group are not generally noted for their prowess in a wet element, but there is one record of a Boston terrier named 'Jumbo' swimming 1½ miles, 2.4 km.

And finally, we mustn't forget to mention the dog that swims like a frog, dives like a duck, herds cattle, eats fish and understands Portuguese!

The canine in question is the poodle-like Portuguese water dog (Cao d'Agua) of the Algarve region, which was originally bred to herd sheep and cattle. Today, however, its excellent swimming and retrieving capabilities are of incalculable benefit to the fishermen of the Algarve. It will dive as deep as 15 ft, 4.57 m to catch a fish that has escaped from a net or recover tackle that has been swept overboard and, before the advent of modern techniques utilizing radio and radar, these dogs would swim up to 5 miles, 8 km in the open sea tracking schools of fish or carrying messages from boats to the shore. It is an historical fact that half of the ships of the Spanish Armada carried Portuguese water dogs on board for use as couriers and, when the Armada was defeated and many of its ships sunk off the Irish coast, these dogs swam to shore where they allegedly mixed with the local breeds to form the present day Irish water spaniel. Unlike other water dogs the Cao d'Agua churns its webbed feet like a frog and uses its tail as a rudder. It also has very powerful hind legs and is able to propel itself from the sea unaided into a fishing boat!

An amusing story concerning a Portuguese water dog named 'Nell' and her litter of seven puppies comes from Nantucket Island, Massachusetts, USA. Early one morning their owner, Mrs Judith Bartsch, ushered the mother and her offspring out into the backyard so that they could obey the call of nature. A few minutes later, when she opened the door again to let in the ravenous horde for breakfast, there was no sign of the dogs, and a quick search revealed that the family had hot-footed it through an open gate leading into the road. Diving into her car, Mrs Bartsch headed along a familiar route Nell might have taken but, apart from seeing a duck and her seven ducklings swimming in a cattle pond, she saw no other signs of animal life. By now she was in black despair but, just as she was about to go further afield, the image of the duck and her brood suddenly came back into her mind ... and then the penny dropped! With a muttered oath she slammed on the brakes, did a quick u-turn and tore back to the pond—where she angrily ordered out Nellie and her bedraggled puppies, who were all none the worse for their adventure.

The only other water dogs known to dive deeply and bring up sunken objects are the Newfoundland, the Labrador retriever and the Irish water spaniel. At the water trials held at Maidstone, Kent, in May 1876 one of the tests was 'diving' in which the dogs had to retrieve a basket of stones from the bottom of the River Medway. The winning competitor in this event was a Newfoundland. Recently there have been stories of Labrador retrievers diving into rivers to pick up bricks and stones, and one woman living in West Sussex says she owns a bitch which can stay submerged for anything up to a minute at a time. The Irish water spaniel is also an expert diver, and one dog owned by breeder Mrs Barbara McKenzie of Basingstoke, Hampshire, has made a career out of recovering balls from the bottom of the lake at the local golf course!

In order to save lives the Newfoundland must also be able to jump from considerable heights into the sea below without flinching. Probably the most incredible performer in this field was a fun-loving Newfoundland kept aboard the *Great Eastern*, the prototype for the modern ocean liner. When this huge steamship was in dock the fearless dog would regularly climb on to the top of the paddle box situated some 50 ft, 15 m above water level—and then launch himself out into space!

An interesting spin-off from the Newfoundland's role as an emergency rescue dog has been the size of an object it can move through the water. As a matter of course during their frequent water rescue trials the dogs tow a boat 12 ft, 3.65 m in length with two adults in it for a moderate distance and beach the boat by single dog power. Under the British Water Trial Rules of 1876 a line 15 ft long is attached to the boat and a bumper or piece of wood fixed to the opposite end of the line to facilitate the rescue.

The heaviest object ever towed and beached by a dog was a 25 ft, 7.62 m cabin cruiser weighing 4481 lb, 2033 kg brought ashore by 'Barbara-Allen's Beau Brummel' on 5 November 1980.

Richest and most valuable

A number of dogs have been left large sums of money or valuable property in their owners' wills, although many of these legacies have later been contested by angry relatives of the deceased.

The richest dog on record was a standard poodle named 'Toby', who was left the modern equivalent of £15 million in the will of his eccentric American owner, Miss Ella Wendel, who died in New York in 1931. This dog had a fortune lavished upon him during his lifetime, and he slept on expensive silk linen in a special room of his own. Every morning his doting mistress would bring him breakfast in bed, and a butler was specially employed to wait upon the dog's every need. When Miss Wendel died there were many claims to the vast estate, and things were never quite the same again for Toby. The butler no longer pampered him, and he was forced to sleep in a plain wooden basket in the kitchen and eat his food like any ordinary dog from a bowl instead of from silver plates. In 1933 Toby was put to sleep by the order of the executors of the will but, as one cynic said at the time, if the dog had not been put down he would have died from disillusionment anyway!

When Miss Eleanor Ritchey, an American oil heiress, died in 1968 aged 58 years, she passed on her $4.5 million, £1 878 000 fortune to the 150 stray dogs she kept on her ranch at Fort Lauderdale, Florida. The will, however, was contested, and when the estate was finally settled in favour of the dogs in 1973 the fortune had increased in value to $9 million. Four years later it jumped again to $14 million, but by this time only 73 of the original inheritors were still alive. The remaining dogs were tattooed for identification purposes, and the sexes kept separate just in case any more heirs suddenly arrived on the scene! In 1982 only eight of the dogs were still alive (the ashes of the other 142 had been deposited in carefully labelled bottles), and their needs were catered for by a personal vet and the ranch manager, who was formerly Miss Ritchey's chauffeur and had driven her around in a Cadillac when she was looking for strays. When the last of the remaining dogs, 'Musketeer', died in June 1984 the $12 million, £8.5 million estate went to the Auburn University Research Foundation in Alabama for research into animal diseases.

Since the early 1970s some astonishing prices have been paid for top dogs of certain breeds, particularly German shepherds, labrador retrievers, Akitas and greyhounds, and it is amazing just how much money people are prepared to hand over for a dog they specifically want.

On 27 June 1972 Mr August Belmont of Easton, Maryland, USA, paid $22 000 (£8500) for a labrador retriever puppy named 'Wanapum Lucky Yo Yo', bred by Mr Eddie Dewitt of Redmond, Washington. The following year Mr and Mrs Vic Colic of Mona Vale, near Sydney, New South Wales, Australia, handed over A$24 000 (£11 156) for a VA (Vorzügliche Auslese) German shepherd named 'Ingo von Hafenlohtal' bred in Germany, and in October 1974 Mr and Mrs Graham Brayne of Patumahoe, New Zealand, paid $11 000 (£5500) for 'Ch. Rossfort Premonition', said to be the finest German shepherd ever produced in England. Two weeks after their purchase the Braynes turned down an offer of $14 850 (£7500) for the dog, but this sum was easily eclipsed in 1981 when a Japanese consortium paid DM 120 000 (£25 000) for another VA German shepherd imported from Germany. Sums in excess of £10 000 have also been paid for Akitas, and recently two Japanese champions were reportedly sold for £50 000.

The prices charged by British breeders for their top dogs are, somewhat surprisingly, well below those of their American and European counterparts.

The highest price paid so far for a British breed of dog (excluding secret deals) is £4500 for a Yorkshire terrier which was exported to Australia in 1978. A few months later it was resold for £7000 in Malaysia.

The highest price ever paid for a dog is 'more than £40 000' by Mr Alf McLean, a Belfast bookmaker, for 'Indian Joe', winner of the 50th Greyhound Derby at White City Stadium, London, on 28 June 1980. The dog, owned and bred by Mr Kevin Frost of Co Clare, Eire, was whelped in September 1977. Since then a Brazilian millionaire has reportedly paid out £45 000 for a VA German shepherd imported from Germany, but this extreme figure has not yet been confirmed.

When dog shows were in their infancy, many breeders put totally unrealistic price tags on their animals for the benefit of the catalogue, although they had no intention of selling them. One famous St Bernard named 'Tell' was priced at £10 000, and the same figure was quoted by Mrs Mabel Tottie of Coniston Hall, Hellifield, Yorkshire, for each of the five basset hounds entered by her at the 1900 Birmingham National Show!

By way of comparison, Mrs V Mannooch's famous chow chow 'Ch. Choonam Hung Kwong', winner of 44 Challenge Certificates and Best in Show at Cruft's in 1936, was valued at £5250, while Mrs Lesley-Ann Howard of Godstone, Surrey, owner of the toy poodle 'Ch. Grayco Hazelnut', Cruft's Supreme Champion in 1982 (see page 55) turned down an offer of £20 000 for her dog shortly before the show.

The owner of a Cruft's winner can allegedly make up to £75 000 during the following year advertising pet foods and accessories, but this figure probably owes a lot to journalistic licence. Owning a champion is an expensive business, and basic running costs alone add up to at least £7000 a year. On top of this there must be also added the cost of capital outlay, and this could well include an expensive motor home for shows.

The largest sum ever offered for a dog of any breed was the £32 000 tendered by the immensely rich American financier and industrialist J Pierpont Morgan in c 1907 for the Pekingese 'Ch. Ch-êrh of Alderbourne' (1904–fl.1914). When the dog's owner, Mrs Clarice Ashton Cross of Ascot, Berkshire, turned down his offer (equivalent to £865 000 today!) Mr Morgan came back with the offer of an 'open' cheque, but again he was refused. This prompted one newspaper of the day to write that there were three good things in England even Pierpont Morgan could not buy: good weather, a British policeman and Mrs Cross's Pekingese!

Professional retriever trainer Eddie deWitt of Redmond, Washington, USA, with 'Wanapum Lucky Yo Yo', who was sold for $22 000 (then £8500) in 1972.

Rarest

Over the years a small number of breeds have been credited with the 'rarest dog' title, but most of these contenders are no longer on the endangered list, thanks to the splendid efforts made by various enthusiasts to re-establish these strains.

In 1969 there were only 40 known examples of the Löwchen or Little Lion Dog left in the world—all of them in Europe. This dog was originally the drawing-room pet of the nobility of Spain and Italy during the Renaissance, and a number of these affectionate little animals are included in paintings of that and later periods, the most famous being Goya's portrait of the Duchess of Alba. They started to become scarce during the 19th century, and the breed declined so rapidly that, shortly before the outbreak of the First World War, there were probably fewer than a dozen individuals left. The dog was saved from extinction only by the timely intervention of a Belgian woman who set about re-establishing the breed. Through her efforts, and those of a German veterinary surgeon, the lowchen is no longer on the danger list. The precise origin of this 'living antique', which has been described as the missing link between the poodle and the Maltese terrier (or the early toy dog breeds Teneriffe and Bolognese) is not known, but it probably evolved in Spain or Portugal during the 15th century. From there the breed spread to France, Italy, Germany and Belgium.

The Chinese crested dog (now extinct in China, although this is probably not its country of origin) was in an even worse plight at one time. Up until 1966 the only known examples of this breed were all owned by an American woman, Mrs Ruth Harris, of Florida, but that year she exported four to Britain. By October 1971 the population had increased to 55–60, including 22 in Britain, and today there are well over 1000 Chinese crested dogs living in the USA alone.

The Chinook, a popular American breed of sled dog developed by Arthur T Walden, the father of New England sled dog racing, in c 1909 from a litter

The Shar-pei, formerly the world's rarest breed of dog, with only 14 known examples surviving in 1974.

of puppies born of a mongrel father and a husky mother, reportedly became extinct in the early 1970s, but these floppy-eared yellow dogs are still bred in small numbers at a kennel in Maine where they are mainly sold as pets.

In January 1974 only 14 examples of the Shar-pei or Chinese fighting dogs were still known to survive (four in Hong Kong and the rest in the USA); by May 1977, however, their numbers had increased to 60, all of them in North America, as a result of planned breeding programmes. Today the world population has soared to over 4000 (c 100 in Britain), but not all these dogs are pure-bred. There have been a number of out-crossings with the chow chow, which is closely related, and recently the fighting dog fraternity in the USA has started introducing bull terrier and bull mastiff blood as well.

The Broholmer, a breed only recognised in Denmark, reportedly became extinct in the late 1960s but, in December 1974, a dog turned up at the home of a pharmacist in Helsinki. The Danish Royal Veterinary College in Copenhagen tried to set up a frozen sperm bank for 'Bjoern', as he was called, in the hope that a bitch would eventually be found to continue the line, but the experiment was unsuccessful. The dog died on 4 January 1975.

The world's rarest breed of dog is now the Tahltan bear dog, which was formerly used by the Tahltan Indians of western Canada for hunting bear, lynx and porcupine. The Indians used to carry these medium-sized dogs (weight about 30 lb, 13 kg) on their backs in hide sacks in order to conserve their strength preparatory to hunting, and would release them when the quarry was sighted. The plucky dogs would then circle the prey and hold it at bay until their masters moved in for the kill. Up until very recently only five known examples of this breed still survived (the last registration with the Canadian Kennel Club was in 1948), and four of these were spayed bitches; this meant the Tahltan bear dog had already passed the point of no return. The solitary dog, 'Iskut' (whelped on 14 March 1967), owned by Mrs Winnie Acheson of Atlin, British Columbia, where three of the bitches also resided, died on 20 April 1982. Ten weeks later two of the remaining bitches named 'Snoopy' and 'Sam' belonging to a Mrs Connally were put to sleep on account of their advancing senility, leaving just one other bitch in Atlin and another in Carcross, some 60 miles, 96 km further to the north.

Another breed now reported to be in danger of becoming extinct is the Podengo Portugues Grande, the largest of the Portuguese warren hounds, which is not recognised outside its own country. This greyhound-type dog closely resembles the Ibizan hound in appearance.

Dog shows

The first recorded dog show was held in the New Cornmarket, Newcastle upon Tyne, Northumberland, on 28–29 June 1859. There were only two classes, one for setters and the other for pointers, and the total number of entries was 59. A judge in the pointer class, Mr William Jobling, won the first prize for setters, and a setter judge, Mr J Brailsford, took the honours in the pointer class! The two winning owners were each presented with a double-barrelled shotgun donated by a local gunsmith, Mr W R Pape, who had helped to organise the show. As dog shows increased in popularity it was decided to bring in some kind of regulating committee that would make rules and enforce them; to fill this need the Kennel Club, the governing body of dog breeders' associations in Britain, was founded in 1873.

The first official dog show staged in the USA was held at the Hippodrome in Gilmore Gardens, New York City, on 8–10 May 1877, and was sponsored by the Westminster Kennel Club. There were 1177 entries but only 20 classes. The American Kennel Club came into being on 17 September 1884.

More dog shows are staged annually in Britain than in any other country in the world. There are 10 000 shows throughout the year, including 26 General Championships and 200 Breed Shows.

The world's largest dog show is Cruft's, which has been held annually in London since 1886, apart from the years 1918–20 and 1940–47 when the event was cancelled. The first show at the Royal Aquarium, Westminster, was restricted to terriers (600 entries and 57 classes), but four years later other breeds were added, including collies and toy dogs. At the Golden Jubilee Show held at the Royal Agricultural Hall, Islington, in 1936 there were a record 10 650 entries and 4388 dogs, but this was before entries were restricted to prize-winners. The Kennel Club has run Cruft's since 1948. At the 1984 show held over three days at Olympia, Earls Court, there were 10 272 entries, a big increase on the previous year. The largest entry came from the Afghan hound with 234 competitors.

Before a dog can become a Champion in its Breed Class, it must win three Kennel Club Challenge Certificates under three different judges. The only exceptions are gundogs, which are designated Show Champions until they win a Qualifying Certificate in the field. An Obedience Champion also requires three Obedience Certificates, although the winner of the Obedience Championship at Cruft's is allowed to use this coveted title as well.

The greatest number of CCs won by a British dog is the 78 compiled by the famous chow chow 'Ch. U'Kwong King Solomon' (whelped 21 June

Table 6. Cruft's roll of honour (Best-in-Show winners since 1928★)

Date	Breed	Name of Dog	Name of Owner
1928	Greyhound	Primeley Sceptre	H Whitley
1929	Scottish Terrier	Heather Necessity	E Chapman
1930	Spaniel (Cocker)	Luckystar of Ware	H S Lloyd
1931	Spaniel (Cocker)	Luckystar of Ware	H S Lloyd
1932	Retriever (Labrador)	Bramshaw Bob	Lorna Countess Howe
1933	Retriever (Labrador)	Bramshaw Bob	Lorna Countess Howe
1934	Greyhound	Southball Moonstone	B Hartland Worden
1935	Pointer	Pennine Prima Donna	A Eggleston
1936	Chow Chow	Ch. Choonam Hung Kwong	V A M Mannooch
1937	Retriever (Labrador)	Ch. Cheveralla Ben of Banchory	Lorna Countess Howe
1938	Spaniel (Cocker)	Exquisite Model of Ware	H S Lloyd
1939	Spaniel (Cocker)	Exquisite Model of Ware	H S Lloyd
1948	Spaniel (Cocker)	Tracey Witch of Ware	H S Lloyd
1949	No show due to change of date from October to February		
1950	Spaniel (Cocker)	Tracey Witch of Ware	H S Lloyd
1951	Welsh Terrier	Twynstar Dyma-Fi	Capt & Mrs I M Thomas
1952	Bulldog	Ch. Noways Chuckles	J T Barnard
1953	Great Dane	Ch. Elch Elder of Ouborough	W G Siggers
1954	Cancelled		
1955	Poodle (Standard)	Ch. Tzigane Aggri of Nashend	Mrs A Proctor
1956	Greyhound	Treetops Golden Falcon	Mrs W de Casembroot & Miss H Greenish
1957	Keeshond	Ch. Volkrijk of Vorden	I M Tucker
1958	Pointer	Ch. Chiming Bells	Mrs W Parkinson
1959	Welsh Terrier	Ch. Sandstorm Saracen	Mesdames Leach and Thomas
1960	Irish Wolfhound	Sulhamstead Merman	Mrs Nagle and Miss Clark
1961	Airedale Terrier	Ch. Riverina Tweedsbairn	Miss P McCaughey & Mrs D Schuth
1962	Fox Terrier (Wire)	Ch. Crackwyn Cockspur	H L Gill
1963	Lakeland Terrier	Rogerholm Recruit	W Rogers
1964	English Setter SH	Ch. Silbury Soames of Madavale	Mrs A Williams
1965	Alsatian (GSD)	Ch. Fenton of Kentwood	Miss S H Godden
1966	Poodle (Toy)	Oakington Puckshill Amber Sunblush	C E Perry
1967	Lakeland Terrier	Ch. Stingray of Derryabah	Mr & Mrs W Postlewaite
1968	Dalmatian	Ch. Fanhill Faune	Mrs E J Woodyatt
1969	Alsatian (GSD)	Ch. Hendrawen's Nibelung of Charavigne	Mr & Mrs E J White
1970	Pyrenean Mountain Dog	Bergerie Knur	Mr & Mrs F S Prince
1971	Alsatian (GSD)	Ch. Ramacon Swashbuckler	Prince Ahmed Husain
1972	Bull Terrier	Ch. Abraxas Audacity	Miss V Drummond-Dick
1973	Cavalier King Charles Spaniel	Alansmere Aquarius	Messrs Hall & Evans
1974	St Bernard	Ch. Burtonswood Bossy Boots	Miss M Hindes
1975	Fox Terrier (Wire)	Ch. Brookewire Brandy of Layven	Messrs Benelli & Dondina
1976	West Highland White Terrier	Ch. Dianthus Buttons	Mrs K Newstead
1977	English Setter	Bournehouse Dancing Master	Mr G F Williams
1978	Fox Terrier (Wire)	Ch. Harrowhill Huntsman	Miss E Howles
1979	Kerry Blue Terrier	Eng Am Ch. Callaghan of Leander	Mrs W Streatfield
1980	Retriever (Flat-coated)	Ch. Shargleam Blackcap	Miss P Chapman
1981	Irish Setter	Ch. Astley's Portia of Rua	Mrs & Miss Tuite
1982	Poodle (Toy)	Ch. Grayco Hazelnut	Mrs L A Howard
1983	Afghan Hound	Ch. Montravia Kaskarak Hitari	Mrs P Gibbs
1984	Lhasa Apso	Ch. Saxonsprings Hackensack	Mrs Jean Blyth

★ Before 1928 there was no award of Best-in-Show at Cruft's.

1968). Owned and bred by Mrs Joan Egerton of Bramhall, Cheshire, 'Solly' won his first CC at The Cheshire Agricultural Society Championship Show on 4 June 1969, and his 78th CC was awarded at the City of Birmingham Championship Show on 4 September 1976. He also notched up six Supreme Bests in Show, six Reserve Bests in Show, 23 Bests of Group and 22 Reserve Bests of Group, and was Top Dog All Breeds for the two years 1970–71, Top Utility in the *Dog World* Dog Competition 1973 and winner of the Chow of the Year Show for four consecutive years (1973–76). Solly died on 3 April 1978.

The only other dog with a career total in excess of 60 was Mrs Betty Farrand's standard wire-haired dachshund 'Ch. Gisbourne Inca' with 62, the last won in 1972.

In the USA they use an entirely different system to that employed by the Kennel Club. To become a Champion there a dog must win 15 championship points awarded on a scale drawn up by the American Kennel Club. The points can only be earned by placing first in the Winner Class, and five points is the largest number that can be won at any given show. The total must also include two wins at 'majors' (shows carrying ratings of three points or more) under different judges.

The greatest number of All-Breed Best-in-Show awards won by an American dog is the 140 compiled by the standard white poodle bitch 'Ch. Lou-Gins Kiss Me Kate' (whelped 23 May 1976), whose campaign lasted from May 1977 to mid-1980. She is owned by Jack and Paulann Phelan of Manhattan, Illinois, USA. The previous record-holder was the famous Pekingese 'Ch. Chik T'Sun

The veteran show-dog 'Ryepiece Rambler' who was still winning titles at the age of 21 years.

of Caversham' (1954–60) who won 127 All-Breed BIS and 125 Best-in-Show during the period January 1957 to February 1960. His campaign included 14 consecutive All-Breed BIS three different times, and his final BIS win at Westminster in February 1960 was over 2546 entries. Born and bred in England 'Gossy', as he was known, was exported to Canada at the age of 11 months and was purchased by Mr and Mrs Charles C Venable of Marietta, Georgia, in November 1956. On 4 March 1984 a Scottish terrier bitch named 'Ch. Braeburn's Close Encounter' (whelped on 22 October 1978), owned by Sonnie and Alan Novick of Plantation Acres, Florida, notched up her 120th All-Breed BIS in Mobile, Alabama, and appeared to be heading for a new world record by the end of July.★

The only other two dogs with a career total of 100 or more All-Breed BIS wins were the boxer 'Ch. Bangaway of Sirrah Crest', owned by Dr and Mrs R C Harris, who won 121 in the years 1950–55, and the English setter 'Ch. Rock Fall's Colonel', owned by Mr William T Holt, who won 100 during the same period, often in competition with Bangaway.

The greatest number of dogs entered by one person in a single show anywhere in the world was the 101 that Dr A P Munn of Long Branch, New Jersey, USA, put in the Morris and Essex Show at Madison, New Jersey, in 1936.

The oldest *active* show-dog on record was a beagle named 'Ryepiece Rambler' (whelped on 20 July 1957), who was hunted regularly with the West Wales Farmers Hounds for a number of years. When he was retired from the pack in 1971 aged 14 years his owner, Mrs Sylvia Britt of Lampeter, Dyfed, started to show him in Veteran Classes against other beagles—and so began his second career. But it was not until 1977 that he was shown in 'Any Variety Veteran Classes', winning on innumerable occasions. He won the Veteran Class for three successive years at the Open Shows of the Welsh Beagle Club, all of them under different judges, and took his first title at Pontypool on 26 November 1978. On 10 February 1979 Rambler was scheduled to take part with other 'greats' in the Personality Parade at Cruft's, but he died suddenly from heart failure on 18 January 1979. Despite his tragic death the beagle was still paid a special tribute at the world's most prestigious dog show, and his Personality Parade rosette was later forwarded to Mrs Britt.

The unluckiest show-dog on record was probably a champion pug named 'Penny' whose owner, Miss Joanne Massey aged ten, was the youngest breeder ever to win a major Cruft's trophy. The little girl was hoping to turn her dog into a double prizewinner at the 1983 Show but, a few days before the competition, Penny dozed off in front of a gas fire and her chances went up in smoke! When Joanne's mother caught the smell of burning she dashed into the lounge—where to her horror she found the dog snoring blissfully unaware and turning a dark shade of brown all down one side! Frantic efforts were made to try and comb over the singed hair, but the affected area was too large to camouflage, and it completely ruled out the chance of Penny winning anything that year.

Population

The world's domestic dog population is estimated to be 150 million. The country with the largest canine population is the USA (*c* 40 million), while Britain has 5.5 million including 2.5 million mongrels.

Dog lovers

The greatest number of dogs ever owned by one person were the 5000 mastiffs which the great Mogul Emperor Kublai Khan (1215–94) kept for the purpose of fighting in the arenas. Ptolemy II (308–247 BC) of Egypt was another over-the-top dog-fight *aficionado* and retained 2400 dogs of the mastiff type, while the 13th century Emperor Takatoko of Japan kept 2000 fighting dogs and staged 12 fights a month. The winners were led through the streets so that the populace could pay homage to them. Mention should also be made of a 7th century AD Emperor of the T'ang Dynasty of China who thought so highly of his chow chows that his kennels housed 2500 braces of them for his huntsmen.

The most fanatical dog-lover of all time was probably Henry III (1551–89) of France. He collected dogs like other people collect stamps and, when he saw one that took his fancy and it wasn't for sale, he would think nothing of arranging for someone to steal it for him. He had at least 2000 dogs spread around his palaces, and when he was in residence he rarely had less than 100 of his pets (mostly toy-dogs) within patting distance. Deciding which ones to take on his daily walk was a constant problem; in the end one of his enterprising courtiers designed a special container for 20 small dogs which the King slung around his neck when he went out on his constitutionals!

Bones

In June 1979 Mr Jack Stoltz of Wellesley, Missouri, USA, claimed a world record when he uncovered 308 dog bones weighing 102 lb, 46 kg in his back yard. They had been stockpiled by his black labrador retriever 'Happy'.

★ Won 141st All-Breed BIS 30 June 1984

Jaw strength

In a test carried out on a 44 lb, 20 kg mongrel it was found that it could exert a bite of 363 lbf, 1.62 kN at the tips of the teeth (cf. 65 lbf, 0.29 kN for an average adult man weighing 154 lb, 70 kg and 1540 lbf, 6.85 kN for a 120 lb, 54 kg crocodile).

The greatest jaw pressure ever recorded for any breed of dog is 1200 lbf, 5.34 kN in the case of a 160 lb, 72.5 kg Bouvier de Flandres tested on a 'Bite-o-Meter' in the USA, which would probably explain why professional burglars are extremely reluctant to break into premises known to harbour one of these four-legged pulverisers!

The dogs in the bull terrier group are also noted for their tremendous jaw muscles, and the author's father once owned a 43 lb, 19.5 kg Staffordshire bull terrier which used to hang from a springy tree branch for anything up to five minutes at a time with its eyes shut in complete bliss!

But jaw power does not necessarily equate with bellicosity. In 1980 animal behaviourist Dr Roger Mugford compiled an Aggression League Table after studying 300 cases of dogs suffering from what he called 'rage syndrome' (temperamental difficulties of genetic origin) and came up with some very interesting results.

According to his findings the labrador retriever, the German shepherd and the cocker spaniel, three of Britain's most popular breeds, were the leading villains, while the notorious Dobermann pinscher could only manage 12th place! In other words, dogs today are largely bred for looks rather than temperament. The top ten, in order of nastiness, were: labrador retriever, German shepherd, cocker spaniel, dachshund, poodle (both miniature and toy), golden retriever, border collie, Yorkshire terrier, old English sheepdog and the Jack Russell terrier.

The high placing of the harmless-looking cocker spaniel is also confirmed by British vets who, in a recent survey, revealed that this so-called 'cheerful and sweet' dog causes more mayhem in their surgeries than any other breed!

In another study of the canine population of New York City, carried out by Dr Robert Oleson of the US Public Health Service over a period of 27 years, he found that the nine breeds most likely to take a chunk out of mankind were, in order of biting averages: the German shepherd, the chow chow, the poodle (toy), the Italian bulldog, the fox terrier, the chow chow cross, the airedale, the Pekingese and what he described as a 'crossed German police dog', which could be a reference to the Dobermann pinscher. Dr Oleson also discovered that the most dangerous time of the year for dog aggression was not on the so-called 'dog days', the period between early July and early September when the hot sultry weather of summer usually occurs, but in the middle of June.

In Britain dog attacks on postmen now average more than 5000 a year and account for 15 per cent of all staff accidents. The worst culprits are the German shepherd and little terriers like the Jack Russell, which like to hide in bushes waiting for their unsuspecting victim—but, if it is any consolation to postmen, one aggressive dog in every four prefers to sink its teeth into its own master or mistress rather than a visitor to the house!

Toughest

The toughest dogs in the world in terms of their ability to face up to extreme hardship are the Spitz types found in the Northern Group. They include the Alaskan and Siberian huskies, the Canadian and Greenland Eskimo dogs and the Alaskan malamute, all of which will survive in conditions to which other breeds of dog would quickly succumb. The largest and toughest of them all, however, with exceptional powers of endurance, amazing strength and courage, is the Alaskan malamute, which can exist in temperatures as low as 94°F (34.6°C) below zero, and pull loads weighing several hundreds of pounds all day with very little rest.

The title of 'toughest dog in the world' is open to various interpretations, but one of the strongest contenders must be a friendly little beagle cross named 'Dumpy', who stood up to everything the human race could throw at him, and still managed to come out ahead. Dumpy's horrific ordeal started early one morning in July 1973 when a patrolling dog warden spotted him walking the streets of Salem, Ohio, USA, and picked him up as a stray. He was thrown into the back of the van, given a supposedly lethal dose of gas, and then taken to the local refuse dump for disposal.

When he arrived at the site the dog-catcher, thinking Dumpy was dead, threw him into a ditch in front of an oncoming bulldozer. To the man's astonishment the dog suddenly started crawling out of his intended grave, so he quickly pumped four bullets into the pitiful creature, hitting him in the leg and chest as he wobbled out of the path of the machine bearing down on him. Even then the gallant little beagle was still not finished, and somehow managed to stagger on despite his serious injuries. By now the bulldozer driver, James Gilbert, who couldn't believe what he was seeing, had stopped work. With tears in his eyes he begged the dog warden to follow the suffering animal and put him out of his misery. The man refused, saying he didn't want to get his boots muddy and the dog was going to die anyway, and drove off. Gilbert was so upset he telephoned a relative to tell her what had happened. Within minutes two of her friends, Joyce Guiler and Jean Fluharty, were on the scene and they began searching in the pouring rain for the dog. When darkness fell they used a flash-light and, later that night, they found the poor little dog in a dilapidated shed sheltering from the rain. 'Every hair on that dog was on end', said Mrs Guiler afterwards. 'He was scared to death after all that had happened to him . . . his eyes were glazed . . . and he was nothing but mud and blood. He didn't try to bite us . . . he didn't make a sound.' The two women took Dumpy—as they christened him—to a local vet who cleaned up the horrific wounds and carried out general repairs.

When the animal-lovers of Salem heard what had happened they were outraged. The dog warden responsible for Dumpy's torment was immediately suspended pending an investigation, and he was also given police protection after receiving threats to his life. Eventually he was forced to leave town, but no investigation will ever reveal how this courageous little dog managed to survive one man's relentless drive to snuff out his life.

Fortunately the story had a happy ending. Despite his terrifying experience, Dumpy made a full recovery and was later adopted by one of the 500 families in Salem who had begged for the chance to give the dog a good home and restore his faith in human nature. It was no more than the little beagle deserved, and it is gratifying to know that Dumpy spent the rest of his life in comfort.

Another little dog who refused to give up the good fight when all the odds were stacked up against him was a long-haired dachshund called 'Maxi', who survived for six weeks in Chile's notorious Atacama Desert the world's driest place. This fun-loving extrovert, owned by a former West German press attaché, Raban von Mentzingen, strayed from the family in January 1977 when they were visiting the El Salvador copper mine in the heart of the desert as part of a final tourist trip before they were transferred back to Bonn. The family could not wait to search for Maxi, so the Chilean police were alerted to look out for the black sausage dog. There was no sign of him, however, and after a month the animal was given up for dead. Then, early in March, a Chilean prospector spotted an exhausted and extremely skinny dachshund staggering through some barren hills 48 miles, 76.8 km from the spot where he had disappeared. The dog was later flown to Santiago for medical treatment, and from there was sent on to Bonn for a joyful reunion with the von Mentzingens. How Maxi survived in an area where there is very little food and no water, and where the temperature sizzles in the daytime and drops to below freezing at night, will remain one of life's mysteries.

Although dogs cannot live much more than a few days without adequate supplies of water or other forms of liquid, they can keep going for much longer periods without food.

In December 1972 Mr and Mrs Ernest Nechvatal of San Leandro, California, USA, were reunited with their mongrel dog 'Cindy' after she had apparently spent an amazing 73 days without food locked in an abandoned car in a parking lot at Stateline, Nevada. The vehicle had been stolen from the same spot—with Cindy inside—on 28 September, and was discovered later when a snowplough operator was brought in to clear the area after some heavy falls of snow. Fortunately one of the windows had been left slightly open, which allowed moisture to seep in, but during her ordeal Cindy's weight fell from a regular 30 lb, 13.6 kg to an emaciated 12 lb, 5.44 kg.

Just over eight years later, in January 1981, a wire-haired pointer named 'Reno' was dug out alive after being trapped under rubble for 43 days following an earthquake in southern Italy. When the dog's owner returned to her shattered home in Aveillino for the first time after the disaster, she suddenly heard her pet yelping and called in a fire rescue squad, who found Reno in a shaft of fallen beams. He had apparently survived by drinking rainwater.

Mother love

The bond between a bitch and her puppies is very strong, and some incredible stories have been told of the devotion shown by mothers to their young. One of the most remarkable episodes occurred in March 1977 when a mongrel named 'Beauty' and her puppy were accidentally imprisoned when workmen boarded up an empty house in Redditch, Worcestershire. For three days the two dogs languished without heat, food or water before Beauty, now suffering badly from thirst, decided to make a desperate bid for freedom. Wedging herself into the chimney she slowly started to inch her way up the 45 ft, 20.4 m stack and, after what must have seemed an eternity, she finally emerged triumphantly into the fresh air. Beauty then started barking furiously to attract attention, and the soot-covered dog was spotted on the roof by a passer-by, who quickly raised the alarm. Mother and son were later reunited with their relieved owners, who said the pair had vanished after squeezing through a gap in a fence at their home.

Another heart-warming account of a fox terrier's devotion to her puppies appeared in the old *Bath Journal*. Apparently a 'gentleman' in that neighbourhood ordered the runt of a litter of four puppies to be thrown into a pail of water and drowned. It was kept down by a mop and remained submerged for a considerable time. Afterwards the pathetic little bundle was dropped into a dust box and covered with ashes. The following morning the servant who had carried out the so-called execution was surprised to find that the bitch still had four puppies. It appeared the little mother had raked her missing offspring out of the ashes and had put it back with the rest, where it had been resuscitated with liberal supplies of warmth and milk.

Both these stories had happy endings, but fate doesn't always show a smiling face. One of the saddest stories comes from Belfast, Northern Ireland, where a young retriever produced a litter of unwanted puppies. These were destroyed at birth, put in a weighted sack, and taken to a deep dam 15 miles, 24 km away where they were thrown in the middle. The bitch was closely confined to the house for 14 days but, when she was let out for the first time, she disappeared. Her owner found her two days later at the dam, swimming around the spot where her puppies lay at the bottom, and judging from her exhausted condition she had tried long and hard to reach them. Deeply touched by such devotion, the man vowed never again to destroy another puppy.

The most expensive dog collar on record was one sold at Christie's, London, on 9 December 1982 for £4100. Composed of leather and crimson velvet, and decorated with gilded brass or bronze masks, it was made in France in *c* 1700. The collar, which had been put up for sale by a 'titled lady', was purchased by the antique dealers Ward Jackson.

In June 1983 a 'dog bowl' was sold for £6200 at Sotheby's, London, after experts told the owner it was a rare Chinese vase! When Mrs Lesley Jacob took the blue and white bowl used for drinking by her Shetland collie 'Twig' to the village hall at Grayshott, Hampshire, where Sotheby's were carrying out valuations, she was informed it was a piece of porcelain which had been fired during the Wan Li period (1573–1619). The purchaser of the vase, Hong Kong dealer Mr Robert Chang, later said he would have bid up to £10 000 for this piece.

Since 1976 an 'ugliest dog' competition has been staged annually at Petaluma, California, USA. Past winners have included a mongrel of undetermined parentage, a Chihuahua, an English bulldog, a Chinese crested dog and a shar-pei, but these dogs were positively handsome compared to the now-extinct Izcuintlipotzotli of Mexico. This hideous monstrosity, first described in 1780, was about the size of a Maltese (*c* 3 kg, 6.6 lb) and had a skin with white, black and brown spots. It also had a relatively small wolf-like head, an almost non-existent neck and a nose which had a strange prominence in the centre. But the most peculiar thing of all was the grotesque hump on its back which stretched from a point behind the head to the hindquarters. This affront to Mother Nature lived mainly in the Taracan area in the State of Michoacan, and was last recorded in *c* 1843.

The grotesque Izcuintlipotzotli of Mexico, which has been extinct since circa 1843.

'Trixie', easy winner of the 'Ugliest Dog' Competition held at Petaluma, California, USA, in 1979. According to her owners she is part Pekingese and part Chihuahua.

One of the most enterprising dog-owners on record must be Hans Roehm, who bred German shepherds at his kennels in Hamburg. Every time he sold a dog it headed straight back to him like an arrow the first time it was let off the lead, and police proved that one dog turned up at the kennels from nine different buyers!

The most naive 'dog-owner' on record was probably a man named Bruno Alti, who bought a tiny, fluffy 'pedigree' puppy from a gipsy travelling fair in Brescia, northern Italy. He thought it was a bargain at £20, but a month later he began wonder-ing why the dog didn't yap or bark and took it to a vet . . . who told him it was a lion cub!

The runners-up were the police force in Wayne, New Jersey, USA, who paid out £2100 in 1983 for a highly-trained German shepherd specially imported from West Germany—only to discover too late that the dog didn't understand a word of English!

Oddities

A small number of dogs have certain physical pe-culiarities which are unique to their breed.

The remarkable Lundehund of Norway, which has fewer teeth and more toes than any other breed of dog.

The most curious of them all is the Mexican hairless dog (Xoloitzcuintli), which is the only breed that perspires through the pores of its skin instead of through the tongue or paws, has no pre-molar teeth and sheds tears like a human being when it is upset. It also has the highest body temperature of any dog (40°C, 104°F), and in cold weather Indians take these canine equivalents of the hot-water bottle to bed with them. Another oddity of the Mexican hairless dog is that its normal diet is fruit and vegetables, although it can adapt to meat.

The only breed of dog to suffer from blackheads during puberty is the Chinese crested dog . . . and the only breed that blushes is the Pharaoh hound: when it is excited or happy its nose and ears change from flesh colour to a rosy red.

The shar-pei is the only breed where the canine teeth are curved like scimitars, and its distinctive bluish-black tongue is only found in one other breed, the chow chow.

The Chihuahua is the only dog with nails that grow into circles if they are neglected . . . and the basenji, apart from being the only dog incapable of barking, is the sole breed where the female comes into season just once a year.

Finally, mention should also be made of the remarkable lundehund, which is indigenous to the Lofoten archipelago north of Norway, and was formerly used to extract puffins (Fratercula arctica) and their eggs from the backs of the small caves and fissures where they nested. This dog has fewer teeth and more toes than any other breed; joints at the nape of the neck which enable it to bend its head right down onto its back (very useful when the dog had to turn round in narrow passages); and ears which can be closed to protect the auditory meatus from dripping water and dust. The four extra toes with additional pads are distinct 'working' toes which help the lundehund to secure a better grip on rocky surfaces, and it also has double dew-claws on all four legs.

In a typical hunt the dog would worm its way into the cave, seize the puffin by the wing and then drag the struggling bird out into the open, and it was not unusual for a good lundehund to catch 70–80 puffins in one night. Sometimes, however, the potential victim would seize hold of one of its companions with its beak in a desperate effort to put up better re-sistance, and this bird in turn would hang on to another. Occasionally a long chain of six to seven birds would be linked up. When this happened, and the dog couldn't get the puffin out by its own strength, the hunter waiting outside would also join in the fray by grabbing hold of the animal's hind legs and pulling as well, and one can only imagine some of the grotesque tugs-of-war that must have taken place in the past.

Devotion

A number of heart-rending stories have been published about dogs who have kept faithful vigil day after day and year after year for masters they would never see again.

The most celebrated case of dog devotion was that of 'Greyfriars Bobby', a small Scottish terrier. He was the faithful companion of a Midlothian farmer named Gray, and every market day the two of them would travel into Edinburgh together. On one such visit in 1858 Gray suddenly collapsed and died and was buried in nearby Greyfriars churchyard. The following morning Bobby was found lying on his master's grave, and was chased away. But he was back again the next day, and after a few more encounters the church warden felt sorry for the wet and shivering terrier huddling under a tombstone for warmth and started to feed him with buns, the only food he would touch. When the people of Greyfriars got to hear about the dog's fidelity many of them offered him a home, but he always made his way back to the churchyard, so they built him a comfortable shelter near the grave instead. The Lord Provost of Edinburgh eventually presented the little terrier with a collar on which was inscribed 'Grey-friars Bobby. Presented to him by the Lord Provost of Edinburgh. 1857'. Bobby kept vigil by his master's grave for the rest of his life, and only deserted his post when he went to a nearby eating house for his daily ration of buns. When he died in 1872 he was buried in the churchyard alongside his beloved master, and a statue was later erected in the town centre commemorating his unfailing loyalty. His collar and his dinner bowl are now in the city's Huntly Museum.

Japan's answer to Greyfriars Bobby was an akita named 'Hachiko', who accompanied his owner to the railway station each morning and met him again at 5 o'clock when he returned from work. One evening in 1925 his master, a professor at Tokyo University, failed to return, having died earlier that afternoon from a heart attack. For the next ten years, until his death in 1935, Hachiko never gave up hope and went to the station every evening at the usual time to wait for his master's homecoming. The people of Japan fell in love with the dog, and honoured his loyalty by putting up a statue of him on the spot at Shibuya station where he had waited. They also sent small replicas of Hachiko to schools all over the country, and even put his portrait on a postage stamp.

The longest canine vigil on record was one lasting more than 15 years carried out by a mongrel called 'Fido' in the little Italian village of Borgo San Lorenzo. His master was killed in a bombing raid in 1943, and every evening from then onwards he trotted along to the bus stop and eagerly scanned the faces of the people returning from their jobs in Florence before he went sadly home. In 1958 the inhabitants of the village erected a memorial to Fido in recognition of his devotion, and also arranged for the mayor to present him with a gold medal. Just as this dignitary was bending down to hang the award round Fido's neck, however, he suddenly took off . . . it was time for the bus!

Heroes

During World War II Britain's own animal VC, the Dickin Medal, instituted by Mrs Maria Dickin, founder of the People's Dispensary for Sick Animals (PDSA) in 1943, was awarded to 18 dogs for displaying conspicuous gallantry and devotion to duty while serving with the Forces or the Civil Defence.

The first dog to win the Dickin Medal was 'Bob', a white cross-bred labrador collie serving with the 6th Queen's Own Royal West Kent Regiment. The episode which won him the award occurred in January 1943 when, camouflaged in black, he led a night patrol into enemy lines at Green Hill in North Africa. Suddenly he froze in his tracks, indicating that the enemy were in the vicinity, but

The pointer bitch 'Judy', the only dog officially registered as a prisoner of war.

after the patrol had waited for a few minutes without hearing anything, the officer in charge decided to press on. Bob still refused to budge, however, and the patrol hesitated. A few seconds later enemy movement was spotted some yards further on, and the patrol was able to retreat to safety without any casualties. In February 1946 arrangements were made for the Royal Army Veterinary Corps to bring Bob back to Britain, but at Milan station he slipped his collar and disappeared into the crowd. The War Office made every effort to trace him, and his description was even circulated throughout Italy, but Bob was never found again and his medal was presented in 1947 to his owner, CQMS Cleggett.

The only dog registered as an official prisoner-of-war, and the only dog member of the British Returned Prisoner-of-War Association, was a pedigree pointer bitch named 'Judy' (b Shanghai 1937). She served in several gunboats before she was appointed mascot to HMS *Grasshopper* in 1942, and took part in a number of actions during the Malay–Singapore campaign. When Singapore fell, the ship headed for Java, but she was bombed by Japanese aircraft and ran aground on a small uninhabited island where she caught fire and blew up. Fortunately Judy and the crew all managed to survive, but no fresh water could be found on the island, and the men were saved from almost certain death from thirst when Judy wandered along the seashore after the tide had gone out and discovered a fresh water spring. Later the castaways managed to commandeer a visiting Chinese fishing junk and sailed for northern Sumatra—but soon after landing they were captured by the Japanese and taken to a prison camp at Medan. It was here that Judy met Leading Aircraftsman Frank Williams, who shared his meagre rice ration with her, and the pair soon became inseparable. During her two years in a POW camp Judy proved her worth on many occasions, acting as lookout and raising the alarm when she spotted venomous animals such as snakes and scorpions. She was also a great morale booster and, when she fell foul of the camp commandant, LAC Williams managed to save her life and get her registered as an official POW. When the prisoners were shipped from Sumatra to Singapore the pointer was ordered to remain behind—but her master was able to smuggle her out of the camp in a rice sack. The following day, however, the ship was torpedoed and Judy was separated from her mentor, but three days later they were miraculously reunited in another prison camp.

Unfortunately their joy was short-lived. Within days they were on their way to yet another prison camp, where the commandant turned out to be the very one they had antagonised at Medan! When he

'King Tut Gunner', making one of
his spectacular long jumps over
water.

The famous chow chow 'Ch.
U'Kwong King Solomon'—winner
of 78 CCs.

The tiny English toy terrier 'Gleam' who only measures $2\frac{1}{2}$ in, 6.3 cm at the shoulder.

'Pudding', the world's most travelled dog, getting a lift from his mistress Jeanette Coltman.

The Newfoundland dog 'Barbara-Allen's Beau Brummel' towing a 25 ft, 7.6 m cabin cruiser which he later beached.

'Himmy', the world's heaviest cat.

'Ginger' and 'Sandy', the oldest twin cats on record.

The part-Persian tom cat 'BC' who made a record 78 trips back to his mistress's old flat.

The Ragdoll, the largest breed of domestic cat.

caught sight of Judy he gave orders for her to be killed and eaten by the prisoners by way of punishment but, before the evil deed could be carried out, Judy was smuggled into hiding. Luckily the war was now almost at its end and the Japanese soldiers were too terrified of reprisals if they carried out the order. After the surrender Judy was repatriated to England and, when she was released from quarantine, it was in a blaze of glory. She was presented with the Dickin Medal in London, and at the same time LAC Frank Williams was awarded the White Cross of St Giles, the highest award made by the PDSA, in recognition of his bravery in bringing Judy safely through her many ordeals.

During her time as a POW she produced a litter of nine puppies, but the high spot of her life was the day she found an elephant's shinbone. According to one eye-witness it took her two hours to bury this much-prized possession.

The only 'civilian' dog to win the Dickin Medal was a collie bitch named 'Sheila' owned by shepherd John Dagg of Kirknewton, Northumberland. She went out in a blinding snow storm with her master in December 1944 and rescued the four-man crew of an American Flying Fortress which had crashed in the Cheviot Hills.

Medical

The dog is subject to a variety of diseases that also afflict humans, including diabetes, rickets and gout. Diabetes mellitus (sugar diabetes) affects about six dogs in every thousand, and is most common after middle-age.

The first dog suffering from diabetes to receive continuous daily injections of insulin was a hound of indeterminate breed treated at the Faculty of Medicine, University of Toronto, Ontario, Canada, in July–August 1921.

The longest-surviving diabetic dog on record was a standard poodle named 'Roger' (whelped 17 January 1971), who lived for 11½ years on a daily course of insulin injections. When he was 15 months old he developed virulent diabetes and soon became painfully thin. For most dogs this would have been a death sentence because ailing animals need constant care and attention. Fortunately Roger's owner, wealthy widow Mrs Katherine Cosmo Cran of Aldwick Bay, Bognor Regis, Sussex, refused to accept that her friendly companion's days were numbered. She consulted a top London veterinary surgeon, who decided to try an experimental form of insulin which had recently been developed in Denmark. Thus began the long and disciplined daily routine that is so familiar to diabetics: the test for sugar in the morning, the careful weighing of the food (mostly protein) in the

John Dagg with his Collie 'Sheila', the only 'civilian' dog to win the Dickin Medal.

special diet, the preparation of the right insulin doses and, in the case of Roger, the keeping of hourly records. Often Mrs Cran was up before five in the morning, and she never took a day's holiday during the dog's illness. Thanks to his mistress's devoted care and attention the poodle's condition quickly improved, and three months later he was back to his normal weight. In 1974 Roger, who by now was living a full and active life, paid the first of many visits to the summer camps for diabetic youngsters run by the British Diabetic Society, where he was the subject of talks and instruction. The children quickly took him to their hearts, and the fact that their big white friend was a fellow sufferer, proved a tremendous source of encouragement to them.

Despite his daily doses of insulin, Roger managed to avoid the side effects that afflict human diabetics; in 1980, however, he developed diabetic retinopathy without cataract, an eye condition never before recorded in a dog, which gave specialists the unique opportunity to try and find out whether diabetes in animals followed the same pattern as in humans. From then onwards Roger was a frequent visitor to the eye clinic at Guy's Hospital, and

The standard poodle 'Roger' with some of his young friends at a Summer Camp run by The British Diabetics Society.

always behaved impeccably when X-rays were taken of his diseased retinae. He was given a special pass for entering and leaving the hospital grounds, but during one visit a formidable-looking matron nearly had a fit when she spotted the poodle—'get that dog out of here' she bellowed at the top of her voice—and refused to believe Mrs Cran's assurance that her pet was a patient at the Hospital. When Roger passed away peacefully in January 1982 it was with the satisfaction that he had helped scientists pioneer a new course of insulin treatment, and had also served as a model for research into diabetic retinopathy.

———————

On 8 January 1977 a three-year-old 80 lb, 36 kg Samoyed-chow bitch named 'Misty Duchess Red' gave birth to a 3 oz, 85 g puppy—a bodyweight ratio unequalled in the dog world. Even more amazing, the tiny creature survived and grew to maturity. According to the dog's owner, Mrs Ginger Ramsburg (*née* Moody) of Hampton, Virginia, USA, 'Duke', as he was called, could not reach his mother's teats, and even when she propped

him up they proved too large for his mouth. In the end she had to feed him with a tiny baby doll's bottle. When Duke was nine days old he developed pneumonia and a vet told his mistress he would not live. But Mrs Ramsburg stayed up all night with the puppy, massaging him and helping him to breathe, and eventually he pulled through. At three weeks his eyes opened for the first time and he began to grow fur, and he eventually finished up looking like a sheltie-sized German shepherd. On 5 January 1982 Duke was dognapped outside his home, and his distraught owner has not seen him since.

———————

The average dog has 42 permanent teeth, but there is some variation amongst the different strains. Bull breeds, for instance, with their short skulls, usually have slightly fewer teeth, while the chow chow has 44.

A dog named 'Miss Noel', owned by Miss Karen Lackey of Cedar Lake, Indiana, USA, was born on 24 December 1976 with double sets of milk teeth in both the top and lower jaws. She has retained them ever since.

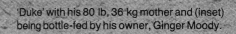

'Duke' with his 80 lb, 36 kg mother and (inset)
being bottle-fed by his owner, Ginger Moody.

Britain's first dog to be fitted with a heart pacemaker was a three-year-old yellow labrador named 'Major Catastrophe', owned by Mrs Vivienne Harcombe of Wellington, Somerset. The 90-minute operation was successfully carried out by Bristol University veterinary surgeons at Musgrove Park Hospital, Taunton, Somerset in February 1980.

When puppies are seized by sudden bouts of overwhelming hunger they will often swallow things that don't normally figure on their menu. The leading exponents in this field are the labrador and the cocker spaniel, and some individuals have been known to gulp down the most amazing objects.

One day Mr Colin Rushforth of Batley, Yorkshire, found his six-month-old labrador 'Dusty' lying on the floor of the garden shed looking decidedly sorry for himself. There was a certain heaviness about the dog's stomach, and he noticed that a sack of DIY materials had fallen from a shelf. Thinking his pet had eaten wallpaper paste he rushed him to the local animal clinic for emergency treatment. On the operating table the vet removed an astonishing collection of hardware from the stricken puppy. First a 3 in, 7.6 cm bolt, then five wood screws and finally 199 1½ inch, 3.8 cm nails. Three days after this superlative feast Dusty was discharged from the clinic apparently none the worse for his experience.

A cocker spaniel named 'Fudge', owned by Mrs Dorothy Thomas of Llanishen near Cardiff, Wales, is also in the same league. On one occasion he was rushed to the vet almost rigid with severe stomach pains and yielded up a full-sized plastic football, a handful of golf balls, a whole melon and a chicken carcase!

Oh, and we mustn't forget the two poodle crosses named 'Amadeus' and 'Amelia' who munched their way through milk bottles, cigarette lighters, barbed wire and even three hearing aids, and Bertie the bull terrier who has a fetish for rubber and likes to dine off tyres while they are still attached to the car!

My Hero!

CATS

The lineage of the domestic cat *Felis catus*, like the dog, can be traced back to the civet-like Miacis. The first cat-like carnivores appeared in the early Oligocene period (*c* 38 million years BP), and their descendants evolved into two distinct groups: *Hoplophoneus* and *Dinictis*. The former included the now extinct sabre-tooth tiger (*Smilodon*), but it was from the second group, which had smaller canine teeth, that the true cats eventually emerged about 13 million years ago. The modern domestic cat has its origin in the African wild-cat or Kaffir cat (*F. lybica*), which later hybridised with the European wild-cat (*F. silvestris*) and possibly the Jungle cat (*F. chaus*) to give it a mixed inheritance.

The earliest record of cats comes from a site in Jericho, Palestine, dating back to *c* 6700 BC, but the skeletons were almost certainly those of kaffir cats. Cats are also mentioned in Sanskrit, the classical language of the Hindus in India, as early as 3000 BC, but the general consensus of opinion is that the cat was first domesticated in ancient Egypt. The earliest indisputable evidence for *F. catus* in that country dates from only *c* 1900 BC, but some zoologists maintain that cats were already household pets at the beginning of the previous millennium. An Egyptian tomb painting showing one of these animals wearing a collar has been dated back to 2600 BC, but this picture—the earliest known of a cat—could just as easily have been that of a Nubian wild-cat, which is very similar in appearance.

In 1888 more than 300 000 mummified cats were found in a necropolis at Bubastis (modern name Tel Basta), one of the six major cities of Lower Egypt. One consignment of 19 tons was pulverised and shipped to England for use by farmers as a crop fertiliser.

It is difficult to trace the ancestry of individual breeds, because the wide variety of pedigree cats seen today are largely the result of careful selective breeding going back only a hundred years or so. Of the few naturally occurring breeds, however, the oldest are probably the short-haired spotted and Siamese types, both of which came originally from Egypt and closely resemble the sacred cats featured in many of the ancient statuettes and paintings. Their role before they became temple cats, and were elevated to the level of gods, was to keep down the rodent populations in the huge granaries along the banks of the Nile, but they were also used to protect gardens from venomous snakes, and even trained to retrieve wildfowl in the marshes. The Abyssinian and the Egyptian Mau (oriental spotted tabby), which is just a Siamese in disguise, also look remarkably like the cats of the Pharaohs but, unlike the spotted and Siamese varieties, they owe their appearance more to contemporary breeding methods rather than natural descendancy from ancient Egyptian lines.

Although domestic cats were probably brought to Britain by early Phoenician traders, and their remains have been discovered on several Roman sites including a skeleton found in the ruins of a villa at Lullingstone, Kent in AD 200, they were not identified as such until much later.

The earliest record of cats in Britain dates from AD 936 when Hoel Dha (Hywel the Good), a Prince of Wales, brought in laws for their protection. They were probably of the British shorthair variety.

The oldest breed found in North America is the American shorthair (domestic shorthair), the ancestors of which crossed the Atlantic with the early settlers. At least one cat is reported to have sailed with the Pilgrim Fathers on the Mayflower in 1620.

Pure-bred cats are divided into three broad groups according to body shape, colour, pattern and length of fur, and are listed under the following headings: shorthair (British and American), foreign or oriental shorthairs and longhairs. In addition, there are some other breeds which have intermediate status such as the foreign longhaired Turkish, and mention should also be made of the two hairless breeds, the Mexican hairless (now extinct) and the sphynx or Canadian hairless, which is not recognised outside of North America.

Largest

In the majority of domestic cats, the average weight of the male (tom) at maturity is 6.2 lb, 2.81 kg, compared to 5.4 lb, 2.45 kg for the adult female or queen. Neuters and spays average out somewhat heavier, their weights ranging from 7 to 11 lb, 3.17–4.98 kg.

The largest domestic breeds of cat (up to 330 types have been described so far) are the ragdoll and the Maine coon, both of the USA. In these two breeds the males have muscular, powerful bodies on substantial legs and they are extremely heavy. There is some controversy as to which of these cats is actually the largest, but the ragdoll would appear to have the edge in terms of *highest average weight* (both sexes), although the Maine coon looks more impressive thanks to its shaggy appearance.

At maturity the average male ragdoll weighs 15–20 lb, 6.8–9.07 kg with a 3 ft, 90 cm leg span, while the female tips the scales at 12–15 lb, 5.44–6.8 kg. The average male Maine coon weighs 12–18 lb, 5.44–8.16 kg and the female 8–10 lb, 3.63–4.53 kg, but males scaling from 15 lb, 6.8 kg to 20 lb, 9.07 kg are not uncommon, and there are a small number of records of neutered 'mooses' weighing between 25 lb, 11.33 kg and 30 lb, 13.6 kg (the 40 lb, 18.14 kg Maine coon must be considered a myth).

Some of the chunky longhaired Persian types have also been known to exceed 20 lb, 9.07 kg. In February 1952 a woman living in Southsea, Hampshire, reported that her 35 lb, 15.8 kg black Persian cat 'Khita' had three brothers who all weighed more than 20 lb, 9.07 kg, and the winner of the 'heaviest cat' title at the first cat show held in London's Crystal Palace in July 1871 (see page 93) was a tabby weighing 21 lb, 9.52 kg. Siamese male cats can also reach a considerable size, despite their long slim bodies and legs. In 1977 a weight of 20 lb, 9.07 kg was reported for a five-year-old neutered chocolate point named 'Sam' owned by Miss Vicky Bisby of Raytown, Missouri, USA, but the cat was already this weight before he was doctored. In October 1981 a weight of 25 lb, 11.3 kg was reported for a ten-year-old male Russian blue named 'Kasha' belonging to Miss Nettie Sohmers of Yonkers, NY, USA.

The heaviest domestic cat ever recorded is a neutered male tabby named 'Himmy' (b January 1976) owned by Mr Thomas Vyse of Redlynch, Cairns, Queensland, Australia. This feline colossus weighed 42 lb 10.9 oz, 19.4 kg on his fifth birthday, 45 lb 1.6 oz, 20.5 kg at the age of six years and 45 lb 10 oz, 20.7 kg on 23 June 1982. Other statistics include a neck circumference of 15 in, 38.1 cm, a waist of 32 in, 81.2 cm and a total length of 38 in, 96.5 cm. According to his owner Himmy is a moderate eater, and a normal meal consists of meat, kidney, hearts or fish.

Britain's heaviest domestic cat is an outsized tabby named 'Poppa' (b 1974) owned by Miss Gwladys Cooper of Newport, Gwent, South Wales, who tipped the scales at a whopping 44 lb, 19.95 kg in March 1983. He shares his mistress's home with two other cats, 'Oggie' and 'Penny', who weigh 24 lb, 10.8 kg and 14 lb, 6.35 kg respectively.

The previous title-holder was a longhaired part-Persian named 'Tiger', owned by Mrs Phyllis Dacey of Billericay, Essex. His abnormal growth started at the age of one year, and during the two-year period ending September 1979 he scaled a constant 42–43 lb, 19.05–19.5 kg (neck 12½ in, 31.75 cm; waist 33 in, 83.8 cm; total length 37 in, 94 cm). Soon afterwards, however, he began receiving treatment for a hormone imbalance and started to lose weight rapidly. When he was put to sleep as a result of kidney trouble on 27 August 1980 aged ten years he was down to 18 lb, 8.16 kg.

Weights in excess of 40 lb, 18.14 kg have also been reliably reported for two other British cats. One of them was a ginger tom named 'Dinkie'

'Gigi', the 42 lb, 19 kg tabby from Carlisle, Cumbria.

owned by Miss K Dowding of Minchinhampton, Gloucestershire, who scaled 42 lb, 19.05 kg in April 1955 when aged eight years (neck 18 in, 46 cm; waist 32 in, 81 cm; total length 40 in, 101 cm). The other feline dreadnought was a female tabby called 'Gigi' (1959–72) belonging to Miss Anne Clark of Carlisle, Cumbria. This cat generally fluctuated between 37 lb, 16.78 kg and 40 lb, 18.14 kg, but in April 1970 she recorded a peak weight of 42 lb, 19.05 kg (waist 37 in, 94 cm; total length 36 in, 91 cm).

The heaviest domestic cat ever recorded in America was a ginger and white calico tom named 'Spice' owned by Mrs Loren Caddell of Ridgefield, Connecticut. He tipped the scales at 43 lb, 19.54 kg on 26 June 1974, and later reportedly shot up to 46 lb, 20.8 kg before he was put on prescribed medication and a special diet, but this latter poundage has not been confirmed. At the time of his death on 17 January 1977 he weighed a more modest 35 lb, 15.8 kg.

Like most of the super-heavyweights already mentioned, Spice's obesity was largely due to an acute hypothyroid condition.

In May 1977 a weight of 53 lb, 24 kg was reported for a male tabby named 'Boots' owned by a woman living in Hamilton, Ontario, Canada, but photographic evidence failed to substantiate this extreme weight.

The winner of the 'Heaviest Cat' competition staged by the American newspaper *The National Enquirer* in 1982 was a neutered tabby called 'Baby', who weighed in at 41 lb 5 oz, 18.73 kg. According to the cat's owner, Mr Maefred Slawson of Constableville, NY, his outsized pet had a gargantuan appetite and was slowly eating him out of house and home.

The most famous 'fat cat' on record was a 32 lb, 14.5 kg tom called 'Tiddles' who lived in the ladies' lavatory at Paddington Station, London, for 13 years.

This celebrated moggy wandered into the loo on

Platform 1 as a tiny, frightened six-week-old kitten in 1970, and was immediately adopted by attendant Mrs June Watson, who shared her lunch-time cheese sandwich with the welcome visitor. From then onwards Tiddles lived in style. Every day he dined on chicken livers, lambs' tongues, kidneys, rabbit or steak brought in by admirers and stored in his own personal fridge. As his girth increased so too did his fame—fan mail started coming in from all over the world, including America, Europe, South Africa, Hong Kong and Australia—and there was always a bulging postbag at Christmas. Mrs Watson kept two scrapbooks with press cuttings about Tiddles for visitors to look at and, on Royal occasions such as birthdays or weddings, she used to decorate the cat's over-sized sleeping basket. All attempts by vets to put Tiddles on a diet failed miserably, and when he beat all contenders to become 'London Fat Cat Champion' in 1982 he tipped the scales at 30 lb, 13.6 kg. Sadly, the legend of Paddington Station died on 2 November 1983. He had been feeling unwell for some days, and a vet put him to sleep when he found fluid round his lungs. Shortly before his death Tiddles was visited by a Canadian film crew, and he had previously been 'interviewed' by several foreign magazines.

The average-sized male cat measures 28–29 in, 71–73 cm in total length (tail *c* 11 in, 28 cm) at maturity, and the average adult female 26 in, 66 cm (tail *c* 9.5 in, 24 cm).

The greatest total length recorded for a domestic cat is 41.5 in, 105.4 cm in the case of a 17 lb, 7.7 kg red-orange longhair called 'Clarence' (b December 1974) owned by Mrs Milinda Los of Burnaby, British Columbia, Canada. He also boasted a 13 in, 33 cm long tail.

The British record holder is a 37 lb, 16.7 kg cat named 'Thomas O'Malley' (b 1972) belonging to Mrs Hilda John of Cardiff, South Wales. He measured 41 in, 104 cm (tail 12 in, 30 cm) at the age of six years.

The longest tail on record appears to be one possessed by a male cat named 'Pinky' belonging to Mr Darren Kreit of Southgate, London. This appendage was measured at 14 in, 35.5 cm in February 1978.

'Pinky', the cat with the 14 in, 35 cm long tail.

The diminutive cat 'Pete' who was fully grown when this picture was taken.

Smallest

Because of the reproduction problems involved there is no recognised 'smallest breed of cat', although the strongest contender for this title must be the Singapura, the small muscular native street cat of Singapore. Adult males and females of this breed weigh only 6 lb, 2.7 kg and 4 lb, 1.8 kg respectively, and the smallness probably owes a lot to its deprived ancestry (these cats live in drains). Some healthy Siamese cats (female) can weigh as little as 5 lb, 2.26 kg when fully grown but, as stated earlier, some males in this group have also been weighed up to 20 lb, 9.07 kg.

In some cases of genuine feline dwarfism due to genetic or congenital failure weights of under 4 lb, 1.81 kg have been reported for some fully-grown cats.

One of the smallest recorded examples was a female shorthair called 'Kitu' owned by Miss Wanda Mitka of Laverton, Victoria, Australia. This cat was examined at the University of Melbourne School of Veterinary Science on 30 July 1979 when aged 20 months, and the following details were obtained: height at shoulder 20 cm, 7.87 in; length (tip of nose to tail base) 33.5 cm, 13.18 in; girth (below shoulder blades) 23.5 cm, 9.25 in; weight 1.18 kg, 2 lb 10 oz. Despite her diminutiveness Kitu is perfectly formed and does not suffer from bad health.

The smallest fully-grown cat on record is a male Siamese/Manx cross called 'Ebony-Eb-Honey-Cat' (b March 1980) owned by Miss Angelina Johnston of Boise, Idaho, USA. In February 1984 he weighed only 1 lb 12 oz, 792 g, although he eats as much as a 12 lb, 5.44 kg cat in the same household.

The smallest cat ever recorded in Britain was a boisterous individual named 'Pete' (b June 1973) owned by Jackie Reed of Bognor Regis, Sussex. This dwarf male weighed only 12 oz, 339 g at the age of 3 months (cf. 3½ lb, 1.58 kg for his brothers and sisters), and never exceeded 2 lb, 907 g when he was fully adult. A dwarf female owned by Mrs M Wildgoose of Gillingham, Kent, tipped the scales at 2 lb 15 oz, 1.33 kg in April 1983 when aged two years.

In another form of dwarfism—achondroplasia—the limbs do not grow at the same rate as the rest of the body but, although this condition is found in certain dog breeds, ie dachshund and the basset hound, it is rarely seen in domestic cats.

The weight of a newly-born kitten normally ranges from 70 to 135 g (2.48–4.77 oz) depending on the breed. A Burmese half-cross named 'Goliath' belonging to Mrs Christine Carter of Newquay, Cornwall, reportedly scaled only 1.5 oz, 42 g at birth in November 1980, and 8 oz, 226 g at three weeks, but further details are lacking.

Most kittens reach full body maturity when they are about one year old, but large-framed breeds like the ragdoll and the Maine coon take at least three years.

Oldest

Cats are the longest-lived of all the small domestic animals. The average life expectancy of entire well-fed males raised under household conditions, and receiving good medical attention, is 13–15 years (15–17 years for intact females) barring accidents, but the highest ranges are reached by neutered males and females which live on the average one to two years longer. Strays (not surprisingly) are much shorter-lived, and few survive more than six to eight years foraging on their own, by which time their teeth are worn down to the gums.

In 1940 Ida M Mellen carried out an investigation into the potential maximum ages of cats by sending out questionnaires to cat-owners in Canada and the USA. She collected 17 cases in which ages between 21 and 31 years were claimed, and they included nine neutered males (21–31 years), three entire males (23–26 years) and four females (21–31 years). These were owners' estimates, but at least one 31-year-old record (an intact female) was fully documented, and 33 years was reported for another individual. In 1956 Dr Alex Comfort, the British gerontologist, carried out a more scientific study and located ten cats aged more than 19 years of age. The oldest animal was an entire male which had been purchased as a weanling kitten in 1927 and was still alive in 1954 aged 27 years.

Unfortunately, without valid proof, it is virtually impossible to assess the age of a mature cat with any degree of accuracy. Unlike their canine counterparts, cats usually retain their permanent teeth well into senescence ... although there may be some discoloration and gum recession, and the fur does not normally turn grey with advancing years. The only signs of extreme ageing are reduced activity, loss of body weight, especially along the back and the hindquarters, and some impairment of hearing and vision (in old cats the lens of the eye tends to turn a milky blue); sometimes, however, none of these conditions are present, even in individuals in their venerable twenties, and in the end the great leveller for the majority of old cats appears to be kidney failure.

Information on the subject is also obscured by the fact that cats of similar size, shape and colour bear the same nickname for several generations in succession, and some owners of long-lived cats are not averse to enhancing their pet's claim by adding on a few years just for good measure!

In November 1972 the American Feline Society received news that a cat living in Hazleton, Pennsylvania, had just celebrated its 37th birthday but, when an official of the AFS made further enquiries, he discovered that the claim was based on the combined life-spans of at least three different cats!

On 2 January 1972 a man living in Dumfriesshire, Scotland, announced that his cat (unnamed) had just passed the 43-year mark, but when Mr W Ferguson, a member of the Scottish Cat Club, wrote to him for further information he received the following reply:

'In reference to the cat, I am sorry to say it was killed this morning by a train. My brother brought it from Millingonbush farm where he worked to Horsolholm in the summer of 1939. I have lived with the cat all my life. We were on the farm for 36 years. My brother who fetched the cat was killed by a train in the same place a month ago. I am the only one left, but I can assure you everything I say is true. I am 64 years old and I gave up farming and bought a house and have lived here ever since.'

The greatest reliable age recorded for a cat is 34 years 5 months for a female tabby named 'Ma' owned by Mrs Alice St George Moore of Drewsteignton, Devon. This feline Methuselah was put to sleep on 5 November 1957.

Another tabby named 'Puss' belonging to Mrs T Holway of Clayhidon, Devon, reportedly celebrated his 36th birthday on 28 November 1939 and died the following day, but this case is not so well documented and some doubts have been cast as to the authenticity of this claim.

The oldest cat of proven age, the tabby 'Ma', of Devon, England, who survived her 34th birthday.

Table 7. Largest cat litters on record

Breed	Number	Date	Owner
Burmese/Siamese ('Tara')	19 (4 stillborn)	7.8.1970	Mrs Valerie Gane Church Westcote Kingham, Oxfordshire
Unknown ('Clementine')	15 (4 died)	14.4.1976	Marc & Natalie Albanese, East Aurora, NY, USA
Siamese ('Tikatoo')	15	25.4.1976	Mr Laurie Roberts Havelock, Ontario, Canada
Unknown	14 (2 stillborn)	6.1.1947	NAAFI, RAF Elsham Wold, Lincolnshire
Calico ('Kelly')	14 (5 stillborn)	19.5.1972	Miss Kim J Bean, Seneca, Missouri, USA
Persian ('Bluebell')	14 (all survived)	16.12.1974	Mrs Elenore Dawson Wellington CP, South Africa
Siamese/Domestic Shorthair ('Anita')	13 (2 died)	1966	Miss Jenny Knoebel Sussex, Wisconsin, USA
Blue-pointed Siamese ('Daniella')	13	13.4.1969	Mrs Helen J Coward, Klenzig, S Australia
Unknown ('Spur')*	13 (11 stillborn)	30.4.1971	Mrs Grace Sutherland Walthamstow London
Sealpoint Siamese ('Chan-Lass')	13 (2 died)	23.4.1972	Mrs Harriet Browne Southsea, Hampshire
Unknown ('Percy')	13 (1 died)	19.7.1978	Miss Betty Gallaway Estevan, Saskatchewan, Canada

* Nine-month mother went blind permanently shortly after giving birth

© Gerald L Wood 1984

In September 1955 the death was reported of a cat in Los Angeles, California, USA, aged 33 years 4 months. The animal was born in Surbiton, Surrey, in 1922, but later emigrated with its owner. Another neutered male named 'Bobby' owned by Miss B Fenlon of Enniscorthy, Co Wexford, Ireland, died on 5 July 1973 aged 32 years 3 weeks, and on 28 August 1983 a shorthair silver tabby named 'Selina' owned by Mrs Margaret Chapman of Wellingborough, Northamptonshire, passed away peacefully in her sleep also aged 32 years.

The greatest reliable age recorded for a purebred cat is 29 years 7 months in the case of a blue Persian called 'Fluff', who died on 15 October 1982. He was owned by Mrs Mary Forster of Dalbeattie, Kirkcudbrightshire, Scotland. A blind Siamese bluepoint belonging to Mr Howard Littel of Redwood City, California, USA, was still alive in November 1975 aged 25 years 8 months.

The oldest twin cats on record were probably 'Ginger' and 'Sandy' (b 18 May 1956) owned by Miss Pat Hillman of Birmingham. Sandy died on 7 January 1977 aged 20 years 5 months 3 weeks, and Ginger was put to sleep on 8 September 1978 aged 21 years 3 months 3 weeks.

On 21 December 1975, a 19-year-old female tabby owned by Mrs F Arnot of St Neots, Huntingdonshire, killed a stoat after a fierce stand-up fight in the garden.

Largest litters

The average gestation period in the cat is 63–65 days, with a normal range of between 60 and 69 days depending on the breed. Kittens born before the 56th day very rarely survive, but terms up to 72 days have been recorded for Siamese or crosses with this type, and the Egyptian Mau is said to have a normal range of 63–73 days.

Litter sizes vary between 1 and 9 according to the breed and age of the mother.

The largest litter (kindle) ever recorded was

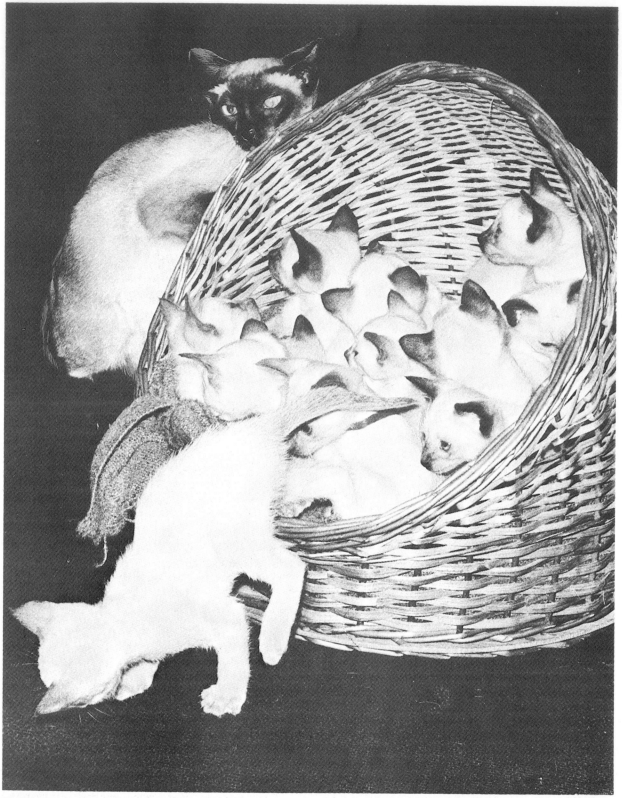

The eleven survivors of 'Chan-Lass's' litter of thirteen.

one of 19 kittens (four incompletely formed) delivered by Caesarean section to 'Tarawood Antigone', a four-year-old brown Burmese on 7 August 1970 after a 70-day gestation period. The cat's owner, Mrs Valerie Gane of Church Westcote, Kingham, Oxfordshire, said the result was a mismating with a half-Siamese in the family barn. 'All the kittens (14 boys and one girl) found good homes where they live as "larger than average" neuters', she added, 'which is not bad work for five minutes in the hay.'

On 14 April 1976, a two-year-old black cat of mixed origin named 'Clementine' owned by Marc and Natalie Albanese of East Aurora, NY, USA, produced a litter of 15 kittens, but four of them died shortly afterwards. A 26-month-old Siamese called 'Tikatoo' belonging to Mr Laurie Robert of Havelock, Ontario, Canada, was also credited with a litter of 15 the previous year (27 April 1975), but further details are lacking.

The largest recorded litter in which all the kittens survived is one of 14 born in December 1974 to a Persian cat named 'Bluebell' owned by Mrs Elenore Dawson of Wellington, Cape Province, South Africa.

Because female cats have only eight teats, exceptionally large litters present a difficult logistical problem. When Percy (see p. 79) gave birth to her litter of 13, 12 of which survived, she cleverly got round her predicament by dividing the litter in two, and placing them in opposite corners of the room used for a nursery. By thus arranging two 'sittings' for meals, she managed them quite efficiently.

The prime years for fertility in females are two to eight years (three to seven years for males), but they may continue to breed throughout their entire lives, although litter size decreases as the parents' ages advance.

On 23 June 1958 a black and white queen (entire female) called 'Tish' owned by Mrs Beatrice Briscoe of Maltby, Yorkshire, gave birth to a litter of two kittens at the incredible age of 25 years and successfully reared them. She had previously produced 99 offspring. In April 1956 a 24-year-old female called 'Tiger' belonging to Mrs Evelyn Bush of Leytonstone, London, gave birth to a single kitten, but it didn't survive. In another case of ancient motherhood, however, the kitten lived—and the mother died. The cat, a tabby named 'Mick' [sic], had been seduced by a Siamese at the ripe old age of 23 years, but the experience proved too much of a shock to her system and she died in June 1980 shortly after she had successfully weaned the kitten.

The oldest cat on record to give birth to a kitten and successfully rear it was a tortoiseshell female named 'Smutty', who produced a handsome and lively black and white kitten on 6 July 1953 at the almost unbelievable age of 28 years! The cat, who never had time to raise a family during her very long and successful rat-catching career, had only recently been retired and her owner, Mrs Eileen Martin of Chacewater, near Truro, Cornwall, had expected her pet to spend the twilight years dozing in front of the fire. Smutty, however, had different ideas . . . and after all it was spring!

At the other end of the scale, some maiden queens (eg the Siamese) are quite capable of becoming mothers as early as five months old, although medically they should not be mated at such an early age.

The birth usually lasts about two hours, but sometimes a cat will produce a litter in two instalments spread over 12–30 hours.

Most prolific

During their peak years of reproduction domestic queens usually average two to three litters a year, but some cats have been known to produce up to five litters within the space of 12 months.

The greatest number of kittens produced by a cat during her breeding life is 420 in the case of a tabby named 'Dusty' (b 1935) living in Bonham, Texas, USA. She gave birth to her last litter (a single kitten) on 12 June 1952.

The British record is held by another tabby named 'Tippy' of Kingston-upon-Hull, Humberside, who produced her 343rd kitten in June 1933 when aged 21 years.

'Minnie', the famous ship's cat of Admiral Nelson's flagship HMS *Victory*, had 98 kittens during her 12-year stay on board in Portsmouth Dockyard, and all the births were recorded in the ship's log. On 7 May 1946, while a court martial was sitting, Minnie brought her latest four kittens into the room, went out, caught a mouse and brought it back for her hungry offspring.

In 1954 a tortoiseshell female named 'Sally' was in the news in Yorkshire when she killed a fox twice as big as herself. The body of the predator was found lying on the cat's dead kittens.

Mousing and ratting

Contrary to popular belief, hungry cats do not make the best rodent exterminators. According to research carried out in West Germany a well-fed cat will notch up more 'kills' than a cat that is left hungry, and even then the best mousers (invariably females of the breeds that possess this instinct) only average 10–15 victims at one sitting before they lose interest in the hunt.

The greatest mouser on record is a tortoiseshell female called 'Towser' (b 21 April 1963), owned by Glenturret Distillery Ltd, near Crieff,

Tayside, Scotland. She averages three mice per day, and in April 1984 she accounted for her 23 000th victim. According to her 'boss', sales manager Mr Peter Fairlie, Towser has been known to become 'tiddly' after breathing in the 130 degree proof alcoholic fumes but he believes the 'heady atmosphere' is responsible for her record-breaking achievement.

Unlike the mouse, the fully-grown rat is a formidable fighter, and a cat employed full-time as a rat-catcher rarely survives more than three years. One of the most impressive performances on record was that of a five-month-old tabby named 'Peter' living at Stonehouse railway station, Gloucestershire, who killed 400 rats during a four-week period in June–July 1938 before his life was prematurely snuffed out under the wheels of a train. Another cat named 'Susie' killed 1033 rats during the seven years she was on duty at an engineering works in Lincoln. While attacking another rat she was severely bitten and died from blood poisoning on 3 April 1919.

The greatest feline ratter of all time was a female tabby called 'Minnie' who, during the six-year period 1927–32, despatched 12 480 rats at the White City Stadium, London. In those days, of course, general standards of hygiene were much less exacting, and rodent poisons were not readily available.

Toughness

Domestic cats are extremely tough animals, and can exist for long periods without food and water.

On 1 November 1955 a cat was discovered emaciated and starving in a crate containing unassembled motor car components in Durban, Natal, South Africa. The packing-case had been sealed at the Morris Works at Cowley, Oxfordshire, on 1 August, which meant the unfortunate moggy had been trapped for three months! Sadly, the feline prisoner died the following morning despite the best medical attention, and a post-mortem revealed that the animal had survived the voyage by living on grease-smeared pieces of paper and an instruction manual!

Another cat accidentally nailed up in a crate with a diesel engine shipped from a factory in Detroit, Michigan, USA to Cairo, Egypt, was more fortunate and managed to survive a journey of 41 days by licking grease from the engine parts. What was even more astonishing, however, was the fact that she had four newly-born kittens with her when the container was opened.

On terra firma, a two-year-old tabby named 'Thumper' belonging to Mrs Reg Buckett of Westminster, London, was rescued on 29 March 1964 after spending 52 days trapped at the bottom of a lift shaft. The cat had survived on sips from a small puddle of oily water, but he never really recovered from his ordeal, and was put to sleep in August 1967 when his vision started to fade.

Cats have also displayed remarkable fortitude in other dangerous situations.

One of the most amazing stories comes from the Netherlands where a three-year-old cat named 'Peter' survived eight days *underwater* in the cabin of the MV *Tjoba* when it capsized and sank in the River Rhine near St Goar on 14 December 1964. The cat, which had managed to keep his head in an air-pocket while the rest of his body was submerged, was rescued when the vessel was raised, and made a full recovery.

Another cat which managed to get itself into a tight spot was a young individual which survived 53 hours of entombment in a concrete wall in Skopje, Yugoslavia, in July 1974. The animal, which had been adopted by the men working on a new cultural hall on the banks of the Vadar River, disappeared one day when the labourers were setting up the planks to mould a concrete wall. When the timber was removed the cat was found jammed between the bottom plank and the cement. It had managed to survive in its prison by breathing through a small crack in the wood. The impression made by the cat's body in the concrete was later preserved so that future generations could marvel at the incident.

In Minerva, Ohio, USA, a cat accidentally locked in a brick kiln one weekend still managed to stagger out alive the following Monday after enduring temperatures up to 600°F, 315°C, and there is also a record of a kitten surviving a journey from New York to London in the unpressurised cargo hold of a jetliner.

On 11 November 1982 a tomcat named 'Sedgewick' strayed into an electricity sub-station near his home in Fulbourn Old Drift, Cambridgeshire, and received a 33 000-volt shock which blacked out 40 000 homes in the area. Miraculously, the badly-singed cat was not killed, but it was five hours before he managed to drag himself the 30 yards, 27 m to the home of his master, Mr Ray Hammond, who said his pet looked like a burnt tyre. Sedgewick was rushed to a vet and, after treatment, made a full recovery—much to everybody's amazement.

Climbing

Individual cats vary a great deal in their climbing ability, and a lot depends on the speed they can build up on the horizontal plane before changing to the vertical.

One of the most incredible feline climbs on record took place on 28 February 1980 when a terrified cat was chased into a dead end with a ferocious dog snapping at her rear. The only way out was up, and the cat certainly rose to the occasion. As tenants looked on in amazement she raced 70 ft, 21.3 m up the sheer wall of a block of flats at Laisterdyke, Bradford, Yorkshire, and took refuge in a gap just below the roof. The cat, who was later rescued by an RSPCA officer and subsequently nicknamed 'Bonnington' after the famous British mountaineer, owed her nine lives to the fact that the building had been pebble-dashed, thus giving her a gripping surface of sorts.

On 7 December 1983 a ginger tom climbed to the top of a 150 ft, 45 m chimney stack at the Wolfenden mill in Bolton, Greater Manchester, and clung terrified to the lip for nearly 30 hours before it was rescued. The cat had scrambled up a ladder while repair work was being carried out on the chimney.

The finest tree-climbing cat is the Norwegian Forest Cat (Norsk Skaugkatt) which, despite its name, is more or less domesticated in the country of its origin. Apart from having extremely powerful legs, this breed also has abnormally large claws, and it loves to climb high trees and then descend by spiralling down head first.

The most eccentric cat on record was a black female named 'Mincho', who ran up a 40 ft, 12 m high tree in Buenos Aires, Argentina, and never came down again! The local people used to push food up to her on a pole and a milkman delivered daily. In 1954 the cat was still going strong after spending six years aloft, and had even managed to produce three litters of kittens during her marathon tree squat!

The greatest feline climber of all time was a cat who became an enthusiastic mountaineer and succeeded in making several ascents of the Blümlisalphorn (12 038 ft, 3668 m) in the Swiss Alps. The animal first appeared at Kandersteg in August 1928 and set up home in the Blümlisalp Club hut at a height of 9000 ft, 2734 m, where the hut guardian supplied her with food. When a party of climbers was starting out for the Blümlisalphorn one morning, the cat decided to tag along, and accompanied the group the whole way to the summit! From then onwards she was 'hooked', and every time a party of climbers left the hut to ascend one of the peaks she accompanied them all the way. On one occasion a mountaineer decided his feline companion would be much better off down in the valley enjoying a milder climate, and placed her in his rucksack while he completed his ascent. When he returned to the spot later on, however, there was no sign of either the rucksack or the cat, and he gave them up for lost. Two days later another party of climbers with a Kandersteg guide was proceeding up the Blümlisalphorn when, to the astonishment of the guide, the cat was seen sitting on the saddle of the peak. The climbers tried to catch her, but she evaded all their efforts, hiding behind rocks and refusing to be made prisoner a second time. Sadly the next day there was a tremendous snowstorm, and the cat must have perished, as she was never seen again.

On 6 September 1950 a four-month-old kitten belonging to Josephine Aufdenblatten of Geneva, Switzerland, followed climbers up to the top of the 14 782 ft, 4505 m Matterhorn, where the incredulous climbing party rewarded her with a share of their meal.

Falling

There are a number of records of cats jumping out of windows or slipping off balconies at great heights, and this often fatal attraction for the wide blue yonder appears to be prevalent among cats living in tower blocks of flats (apartments).

On 7 March 1965 a tom cat named 'Pussycat' owned by Miss Anne Walker suddenly leapt through an open window when he was startled by a cloudburst, and fell 120 ft, 36.5 m from his mistress's 11th-floor flat in Maida Vale, London. He suffered a fractured right femur and internal thoracic damage, but made a full recovery. He was later made a member of the British Parachute Association Ltd for life and granted third party insurance!

This unenviable record stood until 15 July 1972 when a black and white tom called 'Fat Olive' survived a fall of 160 ft, 49 m from a penthouse apartment in Toronto, Ontario, Canada, but the force of the impact broke two of his legs. The following year (21 April) a female cat named 'Quincy' survived a 180 ft, 55 m fall after slipping from a 19th storey balcony in the same city. According to her owner, Mr Peter Thompson, who witnessed the accident, the cat plummeted into shrubs directly beneath his balcony and suffered a broken leg and slight lung bruises which necessitated a nine-day stay in a veterinary hospital. On 24 November 1973 another female named 'Frankie' belonging to Mrs Jane Kneeland of New York City, NY, USA, also lived to tell the tale when she fell 195 ft, 59 m from a 19th-floor terrace and landed in some bushes a few feet above the pavement. She sustained fractures of the pelvis and also had a moderate degree of pulmonary haemorrhage, but eventually made a full recovery.

The greatest height from which a cat has survived a fall from a high-rise block of flats is 200 ft, 61 m for a two-year-old ginger and white tom named 'Gros Minou' owned by orthopaedic surgeon Dr Eugene Trudeau of Outremont, Quebec Province, Canada. On 1 May 1973 the cat fell from the balcony of his master's 20th-floor penthouse into a flower bed, and an X-ray showed an undis-

The tough little black and white shorthair cat 'Patricia', who miraculously survived a fall of 205 ft, 62 m from St John's Bridge, Oregon, USA.

205 feet

placed fracture of the pelvis. He was treated with subcutaneous infusions for three days and started crawling after a week.

It has been calculated that a cat reaches its terminal velocity (40 miles/h, 64 km/h) when it has plunged 60 ft, 18 m. The commonest major injuries associated with violent contacts with the ground are broken jaws (the chin often acts as the fifth impact-absorber after the paws), lung damage and fractures of the limbs and pelvis, and the number of floors fallen can sometimes be estimated by the nature and severity of the injuries sustained. For instance, it takes a minimum of eight storeys to damage the hard palate or roof of the mouth, ten storeys to break a limb and 15 storeys to fracture the pelvic bone. The most life-threatening injuries are chest trauma and rupture of the bladder.

The greatest height from which a cat has survived a fall is 205 ft, 62 m in the case of a pregnant one-year-old black and white shorthair called 'Patricia'. She was thrown from St John's Bridge, Portland, Oregon, USA, by a callous passing motorist into the chilly Willamett River on 8 March 1981, and spent several minutes in the water (temperature 49°F, 9.4°C) before she was rescued by two men who were (ironically) fishing for cat-fish under the bridge. They took the badly concussed cat to Fritz and Mardi Jacob, local directors of Pet Pride of Oregon Inc., a cat advocacy group, and the following morning she aborted two of her kittens. She was rushed to a veterinary clinic where examinations and radiographs revealed shock, multiple contusions and several small tears in the abdomen due to a ruptured uterus. As soon as she was stable enough to risk surgery an abdominal exploratory was performed. All the organs were severely bruised, but there was no major damage other than the ruptured uterus, which was removed with the ovaries as well as a third dead kitten. Recovery was uneventful and, after her discharge, Patricia was adopted by the Jacobs. Since then she has made a number of personal appearances at cat shows around the country.

Speed

Although domestic cats have relatively short legs and are not really designed for speed, they can out-sprint most dogs (apart from the sighthounds) over short distances because their feet are designed for rapid acceleration; however, they cannot sustain this high level of activity for very long.

The top rate of speed is the gallop, which is essentially a series of half-bounds, and there is one authentic record of a frightened cat being timed at 27 miles/h, 43.2 km/h over a distance of 60 yards, 59 m (cf. 25 miles/h, 40 km/h for the fastest human sprinters).

In August 1936 a cat-racing track was opened in the village of Portisham, Dorset, shortly after the electric grid system reached the area. The furry competitors ran over a course of 220 yd, 201 m, chased an electric mouse, and could do half the speed of a greyhound. The scheme had been worked out by the licensee of the local hotel, and at the first two meetings nearly 500 people were present. About 50 cats owned by farmers, farm labourers and village folk were kept in training for the races, and the best runners were said to be two- or three-year-olds.

Cat-racing was also staged twice a week at a Kentish pub called 'The Old Jail' in 1949. All the cats taking part were household pets, and any without tails—whether Manx or not—were banned.

Homing

Although cats generally have a poorer sense of direction than dogs, there are at least four well-documented cases of cats travelling more than 1000 miles, 1600 km through unknown territory to reach a specific destination.

The greatest distance covered by a homing cat is an incredible 1500 miles, 2400 km by a cream-coloured male of Persian ancestry called 'Sugar'. He lived with the Woods family in Anderson, California, USA, and in 1951 they decided to retire to a farm at Gage in Oklahoma. They were forced to leave the cat with a friendly neighbour because Sugar was terrified of cars and refused to have anything to do with them. Just over 13 months later a cat similar in appearance to Sugar jumped on to the shoulder of Mrs Woods as she was doing some weeding outside her new home. At first she found it difficult to believe that the friendly 'stranger' was the old family pet, but her doubts quickly disappeared when she idly stroked the cat and found an unusual deformity on the left hip joint which had plagued Sugar for years. A quick check with their former neighbour in California revealed that the cat had disappeared three weeks after the family he loved had left the district.

This remarkable journey raised a great deal of interest in the USA, and animal behaviourist Dr J B Rhine of Duke University, Durham, North Carolina, paid a special visit to the Woods' farm so that he could observe this super-cat and take notes. He was so impressed by his findings that he arranged for the cat's body to be sent to Duke University after death for examination, but unfortunately fate stepped in first. One day Sugar left home on a routine hunting expedition and never returned, having probably fallen prey to a larger predator than himself.

This record 'walkathon' was almost matched by the 2370 km, 1481 miles travelled by a little ginger tom cat called 'Silky', although this time the journey was made *back* to the family home. In July 1977 Ken Philips and his son took the family pet with them on a caravan tour from Melbourne, Victoria, to Gin Gin, a holiday resort 300 km, 187 miles north of Brisbane, Queensland. When the two men reached their ultimate destination they let Silky out for a stretch, but he did not return and a search failed to find him. Nine months later, in March 1978, the intrepid animal turned up at the Philips' home footsore and emaciated but seemingly in reasonable health; sadly, however, the epic journey had taken its toll physically, and Silky died a week later.

According to one investigator who collected more than 200 cases of cats homing over long distances, most of the journeys were achieved at a speed of about 3 miles, 4.8 km a day, but much higher rates have been recorded by cats who couldn't wait to get back to their old haunts again after their owners had moved—and declined to sleep or hunt on the way.

The British homing record was set by a three-year-old tabby named 'McCavity' who in 1960 walked 500 miles, 800 km back to his old home at Kea, near Truro, Cornwall from Cumbernauld near Glasgow, Scotland, in just three weeks, which means he must have averaged nearly 24 miles a day. The cat was apparently so exhausted after his marathon journey that he was unable even to lap milk and died the following morning. Even more amazing was the 12-year-old tom cat who walked 700 miles, 1120 km from Johannesburg to Port Elizabeth, South Africa, in March 1963. He completed the rugged journey in only ten days, which means he must have averaged an almost unbelievable 70 miles, 112 km daily. On top of this he survived his ordeal and lived for another three years.

The slowest homing cat on record was a Siamese called 'Ching' who vanished from a caravan site at Ammanford, Dyfed, South Wales in 1967 whilst his owners were there on holiday. Three years later he turned up again at the family home in Stow-on-the-Wold, Gloucestershire, having covered the 125 mile, 200 km journey at the miserable rate of only 0.105 miles, 0.168 km a day!

That the vast majority of cats are deeply attached to their home territory and don't like changing addresses is classically illustrated by a part-Persian tom named 'B C', who made a record 78 trips back to the flat in Palmerston North, New Zealand, where his owner, Mrs Marjorie Cummerfield, lived until December 1979. The distance between the new and old addresses was only 2½ miles, 4 km, but the cat had to negotiate four very busy roads to get there, and it usually took him about three hours. On one occasion Mrs Cummerfield managed to intercept her determined pet in the middle of one of his homing trips, but he didn't allow this to happen again. A local vet thought a course of female hormones might curb his wanderlust, but he had to admit failure when B C returned to the flat three times while he was on the contraceptive pill! In view of the hazardous nature of the journey it was generally thought that B C would eventually be killed on the roads, but the old campaigner somehow managed to surmount all the odds and died of natural causes on 8 May 1983.

An even more remarkable story concerns a female cat owned by a family living in a flat in densely-populated Manhattan, New York. One year they rented a summer house 100 miles, 160 km away and took their pet along. The fresh air of the countryside agreed with the cat and, before the end of the summer, she was pregnant. Shortly before she was due to give birth she headed for the secret nest she had prepared, and on departure day there was no sign of her. The family returned home to New York with heavy hearts, but two months later the cat suddenly appeared at the window of their second-storey flat with a kitten in her mouth! Their joy, however, was short-lived. Within a matter of hours the mother cat was gone again, only to turn up two weeks later with another kitten in her mouth. This time, however, the family were better prepared. They put the cat in the car before she could take off again, and drove back to the country house to pick up the rest of the litter!

Travel

Cats have also inadvertently travelled considerable distances under the bonnets of cars, and the warmth and smell of the engine compartment appears to hold a particular fascination for them.

The greatest distance travelled by a cat under the bonnet of a car is the 300+ miles, 490+ km clocked up by an eight-year-old black female named 'Buttons'. In September 1983 she smuggled herself aboard when her owner's neighbour, Mr Fraser Robertson, set off from his home in Great Yarmouth, Norfolk, on a business trip to Aberdeen, Scotland, and was not discovered until six hours later when the electronics engineer pulled into a service station in Newcastle. When he lifted the bonnet of the car to check the oil, Mr Robertson found the cat crouching behind the battery covered in grime and looking extremely sorry for herself. 'How she survived six hours of non-stop driving I will never know', said Mr Robertson afterwards. 'The engine was incredibly hot, and what with the petrol fumes, oil smoke and the noises it must have been a terrifying experience for her.' After giving Buttons a good feed at the cafeteria attached to the service station Mr Robertson continued on his way with his new-found companion curled up on the back seat. When he reached Aberdeen and the news got around about the cat's perilous ride an airline offered to fly Buttons back to Norwich free of charge, and it was there that she was happily reunited with her owner, Mrs Maureen Smith.

The most travelled cat on record was a female Siamese called 'Princess Truman Tao-Tai', who notched up 1 500 000 sea miles, 2 400 000 km during her 16-year career. She joined the crew of the British iron-ore carrier *Sagamire* as a kitten in 1959 and was never allowed ashore because of quarantine regulations. In February 1975 the owners of the ship, Furness-Withy, sold the vessel to an Italian firm on the strict understanding that the buyers would do their best to keep the cat happy in her old age. Unhappily Princess, who had always had a penchant for turkey and chicken, could not stomach the sudden change to Italian food, and a few months after the sale she passed away.

Another cat that travelled more than 1 000 000 documented sea miles, 1 600 000 km was a female named 'Doodles', who lived aboard the White Star liner *Cedric*. When the vessel arrived in a foreign port she would go into town by herself, but she always managed to return just before the ship was due to sail. Doodles was pensioned off in December 1933, and spent her retirement in a country hotel in Bamford in the Derbyshire Peak district.

In 1950 a kitten nicknamed 'Spindle' was taken aboard a British liner in Colombo, Ceylon (now Sri Lanka) and put in a storeroom in the bowels of the ship. During the next eight years and 120 000 miles, 192 000 km of sailing between England and Australia the black tom never left his 'den', and attempts to get him on deck and into the fresh air and sunshine used to turn him into a raging fury.

During World War II a cat named Adolf owned by Ed Stelzig of Seattle, Washington, USA, logged 92 140 documented air miles, 147 424 km. Stelzig was a member of the 5th Squadron Second Combat Cargo Group of the Fifth Air Force. On 17 February 1945 he was sent to Darwin, Northern Territories, Australia, to pick up a group of officers on rest leave, and while he was waiting for his party to arrive a young black and white cat jumped on to his lap. Stelzig gave it some milk, and that was the beginning of a beautiful friendship. Adolf, named after Hitler because of his facial markings, was given a sandbox at the rear of the plane and he slept on radio equipment because it was always warm. When he was on the ground he tended to roam around quite a lot, but when the engines of Stelzig's aircraft started up he appeared as if by magic. Adolf missed only one flight during the entire Pacific campaign, and that was when he boarded the wrong plane and ended up at Hollandia instead of Biak in Dutch New Guinea. Fortunately he was well looked after by a radio operator during the week he went missing, but he never made the same mistake again. When Stelzig received his orders to return home after the war he presented Adolf to the children of a retired Japanese colonel who had fallen in love with the much-travelled cat.

The greatest feline air traveller on record was a black and white cat named 'Hamlet', who flew an astonishing 600 000 miles, 960 000 km in only 52 days!

His marathon journey began on 25 February 1984 in Toronto, Canada, as an official passenger aboard a British Airways Jumbo jet . . . but by the time the airliner had reached London he had vanished from his cage and a search by BA staff failed to find him. Nearly two months later, on 17 April, Hamlet was found thin and bedraggled behind panelling in the hold by an engineer carrying out a routine maintenance check at Heathrow Airport. 'Super Moggy' had survived by sipping condensation, and during his ordeal he had visited such diverse countries as Jamaica, Kuwait, Singapore and Australia. He was later reunited with his owner, Paul Aspland, of Rackheath, Norfolk.

On 8 February 1979 another Siamese cat with the wanderlust identified as 'Wan Ton' by a collar tag was flown back to his owners, an American naval family based at Guam in the south-west Pacific, after Pan Am staff found him in the hold of a jumbo jet at Heathrow Airport. Even more remarkable was the fact that the cat had flown the 11 200 miles, 17 920 km to London via Washington, which means he must have somehow changed planes at Washington Airport for a London flight!

Some cats are also fascinated by rail travel, and one famous character named 'Toby' chalked up several thousand miles before his untimely death. This veteran commuter lived in the refreshment room at Carlisle station, but early in life took to travelling by train. So LMS (London Midland Scottish) gave him a 'season' ticket in the shape of a label round his neck bearing the message 'If found please return to Carlisle Station'. He was always found, and always returned home safely. The station master at Carlisle originally kept an account of Toby's journeys, but when the 50 mark was passed he gave up! The black cat was a good Borderer, and although he took frequent trips to Scotland, nothing would induce him to go south of Carlisle and he always travelled on north-bound trains. On one occasion he turned up at Stranraer, but jibbed at the 40 mile, 64 km steamer crossing to Larne in Ireland. His longest journey was 245 miles, 392 km to Aberdeen and, when he came back, he had attached to his season an urgent invoice for 'halfpenny worth of milk'. He usually patronised fish trains during his travels, but occasionally took to drink and went by milk van. On 12 February 1933 Toby was changing trains at Carlisle and ignored the instruction not to cross the line except by footbridge. Unfortunately a train was just coming into the station—and it cost poor Toby his life.

Mascots

Cat mascots first appeared on the scene during the Crimean War (1854–55) when kittens were found tucked inside the great-coats of captured Russian soldiers.

During the Battle of Stalingrad (August 1942– February 1943) in the Second World War a tom cat named 'Mourka', who had attached himself to a Russian gun crew, was used to carry messages to company headquarters when the journey got too dangerous for human runners. At HQ he was rewarded with food and a friendly pat and then sent back to his comrades. It is not known if Mourka survived the war but, in view of the constant bombardment and the terrible conditions that existed in the beleaguered city, this seems highly unlikely.

The most famous cat mascot on record—and the only one to win the Dickin Medal—was a handsome neutered male named 'Simon', who made world headlines in 1949 when the frigate HMS *Amethyst* escaped down the Yangtse River under the gunfire of Communist troops. The story started in May 1948 when Simon was presented as a kitten to Lt Cdr I R Griffiths, commanding officer of the *Amethyst*, which was then stationed at Hong Kong. He was given the run of the ship and quickly proved himself to be an expert rat-catcher. Just under a year

'Simon', the famous mascot of the frigate HMS *Amethyst*, with a member of the crew.

later, when the army of Red China was sweeping victoriously across the mainland and had captured the Yangtse River area below Nanking, the frigate was sent to the city to protect British lives and property. As the ship steamed to her destination, however, she came under heavy gun-fire from batteries of the Chinese Communist Army stationed on both sides of the river. Before the smoke had cleared 54 of her crew were dead, dying or seriously wounded, and shortly afterwards the crippled *Amethyst* ran aground on a mud bank. One of the shells landed on the captain's table, killing him instantly. Simon was in the same room and suffered injuries to the head and body and a badly singed coat but, after going into hiding for a few days to lick his wounds, he reappeared and started killing off the rats which had been disturbed by the shelling and now threatened the health of the surviving crew members. Inexplicably the Communists did not sink the stricken ship, but entered into long negotiations with the British Government for its release. After three months they were still haggling, by which time life on board was becoming increasingly trying. The weather was very hot, fuel oil was now

running desperately low, and the food situation had deteriorated. Finally Lt Cdr Kerans, who had taken over command, decided to risk the 168 miles, 269 km dash down the Yangtse to the safety of the South China Seas, and set off under cover of darkness. When the frigate arrived back in Hong Kong to a tumultuous welcome two days later, the story of Simon's courage had already preceded him, and he was showered with gifts from admirers all over the world. After a refit the *Amethyst* returned to Plymouth, but sadly the sailor in the black and white furry uniform did not live to enjoy his fame. He died on 28 November 1949 three weeks after he had gone into quarantine, his health apparently undermined by his terrifying battle experience, and badly missing his old ship-mates. The Dickin Medal was presented to him posthumously on 13 April 1950 for 'meritorious and distinguished service' by the Lord Mayor of Plymouth, and the medal is now in the hands of a private collector in Ontario, Canada. Simon was buried in the People's Dispensary for Sick Animals' (PDSA) cemetery at Ilford, Essex.

A previous *Amethyst* cat, a one-eyed tom named

'Nelson', was also a bit of a character. He always jumped ship whenever he got into port, but one day in 1943 he went through his usual routine in Londonderry, Northern Ireland, and rejoined the wrong ship thanks to his 'one eye and a whelk'. As a result he found himself in Gibraltar, and it took a series of top priority cables before he was eventually tracked down and sent back to Londonderry.

The only civilian cat to be awarded a medal for bravery was a beautiful female tabby named 'Faith', who took up residence in the rectory of St Augustine's Church, in the shadow of St Paul's Cathedral, London, shortly before the outbreak of the Second World War. Soon after hostilities broke out there came the nightly bombing raids, and fires raged all around St Paul's. But more important to Faith was the arrival of a small black and white kitten who was christened Panda. One day the rector saw that the cat was worried as she wandered restlessly from room to room—but finally she made up her mind. Taking Panda from his basket on the top floor she carried him down three flights of stairs to the basement and placed him in a recess where piles of music were stored. Three days later, on 9 September 1940, the building received a direct hit from a German bomb. Within minutes it was a blazing inferno but, as masonry and timber crashed down around her and the flames crept nearer and nearer, the brave little mother remained steadfast and calm in the recess shielding her kitten between her front paws. The following morning the rector searched through the smouldering rubble, hopefully calling the cats' names and, when he reached the spot where the recess had been, he heard a faint mewing. He cleared the debris and there, still in the recess, dusty but unhurt, were the two cats. Faith could not be awarded the Dickin Medal because she was not a member of HM Forces or a Civil Defence unit, but a special silver medal was struck and presented to her later in October 1945 by the Director of the PDSA, along with a certificate acknowledging her 'steadfast courage in the Battle of London'. The certificate now hangs in the church alongside a picture of the cat.

The only cat known to have survived three major shipwrecks was a one-year-old male tabby named 'Oscar', who started his adventures on the high seas aboard the mighty battleship *Bismarck*. When the pride of the German navy was sunk 660 miles, 1100 km west of Brest, France, on 27 May 1941 the bedraggled cat was picked up by the British destroyer HMS *Cossack*, but his stay aboard the 'enemy' ship was also short-lived. On 10 November the same year the destroyer was torpedoed in the Atlantic and sent to the bottom. This time Oscar was rescued and transferred to the HMS *Ark Royal*, but three days later he found himself in the water

The brave church cat 'Faith' who guarded her little kitten throughout a terrible night of bombing and fire.

again when the aircraft carrier was torpedoed by a German submarine in the Mediterranean. Luckily he was sighted on a floating plank three hours after the tragedy occurred and was taken by destroyer to Gibraltar. Two weeks later, with only six lives left, he was shipped to a sailors' rest home in Northern Ireland, where the peaceful surroundings were more to his liking.

Another sea-going cat named 'Maizie' serving aboard a US Navy vessel in the Pacific during the Second World War was also torpedoed and spent 45 hours on a life raft keeping up the morale of six shipwrecked sailors. She ate malted milk tablets and went from one man to another, sitting on their laps and comforting them. 'If Maizie hadn't been with us we might have gone nuts', said one of the sailors when they were rescued.

Richest

Cats, like dogs, are sometimes left large sums of money or valuable property in the wills of their owners.

The richest cat on record is a white alley cat named 'Charlie Chan' (b 1970), formerly owned by

Mrs Grace Alma Patterson of Joplin, Missouri, USA, who left her entire estate worth $250 000 (then £131 000) to her 18 lb, 8.16 kg pet when she died in January 1978. When the cat dies the estate, which includes a three-bedroom house, a 7-acre, 2.9 ha pet cemetery and a collection of valuable antiques, will be auctioned off and the proceeds donated to local and national humane societies. Charlie's personal guardian is a woman school-teacher who is allowed to stay rent-free in his house as long as he lives. 'I couldn't ask for a better landlord . . . Charlie is just wonderful company and he is absolutely no trouble', she enthused. 'He has quite simple pleasures and never seems to want anything else but his toys, his armchair and his basket.' And what does the world's richest cat enjoy eating the most? Chicken livers!

When Dr William Grier of San Diego, California, USA, died in June 1963 he left his entire estate of $415 000 (then £148 000) to his two 15-year-old cats 'Hellcat' and 'Brownie'. When the cats died two years later the money went to the George Washington University in Washington, DC.

A Los Angeles cat who inherited $7000 (then £3685) in its owner's will published in 1977 was later ordered to pay $608, £320 tax on the windfall! The cat, who was left the money so that its gourmet-style diet could be continued, was believed to be the first animal in the USA ever to get a tax demand.

Britain's richest cat—until he fell on lean times—was a former stray named 'Blackie', who inherited £20 000 in the will of his owner, Mrs Ivy Black-hurst, in 1975. She also decreed that (1) her pet should stay on at her detached house in Sheffield; (2) that his bills should be paid from the interest on her estate; (3) that he was only to receive his favourite foods—fresh salmon, liver, cod and rabbit and (4) he should have a housekeeper to pander to his every need. Maintaining a detached residence with the employment of a housekeeper, and also eating six (!) square meals a day, eventually proved too much for the purse strings, and in 1978 the trustees of Mrs Blackhurst's estate reluctantly decided that Blackie was living beyond his means. In a drastic effort to cut down on expenses the house was sold and the money invested to provide for the cat's old age (he was born in 1961). When Blackie dies the capital will go to the RSPCA; in the meantime, he is being cared for by the owner of local kennels where the menu is not quite so grand.

Britain's richest cats are now five ordinary moggies named 'Sukie', 'Tessa', 'Pippa', 'Ginger' and 'Jemma', who between them are worth £65 000. They were left the money by their owner, Mr Harry Stivelman of Tottenham Hale, north London, who died on 25 December 1982. The cats are now being looked after at kennels in Waltham Abbey, Essex.

In 1967 Miss Elspeth Sellar of Grafham, Surrey, turned down an offer of 2000 guineas (£2100) from an American breeder for her Grand Champion copper-eyed white Persian tom 'Coylum Marcus', who died on 14 April 1978, aged 13 years.

Earlier, in February 1965, a three-year-old fawn and cream Persian named 'Ming Ling' temporarily eclipsed this price when she swallowed her mistress's diamond and ruby engagement ring valued at £3200. Sensibly the lady refused to allow her pet to be operated on for retrieval of the ring, but merely waited for nature to take its course!

In January 1984 Mrs Josie Farmer of Torquay, Devon, put her white chinchilla cat 'Kasper' up for sale at £39 950—and threw in a three-bedroomed Georgian-style house for nothing! She and her husband Chris were moving to Cheshire, but the cat loved the sea air and the two queens next door so much that they decided it would be cruel to take him with them.

Swimming

Although domestic cats are good swimmers, they lack the dog's oily coat and usually dislike getting wet. Two notable exceptions are the Turkish Van and the Manx, both of which actually enjoy being in the water provided it is not too cold.

Another cat which didn't seem to mind getting a regular soaking was a massive black and white Persian named 'Fluffy', who was renowned throughout the Scilly Isles in the 1950s for his fishing prowess. Every night he used to stand in the shallow water waiting to pounce. When the fish came inshore he hooked them out with his claws and then carried them home to his owners in St Mary's, the main island. One evening he brought back a total of seven fish, some of them over a foot long. On another occasion when his master was sick he brought back a large plaice—still jumping! As a kitten, Fluffy used to swim from the shore to boats which were sometimes anchored more than 300 yards, 275 m away.

Oddities

Cats have a number of unique features and genetic oddities.

The most unusual breed of cat is the sphynx or Canadian hairless. This mutation, the feline equivalent of the Xoloitzcuintli (Mexican hairless dog), dates back to 1966 when a hairless male kitten was found in a normal litter produced by a black and white domestic shorthair in Ontario, Canada. Since then a breeding programme has been set up to maintain this bizarre strain, but it is still not recognised outside of North America. The sphynx is the only breed of cat that sweats, and it has to be sponged periodically to remove the dander on the skin. The Aztecs also had hairless cats (now extinct), and some were recorded in Mexico at the end of the 19th century. In 1902 a Mr Shinick living in New Mexico reportedly owned the last two surviving examples, a brother and sister, which he had bought from some local Indians.

Another very peculiar breed is the controversial ragdoll (see page 74), which looks like a longhaired Siamese. It was developed in the USA in the early 1960s from Angora, Birman and Burmese foundation stock, and was first recognised as a pure breed in 1965. This extremely gentle and docile cat has been described as 'the closest one can get to a real life baby and have an animal' and, when it is picked up and carried, it will immediately go limp and floppy and hang over the person's arm like a ragdoll or bean bag. It also has an exceptionally high tolerance of pain and cannot comprehend danger, which means it will lie down in a busy road and go to sleep if there is no human supervision. This passive and dependent nature is the antithesis of what a cat should be, which would explain why so many people in North America found this animal so fascinating.

Also worthy of mention is the Maine coon (see page 74) if only because its fur looks like a raccoon's coat. At one time many people firmly believed that this animal was a hybrid of the domestic cat and the common raccoon (*Procyon lotor*), and it wasn't so long ago that a popular pet column in an American newspaper carried a cry for help from a woman who had tried to arrange a mating between two of these unsuspecting creatures without success! All she got

The 'cabbit' exhibited in Los Angeles, California, USA, in July 1977.

was one heck of a scrap and a lot of flying fur, because members of different families cannot interbreed. The Maine coon is a hybrid, but the original crossings were probably between American shorthair cats and Angoras or other longhaired breeds brought back to Maine and New England by sailors from Asia Minor.

Other folk are also convinced that there is such a creature as a cabbit (a cross between a cat and a rabbit), but what they really mean is that they have just seen a tail-less Manx-type cat for the first time and also noted that it has long back legs and a rabbit-like hopping gait. One man who claimed he saw a cabbit in Texas but wasn't fast enough to catch it made headlines in a national newspaper in 1917. In January 1977 Val Chapman of New Mexico found a cabbit near his trading post and later exhibited it in Los Angeles.

In August 1975 Mrs Rosemary Morley of Brighton, Sussex, purchased a male Manx from a leading breeder in the Isle of Man, and it was flown to England at the age of 14 weeks. When the patterned orange kitten arrived, its new owner was startled to find that it looked nothing like a Manx—apart from the missing tail. Not only was the general shape of the body all wrong, but the face was pointed instead of round and its claws were as large as those found in an adult specimen. Mrs Morley immediately got in touch with the breeder, who assured her that the sire and dam of this peculiar-looking animal were normal domestic Manx cats born in the Isle of Man, so she called her new acquisition 'Thumper' and left it at that. But Mother Nature still had a few surprises left up her sleeve. As the strangely aloof cat matured, it developed huge whiskers, double canines that were chisel-ended and enormously long claws and, before long, he had adopted the life style of a wild cat. He ate everything he killed while out hunting, and was particularly partial to a snake snack or lizard as second choice, all of which he despatched with a whiplash action: he also inherited a banshee scream which didn't exactly endear him to any neighbours of a nervous disposition! The only thing that seemed to bother Thumper was hot weather, and to get cool quickly he would lie in the fridge with the door open! Veterinary surgeons thought he was either a British feral cat or extremely neurotic but, in June 1978, he was examined by David Taylor the famous 'zoo vet' who identified the 36 in, 91 cm long cat as a rare genetic regression to the African wild-cat (*Felis lybica*) (see page 73). One of the tell-tale signs was the sacred scarab beetle mark on the cat's forehead which distinguishes *F. lybica* from all other wild cats.

In the summer of 1980 Thumper was taken seriously ill after eating poison. He realised instinc-

tively that he risked dehydration by not eating because he normally obtained all his fluids from his kills and assorted vegetation—so he allowed his mistress to drop feed him for as long as he chose to stay in his 'den', which was on top of a 4 ft 6 in, 1.37 m stack of boxes in the attic. Unhappily, however, the poison had already caused irreparable brain damage, and the 'stranger in our midst' died on 4 December 1980.

According to Mrs Morley, the 12 lb, 5.44 kg cat was not dependent on her for anything while he was healthy. He had no need of her companionship and spent most of his life hidden in long grass, shrubs or woodland.

During a visit to China in May 1978 Dr Clayton F Freiheit, an American zoologist, saw four white Persian cats exhibited in a cage at Nanking Zoo which were described as 'exotic animals'.

The most fanatical collector of cats on record was purportedly a 72-year-old man living in Austin, Texas, USA, who had over 1100 examples on his farm in 1982. At one time he was said to have owned 1400!

Shows

The world's first cat show was staged at the Crystal Palace, London, on 13 July 1871. There were 170 entries and 25 classes, and the cats were grouped according to colour. The judges were the well-known naturalist Harrison Weir (who organised the show), his brother Jenner Weir and the Rev. Cumming Macdona, and the meeting was so successful that it became an annual event. The National Cat Club was founded in 1887, followed by The Cat Club in 1898, and the two combined to form The Governing Council of the Cat Fancy—roughly equivalent to The Kennel Club—in 1910.

The first official cat show staged in the USA was held in Madison Square Garden, New York, in 1895 and the first Governing Body, the American Cat Association, was founded in 1901. Today the largest of the eight Governing Bodies in the USA is The Cat Fanciers Association (CFA)

To become a Champion in Britain, a cat must win three Challenge Certificates at three different shows under three separate judges. In North America the requirement is four Winners Ribbons awarded at four different shows under at least three separate judges. To become a Grand Champion, or in the case of neuters a Grand Premier, a cat must win three Grand Challenge Certificates competing against other Champions, while an International Champion (a cat that has won a Champion Certificate in more than one country) can progress to International Grand Champion by a similar route.

The oldest cat to win a top award was probably the Manx Grand Champion 'Wila-Blite Pola of Sylva-Wyte' who, at the remarkable age of 13 years, won a Best in Show in the USA.

Medical

The cat is subject to a wide variety of medical curiosities and anomalies.

In 1899 the *Strand Magazine* carried a report about a 'winged cat' belonging to a woman living in Wiveliscombe, Somerset. The animal was normal in every way, except for two fur-covered growths sprouting out of its back, which flapped about like the wings of a scurrying chicken whenever the cat moved.

Another cat with wings was captured in the garden of a private house in Oxford in 1933 and taken to the city's zoo for exhibition purposes, and six years later a black and white example from Attercliffe, Sheffield, was sold by its owner, Mrs M Roebuck, to a museum in Blackpool exhibiting freaks.

Several cases have also been recorded in North America, including one cat caught near Pinesville, West Virginia, USA, in May 1959 which allegedly shed its wings two months later!

The largest 'wing-span' recorded for one of these cats is 23 in, 58.4 cm in the case of an individual shot and killed in northern Sweden in June 1949. The man shot the 20 lb, 9.07 kg creature after it had 'swooped' down on a child, and later gave the body to the local museum.

These appendages are deformities of the skin which just happen to take the shape of wings. The afflicted cat has no control over them, and they certainly cannot be used for flight as some people have claimed.

Cats normally have five toes on each of their front feet and four on the back, making a grand total of 18, but extra toes (polydactylism) are quite common thanks to an hereditary trait carried by a dominant gene. Usually only the front feet are affected, but sometimes the cat's hind feet have extra toes as well.

A pure-bred Siamese named 'Big Foot' (b June 1978) owned by Miss Joan Conerly of Wauchula, Florida, USA, has 26 toes (7×7×6×6), while his mother has 22 toes, a sister 22 and a brother 24.

The greatest number of toes found on a cat is

The magnificent 'Thumper'—one of Mother Nature's little surprises!

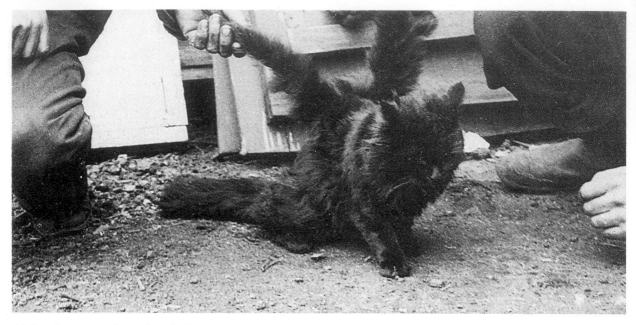

A 'winged' cat—one of nature's curiosities.

32 (8×8×8×8) reported in October 1974 for a tom named 'Mickey Mouse' owned by Mrs Renee Delgade of Westlake Village, California, USA.

A female cat named 'Triple' (b 5 March 1976) belonging to Mr and Mrs Bertram Bobnock of Iron River, Michigan, USA, has 30 toes, but these are backed up by five legs and six paws! The back left leg has two complete extensions from the knee down, and one of these has two paws.

In December 1978 a cat with four ears was reported in Chattanooga, Tennessee, USA, and there are several records of cats with double tails!

Kittens often swallow needles by accident when playing with bits of wool or cotton but, apart from that, very few foreign bodies are found in cats. One of the more bizarre cases involved a female cat who developed an enlarged abdomen and was taken to the vet for examination by her worried owner. When a stomach tube was inserted the feline patient expelled the remains of several hundred grasshoppers!

Another curious phenomenon in the cat is the development of hair balls in the stomach. This infrequent condition occurs mainly among long-haired varieties, because they swallow more hair during their routine grooming operations. The hair becomes matted in the stomach and is usually regurgitated every few weeks in the form of cylindrical rolls, but sometimes the hair ball starts to move from the stomach into the intestine and cannot be voided. When this happens the cat stops eating, and major surgery may be necessary to remove the offending material.

The largest hair ball on record was one removed from a 14-year-old female cat named 'Bushie' by veterinary surgeon W Richards in Brighton, Sussex, on 2 January 1975. The lump of matted fur measured 3.5 in, 89 mm in length, 2 in, 50.8 mm in width and had a thickness of 1.125 in, 28.4 mm. It weighed 2 oz, 56.6 g. According to Bushie's owner, Mrs Rosemary Morley (see page 91), her pet made a full recovery after a year of intensive care, although on three separate occasions after the operation vets described her condition as 'critical and hopeless'.

HORSES, PONIES AND DONKEYS

The evolution of the horse, *Equus caballus*, can be traced back to the fox-sized *Hyracotherium (Eohippus)*, which browsed in the forests of what is now North America about 60 million years ago. It had toes and padded feet, and its neck, head and limbs were proportionally much shorter than their equivalents in modern horses. These 'dawn horses', as they are popularly known, died out 15 million years later after failing to adapt to environmental and climatic changes, and were succeeded in the main evolutionary line of horses by the somewhat bigger genera *Orophippus, Epihippus* and then *Meohippus*, all of which had more efficient teeth than their predecessor—although they were still browsers. During the Miocene period (27–7 million years BP) a new phase in horse evolution occurred with the appearance of the plains-grazing *Merychippus* and other types which had teeth designed for grinding and long wear. Five million years later *Pliohippus*, the first single-toed member of the family, emerged. Its direct descendants, which by then were the size of small ponies, migrated from the Americas to the Old World via the Bering bridge about one million years ago, and the final development of the horse took place in Eurasia about 800 000 years later, ie 180 000 BP. From the horses that survived the last glacial period *c* 10 000 BC four basic types evolved. These were the Forest Horse, the Steppe Horse, the Plateau Horse and the Tundra Horse, and all modern breeds and varieties can be traced back to these animals of prehistory.

The first domestication of the horse reportedly occurred in the Ukraine, USSR, in 4350 BC when paleolithic hunters tamed some for their flesh and milk (the horse was not ridden until c 1600 BC). Recently, however, Paul Bahn, a research fellow at the University of London, examined a number of damaged equine teeth which had been excavated from a 12 000-year-old prehistoric site in southern France in 1911 and they showed definite signs of crib-biting. This vice of biting the edge of a manger or any other firm object is caused by lack of exercise and boredom, and Bahn concluded from his findings that Stone Age man had domesticated these animals at least as early as 10 000 BC.

The oldest breed of horse in the world is the spotted Appaloosa, which has six basic patterns. It originated in China and is believed to be at least 3000 years old. (Spotted horses have existed in Asia and Europe for nearly 20 000 years.)

The Arabian horse has been credited with an ancestry dating back nearly 5000 years by enthusiasts of this handsome breed but, as the Arabs did not start breeding horses until AD 50–100, this claim can be discounted.

The oldest of the four native British breeds of horse is the Suffolk Punch, which dates back to 1506.

Largest

The largest horses in the world (114 recognised strains) are found in the 'cold-blooded' heavy draught group, and the most outstanding breeds in terms of average size and weight at maturity (six

---

Table 8. The heaviest and tallest horses on record (In descending order of size down to 2800 lb, 1270 kg or 20 hands)

HEAVIEST

Name	Breed	Weight	Dates	Owner
Brooklyn Supreme	Belgian (S)	3200 lb 1451 kg	1928–48	G C Good & Sons, Ogden, Iowa, USA
Colossus	Belgian (G)	3151 lb 1429 kg	c 1947	Jack Shelly, Butte, Montana, USA
Lubber	Percheron/Belgian (G)	3120 lb 1415 kg	1929– fl.1934	A E Ponton & Sons, Winsor, Nebraska, USA
Nebraska Queen[a]	Shire (M)	3100 lb 1406 kg	c 1930	Nebraska, USA
Wilma du Bos	Belgian (M)	3086 lb[b] 1400 kg	1966– fl.1983	Mrs Virgie Arden, Reno, Nevada, USA
Hiram	Belgian (G)	3065 lb 1390 kg	c 1906	Unknown, Danbury, Connecticut, USA
Thunderation	Percheron (S)	3000 lb[c] 1360 kg	c 1926	Unknown. Chicago, Illinois, USA
Texas	Belgian (G)	3000 lb[c] 1360 kg	c 1974	Unknown. Richardson, Texas, USA
Dr Le Gear	Percheron (G)	2995 lb 1358 kg	1902–19	Dr L D Le Gear, St Louis, Missouri, USA
Firpon[d]	Shire/Anglo Norman (G)	2976 lb 1350 kg	1959–72	Julio Falabella, Recco de Roca, Argentina
Honest Tom	Shire (S)	2910 lb 1320 kg	1884– fl.1891	James Forshaw, Littleport, Cambs, England
Morocco	Shire (G)	2835 lb 1286 kg	c 1908	Charles L Gamets, Allentown, Pennsylvania, USA
Pat	Suffolk (S)	2810 lb 1274 kg	1925–40	R J Connors, Phelps, NY, USA
Sandycroft Tom	Shire (S)	2800 lb 1270 kg	c 1892	T J Dutton, Cheshire, England
Goliath	Unknown (G)	2800 lb 1270 kg	c 1955	Robert E Jones, Pleasantville, New Jersey, USA
Laddie	Clydesdale (G)	2800 lb 1270 kg	1963– fl.1973	Bill Rieske, Salt Lake City, Utah, USA

years) are the Shire, the Belgian, the Percheron, the Clydesdale and the Suffolk Punch.

The largest of the heavy modern horse breeds both in height and weight—but not bulk—is the Shire, which is also the largest pure-bred horse in the world. Stallions stand 17–17.2 hands high—a hand is equivalent to 4 in or 10.16 cm—and usually weigh between 18 and 21½ cwt, 914–1091 kg (girth 7–8 ft, 2.13–2.43 m), compared to 16–16.2 hh and 17–19 cwt, 863–965 kg for mares and 16.2 hh upwards and 17–22 cwt, 863–1117 kg for geldings.

The heaviest recorded Shire on which there is definite information was 'Honest Tom 5123' (foaled 1884), owned by James Forshaw of Littleport, Cambridgeshire. This horse scaled 1 ton 6 cwt, 1313 kg in 1891, and his son 'Sandycroft Tom 14850' bred by T J Dutton in Cheshire in 1892,

was only 1 cwt, 51 kg lighter. Both stallions stood 17.2 hh, and may have been the heaviest 'normal' horses ever bred. Another possible contender was 'Blaisdon Conqueror 15989', bred by Peter Stubs at Blaisdon, Gloucestershire, on the eastern edge of the Forest of Dean, in 1894. According to one writer of the day he was 'the biggest horse in the world', and was described as such when he made a successful tour of the USA but, although he stood 17.2 hh and one of his shoes measured an incredible 14 in, 35.5 cm across the widest part (see page 99), no information is available regarding his weight. He died at Blaisdon on 22 October 1904, and his skull and limb-bones are now preserved in the British Museum (Natural History).

'Great Britain 978', bred at Bedwell Bay, Cambridgeshire, by Henry Bultitaft in 1876, was

TALLEST

Name	Breed	Height in hands	Dates	Owner
Mammoth	Shire (G)	21.2½	c 1850	Thomas Cleaver, Toddington Mills, Bedfordshire, England
Morocco	Shire (G)	21.2	c 1908	Charles L Gamets, Allentown, Pennsylvania, USA
Firpon	Shire/Anglo Norman (G)	21.1	1959–72	Julio Falabella, Recco de Roca, Argentina
Dr Le Gear	Percheron (G)	21	1902–19	Dr L D Le Gear, St Louis, Missouri, USA
Hiram	Belgian (G)	21	c 1906	Unknown, Danbury, Connecticut, USA
Pat	Suffolk (G)	21	1925–40	R J Connors, Phelps, NY, USA
Unknown	Clydesdale (G)	20.3	1884– fl.1889	Unknown, USA
Lubber	Percheron/Belgian (G)	20	1929– fl.1934	A E Ponton & Sons, Winsor, Nebraska, USA
Goliath	Unknown (G)	20	c 1955	Robert E Jones, Pleasantville, New Jersey, USA
Texas	Belgian (G)	20	c 1974	Unknown. Richardson, Texas, USA
Laddie	Clydesdale (G)	20	1963– fl.1973	Bill Rieske, Salt Lake City, Utah, USA
Sir John[e]	Clydesdale (G)	20	1950–57	Anheuser-Busch Brewery, St Louis, Missouri, USA

S = Stallion   G = Gelding   M = Mare

a Photographic evidence proves Nebraska Queen and Lubber were not one and the same horse
b Credited with weight of just over 3200 lb, 1451 kg shortly before she was shipped to the USA
c Unconfirmed
d Also called Goliath
e Earlier credited with a height of 21.1 hands

© Gerald L Wood 1984

another exceptionally heavy stallion about whose weight there is no definite information. He lumbered across the fens for 12 years and served many mares before he was sold to Phineas T Barnum, the great American showman, who only went in for the biggest and best!

'Baly', a great roan Shire owned by the brewers Barclay, Perkins and Co in the 1860–70s, reportedly stood 18 hh and tipped the scales at 30 cwt, 1524 kg, but this extreme weight has never been confirmed and the figure may have been a misprint for 20 cwt, 1016 kg. This horse was greatly admired by Giuseppe Garibaldi, the Italian revolutionary, during a visit to London in 1864, and was renamed Garibaldi in his honour.

The heaviest Shire mare on record was the famous 17.1½ hh 'Erfyl Lady Grey', London Show Champion 1924–26, who scaled 22½ cwt, 1143 kg (girth 9 ft, 2.74 m) at the time of her third win. She was bred by William Vaughan of Hafod, Llanerfyl, Montgomeryshire, north Wales in 1915. When Vaughan died in 1919 the grey mare was sold to John Anwyl of Preston Brockhurst, Shrewsbury, Shropshire, for £300 and four years later she came into the hands of George Foster of Anstey Hall,

The famous Shire mare 'Erfyl Lady Grey', London Show Champion 1924–26.

The enormous Belgian stallion 'Brooklyn Supreme' who attained a peak weight of 3200 lb, 1451 kg in 1936.

Trumpington, Cambridgeshire. This outstanding mare, considered by many Shire connoisseurs to have been 'the best ever seen', made her last appearance at the London Show in February 1929 when she was placed second in her class but later disqualified on a technicality. The date of her death is not known.

The tallest documented Shire on record—the height is measured in a straight line from the highest point of the withers (shoulders) to the ground—was a gelding named 'Sampson' (later re-named 'Mammoth'), bred by Thomas Cleaver of Toddington Mills, Bedfordshire. This equine colossus measured 21.2½ hh in 1850 when he was four years old, and was said to have weighed nearly 30 cwt, 1524 kg when he was later exported to the USA for exhibition purposes.

Another freakishly tall Shire gelding named 'Morocco' living in Allentown, Pennsylvania, USA, was credited with a height of 21.2 hands and a weight of 2835 lb, 1285 kg in 1908, and a published photograph showing this horse with his owner, Charles H Gamets, certainly confirms this extraordinary height.

The tallest Shire horse bred in Britain in recent years was the stallion 'Ryton Regent' (1971–83), owned by Mr Robert Brickell of Witney, Oxfordshire. He stood 19.2 hh and weighed 21 cwt, 1067 kg. Another stallion named 'Ladbroke Invader' (foaled 17 April 1968) stood 19.1½ hh and weighed 22 cwt, 1118 kg.

The short-coupled Belgian Heavy Draught is the bulkiest and most massively-framed of the heavy horse breeds. There are three recognised types, and the largest is the Brabant, which derives its name from the low-lying area from which it originates. Both stallions and mares alike usually stand 16.2–17 hh and weigh between 17 cwt and 20 cwt, 863–1016 kg at maturity, but these descendants of the old Flemish horse sometimes attain greater weights than those recorded in other draught breeds, thanks to the support of their tree-trunk legs.

The heaviest horse ever recorded was the 19.2 hh red-roan Brabant stallion 'Brooklyn Supreme', who attained a peak weight of 3200 lb, 1451 kg in 1937. This gentle giant, foaled on the farm of Earle Brown of Minneapolis, Minnesota, USA, on 12 April 1928 (another source gives the date as 6 June 1930) and later sold to C G Good & Son of Ogden, Iowa, was a Grand Champion of his breed in many States before he became oversized, and Brown said he was so strong that he was afraid to team him up with other draught horses on his farm in case he worked them to death! Each of Brooklyn Supreme's enormous 7½ lb, 3.4 kg shoes measured 14 in, 35.5 cm across and required 30 in,

76.2 cm of iron. A replica is currently on display in the Guinness World of Records Museum, London. He also boasted a record girth of 10 ft 2 in, 3.09 m and a collar size of 40 in, 101.6 cm, which is equivalent to a neck circumference of 80 in, 203.2 cm. This veritable earth-shaker died in 1948.

'Wilma du Bos' (foaled 15 July 1966), an 18.2 hh Brabant mare rescued from a Belgian slaughterhouse by wealthy horse-lover Mrs Virgie Arden of Reno, Nevada, USA, reportedly weighed just over 3200 lb, 1451 kg when she was shipped from Antwerp in December 1972, but when the red-roan mare arrived in New York just before Christmas she tipped the scales at 3086 lb, 1399 kg. Both these figures, however, are misleading inasmuch as Wilma was in an advanced state of pregnancy at the time and had a girth measurement of 12 ft, 3.65 m! After the birth of her foal 'Little Willy' Wilma's

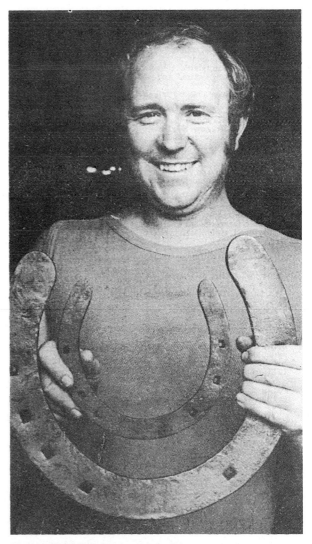

Blacksmith Melvyn Baker posing with an exact replica of a horseshoe made for 'Brooklyn Supreme'.

weight returned to her normal 2400 lb, 1088 kg.

Two other Brabants have also exceeded 3000 lb, 1360 kg. One of them was an unnamed gelding acquired from a German circus by an agent for the Ringling Bros Circus and shipped back to the USA in 1946. When the giant horse disembarked it was sent to the circus's ranch at White Sulphur Springs, Montana, for a period of recuperation, but a new foreman had just taken over and he accidentally sent the animal to a packing combine in Butte, Montana, to be slaughtered for horsemeat. Fortunately Jack Shelley, a citizen of Butte, heard about the outsized horse (height not recorded) and purchased it for 200 dollars (then £50) just before it was due to be killed. The following year he exhibited this colossus at the Salt Lake Centennial State Fair, Utah, where it recorded a weight of 3151 lb, 1430 kg (height to tips of ears 9 ft 3 in, 2.82 m), but further details are lacking. The other Brabant was a gelding called 'Hiram', owned by a man living in Danbury, Connecticut, USA. He weighed 3065 lb, 1390 kg (height 21 hands) in *c* 1906.

The largest horse living today is a Brabant gelding called 'Big Sid' (foaled April 1974), who was officially measured at the home of his owner, Murray Grove, in Stouffville, Ontario, Canada, on 18 January 1983. He stands 19.2½ hh and weighs 2700 lb, 1224 kg. This size was closely matched by another Brabant gelding named 'Big John' (foaled 1963) belonging to Richard Randall of Wyckoff, New Jersey, USA. At the age of ten years this horse stood 19.2 hh and weighed 2640 lb, 1197 kg. Other statistics included a collar size of 34 in, 86 cm and a height from the ground to the tips of the ears of 8 ft 6 in, 2.59 m.

Although the Percheron is shorter in the leg than both the Shire and the Belgian, it possesses tremendous depth of body and has massive quarters. Stallions bred in this country stand upwards of 16.3 hands at maturity (weight 18–20 cwt, 914–1016 kg), and mares upwards of 16.1 hands (16–18 cwt, 813–914 kg). The Percherons of France are not quite so tall at the withers, but they carry more bulk than their British counterparts and average out heavier.

The heaviest British Percheron on record was the champion stallion 'Saltmarsh Silver Crest' (1955–78), who scaled 1 ton 4¾ cwt, 1257 kg in 1967. His 17.2½ hh champion grandson 'Pinchbeck Union Crest' (foaled 27 January 1964), also owned by George E Sneath of Pinchbeck, Lincolnshire; weighed 23½ cwt, 1218 kg in 1977 and boasted a girth of 8 ft 6 in, 2.59 m (cf. 8 ft 4 in, 2.54 m for his famous grandfather), but this stallion usually scales between 22 and 23 cwt, 1117–1168 kg.

On 11 December 1845 an outsized Percheron named 'George Washington' was being led around a room before a large audience at the famous Egyptian Hall in Leicester Square, London, when the floor suddenly gave way and the 2500 lb, 1134 kg horse's legs went into the apartment below, where the porter's wife was sitting. According to a report in *The Times* the woman 'screamed and jumped out of the window, while a clock near her was smashed to atoms by the horse's hoofs!' The animal, whose hind leg was badly bruised in the incident, was extricated with considerable difficulty, and a double floor was subsequently installed.

The Clydesdale, which has been called the Scottish Shire because both breeds are similar in appearance (in the 19th century they were regularly crossed), is a comparatively rangy horse and carries very little excess flesh. The average height of adult stallions is 16–16.2 hands (weight 15–17 cwt, 762–863 kg), while mares stand 15.3–16.1 hh (14½–16 cwt, 737–813 kg) and geldings 17 hh (17–18 cwt, 863–914 kg).

The largest Clydesdale on record was an unnamed gelding (foaled 1884) which was widely exhibited in the USA in 1889. It measured 20.3 hh and reportedly weighed nearly 3000 lb, 1360 kg. Other statistics include a girth of 7 ft 4 in, 2.23 m and a length of 11 ft 4 in, 3.45 m (nostrils to root of tail), and its head was 36 in, 91.4 cm long. A set of shoes made for this horse weighed 32 lb, 14.5 kg.

Another gelding called 'Laddie' (foaled in 1963) weighed 2800 lb, 1270 kg (height 20 hands) at the age of ten years, and was regularly exhibited by his owner, Bill Rieske, of Salt Lake City, Utah, USA.

The tallest Clydesdale recorded in Britain was a gelding called 'Big Jim' (real name 'Clifton Command') bred by Mr Lyall M Anderson of West Broomley, Montrose, Scotland, in 1950. At the age of three years this horse reportedly stood 21.1 hh (weight 2324 lb, 1054 kg) and measured 16 ft 4 in, 4.98 m 'overall'. Big Jim was later acquired by Mr Irvine Holliday of Clifton Hall, Penrith, Cumbria, a well-known exhibitor at Royal Highland Shows, who in turn sold the Clydesdale to the giant Anheuser-Busch brewery in St Louis, Missouri, USA, which was seeking a replacement for a recently deceased member of its famous Budweiser eight-horse hitch of outsized Clydesdales. As the brewery already had a gelding called 'Jim' the new acquisition was renamed 'Sir John'; he was also measured and found to be exactly 20 hh. According to a spokesman for Anheuser-Busch this horse—the tallest ever owned by the brewery—died in 1957.

The heaviest Clydesdale ever bred in Britain was a stallion which tipped the scales at 2688 lb, 1219 kg, despite the fact that it only stood 17.3 hh. The horse was owned by Mr Holliday's father (see above).

The barrel-bodied Suffolk Punch of today is a

The chestnut gelding 'Tic Tac II', the oldest British Thoroughbred on record.

Twin donkey foals of different sex and colour born at Lady Swinfen's donkey stud at Spanish Point, Co Clare, in 1971.

'Saltmarsh Silver Crest', the heaviest
Percheron ever recorded in Britain.

Mrs. Carmen J. Koper with her bay gelding
'Tango Duke', the oldest Thoroughbred
horse on record.

'Butterscotch', the only horse in the world who
can drive a car.

The 20-year-old Chinese silver pheasant
owned by Mr J V Bodenheimer of Kernersville,
North Carolina, USA.

The unigoat 'Lancelot' who has a 10 in, 25 cm
horn sprouting from the middle of his forehead.

Five-year-old 'Smidget', reputedly
the world's smallest living horse,
shown here with a duck for
comparison of size.

'Bobo', the world's oldest monkey.

'Davey Croakett' the world's most athletic
amphibian with his owner Dennis Matasci.

larger animal than early examples of the breed, which measured about 16 hh and weighed 15–16 cwt, 762–813 kg when in working condition. Modern stallions stand 17–17.1 hh at maturity and can weigh anything from 18 to 20 cwt, 914–1016 kg, while mares are 16–16.2 hh and 16–17 cwt, 813–863 kg.

The largest Suffolk on record was a gelding named 'Pat' (1925–40), who stood 21 hh and weighed 2810 lb, 1274 kg at the age of nine years. This extraordinary height—the Suffolk is a notably chunky horse with short, strong legs—was corroborated by his owner, R J Connors of Phelps, NY, USA, who said the horse measured 9 ft, 2.74 m to the top of the head in the normal standing position.

The heaviest Suffolk ever recorded in Britain was the 17.0½ hh champion stallion 'Monarch' (foaled in 1937) owned by W J Newman. This horse weighed 2576 lb, 1168 kg at the Woodbridge Horse Show held in 1942. The heaviest mare at the same show was Mr Gordon Freeman's 16.2½ hh

'Tangham Irene', also foaled in 1937, who scaled 2128 lb, 964 kg.

The eight-horse team of Suffolk geldings owned and exhibited by Mr W C Saunders of Billingford Hall, Diss, Norfolk, at the 1966 Peterborough Show each weighed over 1 ton, 1016 kg.

The only other breeds of heavy horses known to reach or exceed 1 ton, 1016 kg on occasion are the Dutch Heavy Draught, which is largely of Belgian blood; the Rhineland Heavy draught (Rhenish-German), which is built along the lines of the Belgian; and the Ardennes or Ardennais (Trait du Nord) which contains both Belgian and Dutch Draught blood.

Nowadays most breeders of heavy draught horses aim for animals that are not unduly bulky, because they tend to lose the quality of their breeding by being too large. The most efficient weight for a farm draught horse is said to be 1400–1500 lb, 635–680 kg.

Although the heavy horses of today are supposed

The Clydesdale 'Big Jim', the tallest horse recorded in Britain this century.

to represent the pinnacle of size in *Equus*, at least one fossil horse, *Equus giganteus* of the Pleistocene period (1 750 000–50 000 BP) was much larger if the evidence of an enormous upper second molar tooth found in Texas, USA, is anything to go by. The tooth, now in the palaeontological collection of the American Museum of Natural History in New York, measures 41.5×36 mm, 1.63×1.41 in and David P Willoughby, a research worker in vertebrate palaeontology, has calculated from its record-breaking dimensions that the owner must have stood at least 22 hh in life!

Smallest

In 1883 the Hackney Horse Society ruled that all animals standing 14 hands (56 in, 142 cm) or less should be classified as ponies, and this dividing line between horses and ponies has since been adopted on a worldwide basis. The only notable exception is the polo pony which needs to stand at least 15 hh, but some miniature breeds also justify exclusion because they have a predominance of horse characteristics, despite their small size.

Miniature horse breeding dates back to the Han period (206 BC–AD 220), the second great Chinese Imperial Dynasty. They were originally developed for pulling carriages in circuses, and some of these equine pygmies stood only 32 in, 81 cm tall. Miniature horses were also popular with royalty and the aristocracy of 16th and 17th century Europe, having been bred down from crosses between Shetland, Welsh and Mongolian ponies. In 1820 a 33 in, 84 cm mare said to be 'the smallest horse in the kingdom' was exhibited in London.

The smallest breed of horse in the world is the Falabella of Argentina. Most examples stand less than 30 in, 76 cm at maturity, but they can grow to 38 in, 96.5 cm. Stallions are slightly larger than mares because they are more heavily muscled; they average 80–100 lb, 36–45 kg in their prime, but both sexes get correspondingly heavier as they grow older, and weights up to 350 lb, 159 kg have been reported for veteran stallions and some mares who have produced a large number of foals during their breeding life.

In c 1860 an Irishman named Newton discovered a herd of exceptionally small horses in the mountains of southern Argentina, where they had been domesticated by local Indians. He managed to obtain a fertile pair, and then set about trying to develop a miniature horse by inbreeding and crossing with the smallest progeny in an effort to reverse the course of equine evolution. He was only partially successful, however, and the world had to wait until 1932 before his grandson, Julio Cesar Falabella, after whom the horse was named,

A 31 in, 78 crn high 3-year-old pony exhibited in Liverpool in 1898 and claimed to be the smallest ever seen in the UK.

produced the first mini-version at the family's huge Recreo de Roco Ranch near Buenos Aires. The first stallion bred by the Falabella family—with perfect horse conformation—was 'Napoleon', who stood 22 in, 56 cm and weighed 70 lb, 31.7 kg. He sired or was related to most of the miniature horses living today, and died in 1976 aged 42 years (see page 109).

When the Falabella first made news headlines a story went round the world that these horses were descendants of a herd which became trapped in a canyon by a landslide. For generations they were unable to escape, had only cactus to eat—and consequently decreased in size. In the end their plight was discovered by Julio Falabella, who had the hapless creatures winched out of the canyon by crane! Another writer claimed the Falabella was closely related to the little horses of Bolivia and Peru, which had been specially bred to pull ore carts through the narrow tunnels of tin mines, and this explanation is much more plausible because the Falabella is unbelievably strong for its size and can pull 20 times its own weight.

The average Falabella foal stands 20–24 in, 51–61 cm at birth and weighs 14–16 lb, 6.35–7.25 kg. On 2 August 1970 a 35 cm, $17\frac{3}{4}$ in female foal weighing only 3 kg, 6.6 lb was born at Froso Zoo, Sweden, and survived into adulthood. Her sire and dam stood 68.5 cm, 27 in and 64.7 cm, $25\frac{1}{2}$ in respectively. Three weeks later a weight of 10 lb, 4.53 kg was reported for a $11\frac{3}{4}$ in, 30 cm male foal born on the farm of miniature horse breeder Moody Bond at Lavonia, Georgia, USA, but this horse had been bred down from a small Welsh pony. At the age of two years 'Tiny Tim', as he was called, stood 14 in, 35.5 cm and scaled 55 lb, 25 kg. Foals of

12 in, 30 cm have twice been recorded by breeder Norman J Mitchell of Glenorie, NSW, Australia, in the cases of 'Quicksilver' (1975) and 'Tung Dynasty' (8 February 1978).

The smallest adult horse bred by Julio Falabella before his death in 1981 was a mare which stood 15 in, 38 cm and tipped the scales at 26¼ lb, 11.9 kg. Another fully-grown mare named 'Sugardumpling' owned by Smith McVoy of Roderfield, West Virginia, USA, weighed 30 lb, 13.6 kg (height 20 in, 51 cm) at the time of her death in 1965, while the much-publicised 'Smidget' (foaled 13 April 1979) belonging to Ron Boeger of Durham, California, USA, stands 21 in, 53.3 cm and weighs about 50 lb, 22.6 kg.

The smallest fully-grown horse on record is a stallion named 'Little Pumpkin' (foaled 15 April 1973) owned by J C Williams Jr of Della Terra Mini Horse Farm, Inman, South Carolina, USA. On 30 November 1975 this incredibly tiny horse was examined by Dr T H Hamison of the Circle T Veterinary Centre, Spartanburg, SC, who registered a height of 14 in, 35.5 cm and a weight of only 20 lb, 9.07 kg. He also confirmed that this equine midget, which contained a large percentage of Falabella blood, was extremely well-proportioned and had no physical deformities such as stunted legs.

Of the estimated 700–900 pure-bred Falabellas living today, about 300 are to be found in Argentina. They are still bred by the Falabella family, who have about 200 on their ranch, but they are reluctant to sell these much sought after animals, and this tends to keep prices artificially high. As a result, there have been a number of cases of rustling in recent years, and horses have been brought into the USA via Miami, Florida. Of the 100 or so Falabellas living in Britain today, 41 are owned by Ian Pinkerton, who runs the Wick Place Stud at Bulphan, Essex. He purchased his initial herd of six from the Gettysburg Miniature Horse Farm in Pennsylvania, USA, in 1979 and sells his horses for between £1750 and £3000 (£4000–£4500 for a breeding pair),

A dwarf Shetland pony checking to see if it has been mentioned in the *Guinness Book of Records*.

depending on their size, colour and shape. Generally the smaller the horse the higher the price, but appaloosa markings also enhance the value.

About 90 per cent of the world's miniature horse studs are in the USA and, apart from the Falabella, they also cater for mini versions of the Shire, the Clydesdale, the Arabian, the Pinto, the Welsh pony and the American trotter. The standard for the American Miniature Horse Registry reads as follows: 'The American miniature horse shall be, as the name implies, an unusually small equine, not exceeding 34 inches in height at maturity. It shall be perfect in form and normal in function, with head, body and legs presenting a pleasing, well-proportioned appearance. Unsound or unworthy animals should not be presented for registration. Breeders are particularly cautioned to avoid registering, or using for breeding purposes, any animal that possesses characteristics of a dwarf.'

The Caspian and the Skyros have also been described as 'miniature horses' because of their configuration, although neither of them can compete with the Falabella *et al* in terms of smallness.

The Caspian horse, long thought to be extinct until it was rediscovered in small numbers (population *c* 140) in the North Iran/Caspian Sea area in 1965, is considered by some hippologists to be a survivor of the ancient miniature horse of Mesopotamia which supposedly died out in *c* AD 700. This breed stands between 40 and 48 in, 101–122 cm and is reported to be a remarkable jumper. Mrs Elizabeth Hoden, owner of the Caspian stud in Claverley, Shropshire, has at least 18 of these highly-intelligent animals, which can be used in harness or ridden by a child.

The little horse of the Greek island of Skyros is another breed of great antiquity that is also under threat. For centuries this finely-built horse, which stands 37 to 44 in, 94–111 cm tall, was used for agricultural work, but when farm machinery reached the island its services were no longer required and it often went hungry in the bitter winters, because the poor people could not afford an animal that did not earn its keep. The Greek Animal Welfare Fund is now trying to raise money to build a special centre for the 100 or so horses left on the island so that they can be trained for tourists to ride.

The smallest breed of pony is the Shetland, which is built on the lines of a miniature draught horse. Mature examples (both sexes) stand 39–42 in, 99–106 cm tall and weigh 350–385 lb, 159–175 kg, but mini-versions of this breed have been known to measure less than 28 in, 71 cm when fully-grown. The winner of a special 'miniature' class in the National Pony Society Show held at the Royal Agricultural Hall, Islington, London in 1913 was a Shetland which stood 27 in, 68.5 cm. Another

example bred in the USA stood 26 in, 66 cm at the age of five years and weighed 102 lb, 46.2 kg.

In 1983 a height of 21½ in, 54.6 cm was reported for a four-year-old Shetland called 'Fudge' owned by Mrs Sue Maher of Northolt, Middlesex, but as this pony had previously suffered from rickets and the disease had left him bandy in both front legs, this measurement cannot be considered valid.

Recently an undersized Shetland called 'Tiny' went missing in Bradford, Yorkshire, after he had hitched a lift in a car. According to the pony's owner, Mr Sonny Fletcher, his pet had a passion for travel and often jumped into the back seats of cars for a ride. A reward was offered for Tiny's safe return, but it is not known if the money was collected.

The average Shetland foal stands 22 in, 55.8 cm at birth and weighs about 32 lb, 14.5 kg. On 15 August 1977 a standard Shetland mare gave birth to a 12 in, 30.4 cm filly at Malton, Yorkshire. Owner Miss Jacqueline Maw said the 'happy event' had been overdue and everybody had been expecting an enormous foal. She estimated that 'Supermouse', as he was called, would only grow to 24 in, 61 cm. This size was closely matched by another foal born on the farm of Mr and Mrs Dale Carmen near Goshen, Ohio, USA in May 1973. The colt, nicknamed 'Mini Mustang', stood 13 in, 33 cm at birth and 15 in, 38 cm at three weeks.

The lowest birthweight recorded for a Shetland foal is 10 lb, 4.53 kg in the case of a 14 in, 3.5 cm individual named 'Tiny Bit' bred in the 1960s by Mr and Mrs T P Parker of the Royal Crescent Shetland Pony Farm at Arlington, Texas, USA. Tiny's dam stood only 24 in, 61 cm.

Oldest

The age of a horse can be accurately assessed up to eight years by studying changes in the biting surfaces of the lower incisor teeth. From then onwards age definition is based mainly on the length of a dark depression called Galvayne's Groove, which appears at the top of each of the upper corner incisors when the horse is nine years old and grows down with the tooth. At 15 years the groove is halfway down the tooth, and by the age of 30 it has grown out completely leaving only brown lines called dental stars. Other guidelines to age estimations up to 30 years are the alignment of the upper row of incisors and the angle at which the lower incisors project. Unfortunately few domestic horses are allowed to die of old age, and the average life-span is somewhere between 20 and 25 years for most breeds. Riding horses sometimes reach the age of 30, but their value drops steadily from the age of about nine years, and they begin to age at 15 years.

Thoroughbred racehorses don't usually live much beyond 20 years. Those raced on the flat are generally pensioned off before they reach the age of five years, while hurdlers and steeplechasers are rarely run after their 12th birthday, and it is interesting to note that the legs of a horse go before its teeth. When Dr Alex Comfort carried out an investigation of age records in the *General Stud Book* in 1958 he found the average duration of life for all mares reaching four years was 21.2 years. The oldest mare was 'Blue Bell' (by 'Heron' out of 'Jessie'), who was foaled in 1851 and died in 1885 aged 34 years, while another mare died in her 33rd year (1911–43). A stallion named 'Matcham', who sired 354 winners, also lived for 33 years (1749–81), and there is a record of a stallion in an Irish stud which was still vigorous at the age of 33 years.

Because the actual date of birth is not always available, most horses born in the Northern Hemisphere are dated from 1 May. The only exceptions are Thoroughbreds which are dated from 1 January (1 August in the Southern Hemisphere).

The greatest age recorded for a Thoroughbred is 42 years in the case of a chestnut gelding 'Tango Duke' (foaled 1935) owned by Mrs Carmen J Koper of Barongarook, Victoria, Australia. She purchased the animal as an eight-year-old in 1943 when she lived in Melbourne, and used him as a stock horse for many years. Tango Duke died on 25 January 1978.

The oldest British Thoroughbred on record was another gelding named 'Tic Tac II' (by 'Patachon' out of 'Mystique') belonging to Miss Maureen Willis of Wythall, near Birmingham, West Midlands. He was foaled in France in 1944, and was bought by Miss Willis's father in a selling race at Wolverhampton when he was three years old. There were 27 runners and Tic Tac, winner of the race, was ridden by Gordon (later Sir Gordon) Richards. This horse died on 13 July 1978 aged 34 years.

On 5 May 1980 the death was reported of a seven-eighths Thoroughbred gelding named 'Mr Conker' aged 40 years at Kelsall, Cheshire. His owner, Miss Rhoda Stocks, purchased the horse when he was 14 years old from farmer Mr Reg Tongue of Altrincham, Cheshire, and she rode him until he was 26. She attributed her pet's longevity to the excellent treatment he received from various 'caretakers' who looked after him when she was working full-time in business.

According to one writer (1972) the famous 'Eclipse', the fastest of the early English racehorses, was 75 years old [sic] when he died in 1789, but the actual age of this horse was 24 years. He was foaled on the day of a solar eclipse, 1 April 1764, and was bred by the Duke of Cumberland. During his short racing career of 17 months he never lost a race, and his skeleton is now preserved in the racing museum at Newmarket, Suffolk, home of the racing industry.

Although a number of claims have been published, there are less than half a dozen authentic records of horses living for more than 50 years.

In February 1960 an ex-Italian army horse called 'Topolino', foaled in Libya on 24 February 1909, died in Brescia, Italy, aged 51 years. He was of the Salerno breed.

This age was slightly exceeded by a 17 hh light draught gelding named 'Monty', who was foaled at Lavington, NSW, Australia, in October 1917. In his youth he was hitched to the plough or harrow and made regular trips to the local railway station (Albury) with a cartload of packed fruits. In 1926 he came into the possession of Mrs Marjorie Cooper, who owned a farm in Albury, where he remained in a non-working capacity for the rest of his life. Monty was put to sleep on 25 January 1970 aged 52 years because of progressing debility, and his head (skull and mandible) and heart are now preserved in the Museum of the School for Veterinary Sciences at the University of Melbourne.

Another longevity record also considered reliable, although not quite so well-documented, is that of a light draught mare named 'Nellie', who died in Danville, Missouri, USA, on 1 November 1969 aged 53 years. According to the horse's original owner, Mr Leeman Kirk, she had been foaled in Audrain County, Missouri, in March 1916. When Mr Kirk retired in 1968 and moved to Florida he gave the old mare to his friend, Mr Charles O Buchanan. On 31 October 1969 Nellie suffered a heart attack and died the following day. She was buried on the Buchanan farm, and a monument was erected on the spot dedicated to 'the oldest horse in the world'.

Less well-established records include a horse named 'Paramatta', who died in Australia in 1874 aged 53 years, and a horse owned by the Thames Navigation Company, which died in 1822 shortly after its 52nd birthday.

As mentioned earlier, the Falabella is a long-lived animal. The stallion 'Napoleon' was 43 years old at the time of his death, and the maximum life potential for this breed has been put at 50–55 years. The fact that this horse has a larger heart in proportion to its size than any other breed is probably an important factor where life-span is concerned.

The greatest reliable age recorded for a horse is an incredible 62 years in the case of 'Old Billy' (foaled 1760), believed to be a cross between a Cleveland and Eastern blood, who was bred by Mr Edward Robinson of Wildgrave Farm in Woolston, Lancashire. In 1762 or 1763 he was sold to the Mersey and Irwell Navigation Company and

'Old Billy', the world's oldest horse.

remained with them in a working capacity (ie marshalling and towing barges) until 1819, when he was retired to a farm at Latchford, near Warrington, owned by Mr William Earle, a director of the company. In July 1820 an attempt was made to get this equine Methuselah to walk in a procession celebrating the coronation of George IV, but by then the horse was too old and feeble and refused to leave his stable. Old Billy died on 27 November 1822. His skull is preserved in the Manchester Museum and his mounted head (fitted with false teeth!) is now on display in the Bedford Museum.

With the sole exception of the Suffolk, the heavy draught breeds are not noted for their longevity. At one of the early Suffolk Agriculture Association shows a mare was exhibited with a suckling filly by her side whose combined ages added up to 41 years. As the filly was then two years old, this made the dam 39 years of age. Another Suffolk mare reportedly foaled at the age of 42.

Ponies tend to be hardier animals than horses and generally live longer. In the case of the Shetland pony 30 years is a common age, and there have been a number of instances of this pony living between 40 and 45 years.

In October 1974 the death was reported of a Shetland mare named 'Jean' aged 45 years in Dundee, Scotland. The pony, foaled in January 1949, was owned by Miss Irene Sibbald.

This age was exceeded by another Shetland pony named 'Mickey', winner of seven cups and 158 rosettes, who was 50 when he died at Bungalow Farm, Gimingham, Norfolk, in March 1982. Miss June Gotts, a show-jumper who grew up with the pony, said: 'He was a family pet and always had a good life with plenty of food and exercise. He also enjoyed a pint of Guinness, and we were heartbroken when this great little pony passed on.'

The maximum age potential for this breed is c 60 years.

Apart from the Shetland, the only other pony known to have lived longer than 50 years was a grey-faced New Forest cross named 'Nobby'. He was foaled in Medbourne, Rutland, in 1932 and started his working life between the shafts of a butcher's van. When he was pensioned off at the age of 30 his owner, a Mr King, sold him to Mr Colin Crawford, who ran a riding school in Wimbledon, SW London, and it was there that Nobby settled down in happy semi-retirement. On 19 September 1982 he took part in the Horseman's Sunday held at Tattenham Corner, Epsom, but it was the gelding's last public appearance and he handed in his nosebag on 21 December 1982 just short of his 51st birthday. His skeleton is now in the Royal Veterinary College Museum.

Lord Rothschild told Major Stanley Flower, a leading researcher into maximum longevities in animals, that he knew of a pony in France that was still alive in 1906 aged 54 years, and the same age was reported for a pony living in Boyle, Co Roscommon, Eire, in October 1979, but neither of these claims has been fully documented.

A Dartmoor pony named 'White Sox' bred on

The famous New Forest cross 'Nobby' who died in December 1980 just short of his 51st birthday.

Dartmoor and purchased by Mr Francis Meade of Langport, Somerset, in 1870, lived for 41 years, dying in 1909. The same age was also reported for another Dartmoor pony named 'Flash', owned by Miss Elizabeth Lamb of Great Bowden, Market Harborough, Leicestershire, who moved to Jersey in the Channel Islands in 1978. It is not known if she took the pony with her.

Ponies were first used down the mines in the 17th century. When the 1842 Mines Act banned women and children from pulling coal tubs they were replaced by ponies, which were ready for the pits at four years of age and had a working life of 15–20 years before their wind went. Once down a deep shaft mine they were not brought to the surface again until they retired, because it was too risky to expose them to variable weather after the warmth of their underground homes. In 1913, the year of peak coal production, there were 73 000 of these hard-working animals (all males) toiling away for long hours in perpetual twilight and sharing the same conditions as the miners. The National Coal Board originally planned to phase out pit ponies by 1970, but today there are still about 60 of them left, mainly in Durham and Northumberland. Unlike their predecessors, however, they no longer haul coal but are used to carry supplies in pits where the expected life of the seams would not justify expenditure on new machinery. They also have a strictly-controlled working week of 40 hours and are maintained under first-class conditions.

The oldest pit pony on record was a much-loved character named 'Ant', who worked at Blaenavon Colliery, Gwent, Wales, for 24 years. During his time underground he travelled an estimated 70 000 miles, 112 000 km and, when his working life ended in 1966, the 27-year-old pony was given a home by a local man. But his new owner found the pony too expensive to keep (all pit ponies have to be hand-fed because they have never learned to crop grass) and decided to have him put down. When Mr Philip Davies, himself a retired miner, heard that the skewbald Welsh pony was going to be shot he asked Ant's owner if he could buy the animal, and a deal was struck. Mr Davies, who ran the 'Three Horse Shoes Inn', a small pub in the village of Pentwynmawr, near Newbridge, Gwent, was very fond of animals, and he had a field adjoining his premises that he knew would be ideal for the pony in his retirement. Ant arrived at his new home on 6 November 1966, and immediately showed his approval by galloping excitedly round the field, much to everybody's delight. Within days he had built up quite a fan club, because there was a bus stop right next to the field and passengers couldn't resist patting the friendly pony as he leaned over the fence to see what was going on. He was also

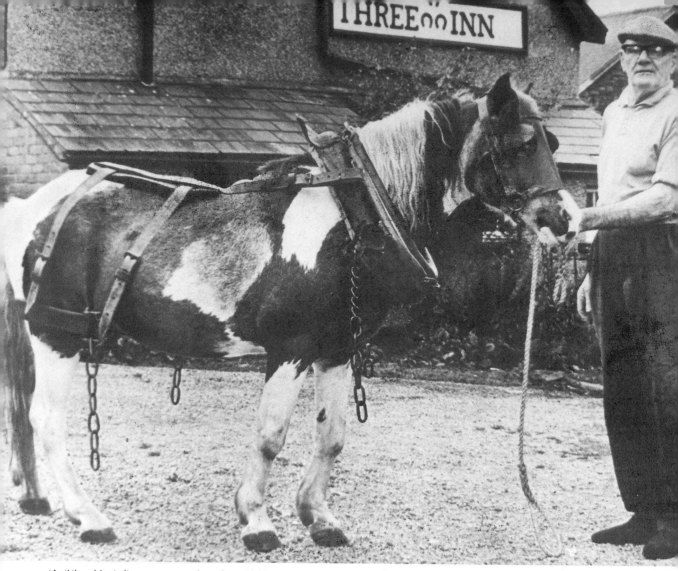

'Ant' the oldest pit pony on record, posing with his owner, retired miner Mr Philip Davies.

an instant hit with the children at the local junior school who, apart from adopting him as a pet and keeping him well supplied with sweets and apples, were later to use him as a model when the weather was sunny and they could go outdoors for their drawing lessons. At the end of term the pictures would be exhibited in the pub.

When Mr Davies died in 1975 his daughter Mrs Tegwyn Rose and her husband took over the running of the pub, because Mrs Davies was now 75 years old and couldn't manage it on her own. They knew nothing about looking after ponies, but they soon got into the swing of things and from then onwards it was a labour of love. Because Ant was now getting very long in the tooth Mrs Rose decided to cook all his food for him in future, and it was given to him daily in three separate meals—the last served at midnight! She also arranged for him to have a pint of nourishing stout after each snack. When a local newspaper got to hear about Ant's 'boozy' antics they sent along a reporter to do a

story, and his fame quickly spread. He even appeared on television, and a woman in Cwmbran wrote a poem in his honour. During the bitterly cold winter of 1978 Ant was taken ill with pneumonia. Every effort was made to save him, and for a while he rallied, but the end was obviously in sight and the gallant little pit pony died in his sleep early in February 1979, aged 40 years. When BBC Wales announced the news of Ant's death it brought a flood of hand-drawn cards of sympathy from the children who had befriended him over the years, and there were also a number of floral tributes. Ant was buried in the field where he had spent so many happy times, and a tree was planted on his grave as a lasting memorial.

Strength

All heavy draught breeds are renowned for their great strength and pulling power, and in the 18th century hauling tests for big wagers were regularly held in England. Horses would often have to pull carts full of sand with the wheels partly sunk in the ground and wood blocks placed in front of them to make the test more difficult.

In c 1810 'an ordinary cattle horse' (probably a Shire type) easily pulled 36 tons/tonnes for a distance of 6 miles, 9.6 km along the Surrey Iron Railway between Wandsworth and Mersham to win a bet for a gentleman named Mr Banks. The horse completed the journey in 1½ hours, despite the fact that it was stopped four times to demonstrate a start from a dead rest. After collecting his winnings the enterprising Mr Banks added four extra wagons and 50 labourers, bringing the weight up to 55 tons 6 cwt 2 qr, 56.5 tonnes, but again the horse moved off comfortably.

Another very impressive display of horse-power which did not involve the advantage of steel to steel contact and good lubrication took place outside the Royal Agricultural Hall, Islington, London on 24 February 1924 when two eight-year-old Shire geldings named 'Vesuvius' and 'Umber' (owned by Liverpool Corporation) yoked tandem-fashion and on slippery granite setts, moved off easily with 18 tons 9½ cwt, 18.7 tonnes behind them, the shaft horse starting the load before the trace horse got into his collar. Six tons/tonnes was moved on the tan in the show ring and 16½ tons/tonnes on the wooden blocks. In an earlier test in Liverpool the same pair (combined weight 3498 lb, 1585 kg) hauled a 20 ton/tonne load of cotton plus the 2 ton/tonne wagon for 50 yd, 45 m over granite setts, but this was an easier load to pull than the deadweight of metal in the other demonstration.

Later the same year (23 April 1924) another weight-pulling test involving Shires (weight range 1708–2100 lb, 774–952 kg) was staged at the British Empire Exhibition at Wembley, but this time the horse had to pull against a dynamometer, attached to an immovable object. One horse, 'Vulcan', exerted a pull equal to a starting load of 29 tons/tonnes, and a pair easily pulled a starting load of 50 tons/tonnes, the maximum registered on the dynamometer.

Today pulling contests are no longer staged in Britain, but they are still popular in North America and Russia, where various methods are used. In the USA two-horse teams usually pull against a special dynamometer which raises weights up a shaft or haul a sledge known as a stone-boat, to which weights are added to an agreed total. The aim of the contest is to find the team that can pull the greatest load over 27½ ft, 8.38 m, which is the calculated distance a draught horse will travel in ten seconds whilst making its maximum effort.

On 24 September 1935 two Belgian geldings named 'Rock' and 'Tom' owned by George H

Statler Farms, Piqua, Ohio, pulled a load weighing 3900 lb, 1769 kg for a distance of 27½ ft, 8.38 m at Hillsdale, Michigan, a leading centre for dynamometer pulling contests. The load was placed on a specially-built wagon with four dual pneumatic-type wheels, chains over the tyres and all wheels locked. The pull exerted by these two powerhouses was said to have been equivalent to the starting of a load weighing 23.15 tons/tonnes on granite setts.

In weight-pulling trials carried out in Russia the loads are moved over much greater distances because the wheels of the wagons used in the competitions are smooth-turning and chains are not used. The four main breeds of heavy horse found in the USSR (in order of size) are the Vladimir Heavy Draught, the Soviet Heavy Draught, the Lithuanian Heavy Draught and the Russian Heavy Draught, and individual horses have recorded some memorable pulls. One Vladimir stallion pulled 10 906 kg, 10.73 tons for 834 m, 912 yd, while a Lithuanian stallion drew 11 438 kg, 11.3 tons over 1397 m, 1529 yd. Both these feats, however, were eclipsed by a six-year-old Soviet stallion which pulled a load weighing 22 990 kg, 22.7 tons for an astonishing 35 km, 21.8 miles.

The greatest load ever moved by a pair of heavy draught horses was allegedly one weighing 144 US short tons (130.9 tonnes) which two Clydes-

The greatest load allegedly pulled by a pair of draught horses.

dales with a combined weight of 3500 lb, 1587 kg pulled on a sledge litter for a distance of 440 yd, 402 m along a frozen road at the Nester Estate near Ewen, Michigan, USA, on 26 February 1893, but this tonnage was exaggerated. The load, which comprised 50 logs of white pine scaling 36 055 board feet, measured 30 ft, 9 m in height, 18 ft, 5.5 m in length and 18 ft, 5.5 m in width. As 36 055 board feet = 3171.25 ft^3, and coniferous sawn lumber normally weighs 32 lb/ft^3, the logs making up this load must have totalled in the region of 101 480 lb, 46.12 tonnes, and even if we add another 3000 lb, 1360 kg for the weight of the sledge and 2000 lb, 907 kg for the 850 ft, 259 m of steel test chain used to secure the load, the total weight is still less than 50 tonnes. After the test, nine railway box cars were required to transport the logs to the World's Fair in Chicago where they were put on display. When the fair ended, a man bought the timber and used it to build himself a home!

The prime pulling age for a draught horse is between 8 and 12 years, but a good horse may last 20 years or even longer on the weight-hauling circuit, provided it is not used in distance events which put additional strain on the heart.

Breeding

The duration of pregnancy in the horse varies according to the breed and the season of foaling. The normal range is 327 to 344 days, with light breeds averaging 337 days, heavy breeds 332 days and Shetland ponies 333 days. Foals born in the spring average 13–14 days longer than those which arrive in the autumn.

On 28 September 1982 a four-year-old Welsh mountain pony named 'Swinford Annabella' belonging to Peter and Elizabeth Sherlock of Birch Farm, Mouldsworth, Cheshire, dropped her first foal after a gestation period of 408 days. A vet was called in twice by the mare's worried owners to induce foaling, but in the end she gave birth on her own. There is also a reliable German record of a horse producing a healthy foal after 419 days.

Foals born before the 328th day are classified as premature. The shortest gestation period reported for a horse is one of 287 days.

The breeding life of mares is normally 16–22 years, with an average of 18 years. One hunter, long retired to grass, broke out of her field at the age of 23 when she spotted a small band of gipsy horses passing by, and produced her *first foal* without difficulty the following year.

On 28 June 1981 a 24-year-old mare named 'Cindy' owned by Mr James McMahon of Newmarket-on-Fergus, Co Clare, Eire, produced her 18th foal in 20 years of breeding. One of her

progeny was 'Ardnacrusha', who won international show-jumping honours. In April 1963 a Thoroughbred racehorse named 'Wayward Miss' belonging to Mr Tom Jones of Atcham Grange, near Shrewsbury, Shropshire, gave birth to her 20th foal at the ripe old age of 27. Nine of her previous foals were later winners on the race-course. Two years later a little Connemara mare called 'Velvet' owned by Mrs Eileen Vard of Booterstown, Co Dublin, Eire, dropped her first foal at the age of 25. The next year she produced another healthy filly, followed by a third in 1967 and a fourth a couple of years later. In 1973, at the age of 33, she surprised everybody by dropping yet another filly, but this time the birth was so painful and exhausting that she died three weeks later.

On 11 January 1980 a 33-year-old mare named 'Miss Vindy' gave birth to twins, both of which survived along with the mother, at the Land of Oz Morgan Horse Farm in Marengo, Illinois, USA. The mare had been seduced by a determined young stallion who had craftily utilised a snow bank to jump a high fence which had previously thwarted its efforts. 'Unusual things happen in the Land of Oz', commented the horses' owners, Nat and Betty Ozman, after the unexpected birth.

The greatest age at which a horse has produced a healthy foal is an astonishing 42 years in the case of an Australian brood mare who dropped her 34th foal (in itself a record) in 1933. This equine matriarch was still alive ('in splendid condition') four years later, although by then she had ceased to breed. Her exceptionally productive life was attributed to the fact that she never did much work!

There is also a record of a Suffolk draught mare dropping a healthy foal at the grand old age of 39 years (see page 110).

A number of cases have been reported of horses producing 18 or more foals during their breeding life, and as already noted the world record stands at 34.

In May 1976 a Shetland pony named 'Express of Netherley' owned by Miss J Burrows of the Buckberry Shetland Pony Stud, Ingoldsby, Grantham, Lincolnshire, gave birth to her 14th foal at the age of 17 years. They had all been sired by a stallion named 'Royal Sovereign'.

Also worthy of mention is a 7.2 hh Shetland mare called 'Judy', who produced a healthy foal on the farm of veteran horse-breeder Mr George Upton at Hinckley, Leicestershire, in August 1982. In this case, however, the sire was not another Shetland but a mighty 16.2 hh stallion called 'Prince', who had been brought into Judy's life originally to keep her company. How the two stablemates managed to carry out this seemingly impossible liaison will remain one of life's mysteries, but it just goes to show that love will always find a way!

Manes and tails

Mane and tail hair is normally cut in the process of grooming; however, if it is allowed to grow unchecked, and the hair is braided and wrapped in cloth to protect it, excessive mane and tail development will sometimes occur.

The longest mane on record was one grown by a horse named 'Maud' owned by George O Zillgitt of Inglewood, California, USA. It was measured at 18 ft, 5.48 m in 1905.

The longest recorded tail belongs to a 15 hh Palomino named 'Belvedere Forest King' (foaled 22 April 1965) belonging to Bill and Louise Grieve of Mission, British Columbia, Canada. In September 1980 it was unbraided and found to measure an amazing 22 ft, 6.7 m in length. In his early years 'Chinook', as he is known locally, was a regular winner of cups and ribbons in harness classes at horse shows, but his career in that department ended when he started getting his tail caught in the wheels of the light vehicle. Instead, he went on to win a parade horse class four years running (1974–78) at the Pacific National Exhibition, and since then he has been shown by his owners in special exhibition classes. The Palomino, incidentally, is not a breed but a colour type, and the size ranges from small ponies to heavy horses.

The longest mane-and-tail combination on record was the 30 ft, 9.14 m (13 ft, 3.96 m mane and 17 ft, 5.18 m tail) credited to a horse named 'Linus' in Oregon, USA, in 1901.

The British record is 23 ft, 7 m for a Percheron measured in Dee, Scotland, in 1891. The mane was 13 ft, 3.96 m long and the tail 10 ft, 3.05 m.

Toughest

The toughest breed of horse or pony in the world is the Yakut of the huge autonomous Soviet Republic of Yakutia. The climate in this region, which lies in NE Siberia and extends beyond the Arctic Circle, is the severest of the inhabited world, and frosts can be as extreme as minus 92°F, −69°C in areas where strong temperature inversions build up. Despite these extremely harsh conditions, the Yakut

The palomino 'Chinook' proudly displays his record-breaking 22 ft, 6.7 m long tail.

lives in the open all the year and forages for its own food.

The most popular breed of horse in the world is the American Quarter horse, which has more than 1 500 000 registrations in the USA alone.

The rarest breeds are the Caspian and the Skyros (see page 108), which have a combined total population of less than 250.

Heroes

Three horses have been awarded the Dickin Medal, the animal equivalent of the VC. They were 'Regal', 'Olga', and 'Upstart', all members of the Mounted Branch of the Metropolitan Police Force.

Regal won his award for two displays of courage in the face of fire. On 19 April 1941 a cluster of German incendiary bombs scored an almost direct hit on the police station at Muswell Hill, north London, and set part of the building alight. The flames quickly spread to the nearby stables where the horses were kept, but Regal showed no signs of panic and waited patiently until help arrived. Three years later, on 20 July 1944, a flying bomb exploded within 20 yd, 18 m of the same building. This time, however, the magnificent bay gelding received minor cuts from bits of flying glass and metal and ended up half-buried in debris when the roof collapsed. Despite the shock to his system Regal 'once again lived up to his name and was not unduly perturbed'.

Olga was in Tooting, south London, on 1 July 1944 when a flying bomb demolished four houses 75 yd, 68 m away and brought a plate-glass window crashing down immediately in front of her. The bay mare panicked briefly but, after being calmed by her rider, PC J E Thwaites, she returned to the scene of devastation and carried out traffic control duties.

The other member of the brave trio, Upstart, was twice involved in enemy action when his stables were bombed, but the chestnut gelding's biggest test came on 22 August 1944 when he was on patrol duty in Bethnal Green, east London, and a flying bomb exploded close by. Both horse and rider were showered with broken glass and debris, but luckily neither was hurt, and they remained on duty keeping the way clear for ambulances and other services.

Driving

The only horse in the world that can drive a car is a palomino gelding named 'Butterscotch' owned by Dr Dorothy Magallon of Louisville, Kentucky, USA. This equine prodigy gets around in a

'Olga', 'Regal' and 'Upstart', the only three horses to be awarded the Dickin Medal.

specially-converted red 1960 Lincoln Continental, which he enters via his own custom-built drawbridge ramp. In the car is a system of rubber control hoses designed by trainer Hamilton Morris. Butterscotch pulls the starter lever until the engine starts, and then pulls the gearshift lever into 'drive'. He then steps on the greatly enlarged gas pedal (accelerator) and away he goes. The other pedal is the brake for stopping, and the horse steers by turning the padded steering-wheel with his nose. Butterscotch knows the difference between Left, Right and Straight, and his favourite piece of apparatus is the centre lever which honks a horn when he bites down on it. For safety reasons the car, which has a top speed of only 5 miles/h, 8 km/h, is equipped with side railings, and Butterscotch always wears an outsized seat belt when he goes through his performance for the public.

Donkeys and mules

Donkeys (asses) differ from horses in their smaller size, longer ears, bigger eyes and shorter neck.

The Common donkey (*Equus asinus*) stands about 10 hh on the average and weighs in the region of 400 lb, 181 kg, but other types vary considerably in size according to their country of origin. In Britain donkeys measuring between 10.2 hh and 12 hh are described as Large Standard, and any animal over this height is called a Spanish donkey. In the USA, however, the upper limit for the latter type is 13.2 hands, and taller individuals are known as Mammoth donkeys. In most strains, the jack (stallion) is about five per cent larger than the jennet (mare).

The largest recognised breed of donkey is the American type, which was developed from Spanish and Maltese strains imported into the USA in large numbers in the early 19th century. Jacks stand at least 15.3 hh and weigh about 1200 lb, 544 kg. The Majorcan donkey is also of comparable size, jacks standing 15.2 hh and weighing 1150 lb, 521 kg.

The largest donkey ever recorded was an outsized jennet called 'Dinah', who reportedly stood a colossal 21 hh! She was exhibited at Glasgow Hippodrome, Scotland, in 1902, and a published photograph substantiates this freakish size.

The smallest breeds of donkey are found on the Mediterranean islands of Sicily and Sardinia, where they are known as miniature donkeys or 'minimokes'. According to the standard of the Donkey Breed Society a miniature donkey must measure less than 36 in, 91 cm. The upper height limit for the American Miniature Donkey Registry is 38 in, 96.5 cm, but most examples are less than 34 in, 86.3 cm, and the average measurement is about 31 in, 78.7 cm; weight 150 lb, 68 kg.

The donkey has a normal gestation period of 345–375 days.

The longest donkey pregnancy on record occurred in 1976 when a jennet owned by Mr Paul Sellers of Bassetts Cowden, near Edenbridge, Kent, produced a healthy foal after 455 days.

Although twins are quite rare in the donkey world, they are much more likely to survive than a pair conceived by a horse. This is because the jennet has a much roomier and better shaped womb in which to accommodate her young, which in turn means the foals are generally born in reasonably good condition. A much more unusual—and almost unique—event, however, is the birth of foals of different sex and colour. In September 1971 a Spanish donkey owned by Mrs Kingsley-Lewis of Caer Dyke Donkey Stud, Waterbeach, Cambridgeshire,

The outsized jennet 'Dinah' who stood a colossal 21 hh (7 ft, 2.13 m).

produced what was believed to be the first recorded twins fitting this description, but the following month this feat was repeated by a donkey named 'Breaffy' belonging to Lady Averil Swinfen, who owns Ireland's largest donkey farm at Spanish Point, Co Clare. The twins, a piebald filly and a black colt, were named 'O'Me' and 'O'Mi'.

Donkeys usually live longer than horses and ponies if they are well-fed and kept warm in the winter, and a number of authentic cases have been reported of this species exceeding 40 years. Two jennets named 'Polly' and 'Flossie' belonging to Mrs Kay Lockwood of Wormley, Surrey, who runs the largest private donkey sanctuary in Britain (600 animals) both died in 1978 aged 55 and 56 years respectively, and another resident named 'Paddington' was put to sleep in 1980 aged 56 years. Five other veterans in Mrs Lockwood's donkey haven also lived for more than 45 years, and the oldest example living there today is a jennet called 'Sarah', who is aged *c* 53 years and is still going strong, despite the fact that her teeth are now worn down to the gum. Earlier, in 1936, the death was reported of a jennet aged 60 years in Yorkshire, and a 65-year-old donkey reportedly died in Stirlingshire, Scotland, in 1941, but further details are lacking.

The rarest breed of donkey in the world is the remarkable Asinara, which is confined to the small Italian island of that name off the north-west extremity of Sardinia. Because the island is a penal colony, very few outsiders have seen this blue-eyed white miniature, but the race is believed to be on the verge of extinction—despite full protection.

The lowest price ever paid for livestock was at a sale at Kuruman, Cape Province, South Africa in 1934 where donkeys were sold for less than 2p each.

A mule is the hybrid offspring of a jack donkey and a mare (horse or pony), and as such is a product of artificial selection by man. Crosses between a jennet and a stallion are much less frequent, and the result is the smaller hinny.

In the ancient world mules were greatly valued for their size and strength, and at the funeral of Alexander the Great in 323 BC the carriage was pulled by 64 of these hefty beasts. The largest mules bred today range from 16 hh to 17.2 hh and weigh between 1200 lb, 544 kg and 1600 lb, 725 kg, which means the males are just as tall but not quite so heavy as many draught breeds of horse. Most of the sires are Majorcan and Poitou types.

Miniature mules are a fairly recent innovation. The first individuals were bred in 1950 by August A Busch, Jr, of the giant Anheuser-Busch brewery in St Louis, Missouri, USA, who crossed miniature Sicilian donkeys with Shetland ponies. The results measure 29–31 in, 73–79 cm in height and weigh 200–250 lb, 91–113 kg.

The smallest mule on record is a 25 in, 63.5 cm male called 'Ulysses Simpson Grant' owned by Ray and Ruby Lee of Shady Acres Miniature Horse Farm near Hardin, Kentucky, USA. This tiny power-house, named after the 18th American President, was foaled on a farm at Missouri in 1975 and weighs less than 100 lb, 45 kg. His sire was a miniature Sicilian donkey and his dam a miniature horse.

Despite their 'hybrid vigour' mules are not as long-lived as donkeys, and there are few authentic records of this animal exceeding 40 years. In 1936 details were published of a 48-year-old mule, and this may well be a record age.

———————

Although she-mules and hinnies (hinnes) are generally considered to be infertile, there have been at least 30 unconfirmed reports of foaling in these hybrids since 1527. The most recent occurred in South Africa in 1982, and the previous year a she-mule allegedly gave birth to a foal in Hunan province, China. As far as is known, there are no records of fertile male mules.

RABBITS AND HARES

Rabbits, hares and pikas (mouse-hares) were once included in the order *Rodentia*, but they have little in common with rodents and now constitute a separate order, *Lagomorpha*.

The history of the rabbit is largely confined to the northern land masses where the earliest representatives appeared in the Mongolian Palaeocene about 60 million years ago. The European rabbit (*Oryctolagus cuniculus*), from which the domestic rabbit is derived, was initially a native of the Iberian Peninsula; later it spread southwards to Morocco and Algeria in NW Africa and northwards through Europe, and Man has kept and reared this very adaptable mammal in a semi-captive state for at least 3000 years. The European rabbit was introduced into Britain by the Normans in the 11th century, and for hundreds of years this species was successfully 'farmed' in enclosed warrens called coneygarths ('rabbit gardens'). The bottom fell out of the market in *c* 1880 when competition from abroad and the wild rabbit population explosion caused prices to slump. Twenty years later the rabbit was one of the commonest animals in England, with the density still rising at an unprecedented rate, and it was round about this time that the selective breeding of modern rabbits really began in earnest.

Domestic rabbits are divided into four main groups for show purposes—Normal Fur Breeds, Rex Breeds, Satin Breeds and Fancy Breeds.

Largest

The largest of the 90 or so recognised breeds of domestic rabbit is the Flemish Giant (also called the Flemish), which originated in Flanders and was later bred on a massive scale in Ghent, where the Belgian standard was established in 1895. The French standard for this Giant Rabbit was set in 1919, but breeders in France were much more interested in length than weight, and in the end this obsessive desire for elongation was pushed to such extremes that the unfortunate strain became known as the 'Accordian Giant'!

German breeders, on the other hand, were much more sensible in their approach and went in for a better-proportioned animal, and today the German Giant, which dates from 1937, is the approved model for international breeders of this fancy rabbit. The weight of an adult Flemish giant ranges from 7 kg, 15.4 lb to 8.5 kg, 18.7 lb (average toe to toe length when fully stretched out 36 in, 91 cm), but bucks weighing up to 21 lb, 9.52 kg have been exhibited. In June 1963 a posthumous weight of 25 lb, 11.3 kg (toe to toe length: 40 in, 101 cm) was reported for an eight-year-old buck named 'Floppy' bred in England, but this rabbit must have been an outsized freak, because the English Flemish Giant is smaller than its continental cousins and does not normally weigh more than 12 lb, 5.44 kg. Other Giant Rabbits known to exceed 15 lb, 6.8 kg occasionally include the Belier Français, the Giant Papillion and the Blanc de Bouscat (all French breeds), and the American Checkered Giant and the American Giant Chinchilla.

The now-extinct Angevin, which originated somewhere in Europe in the 16th century, was also noted for its great size (and huge feet) and regularly reached a length of more than 5 ft ... yes 5 ft!... 1.52 m. This massively framed strain was the forerunner of all the modern Giant Rabbit breeds, and some individuals probably weighed over 30 lb, 13.6 kg.

The largest variety of rabbit bred in Britain is the Giant Rabbit (British). Adults regularly weigh 12–15 lb, 5.4–6.8 kg, and examples over 20 lb, 9.07 kg have been recorded. The English Lop, the oldest of the fancy breeds, was also credited with weights up to 20 lb, 9.07 kg in the 19th century, but the rabbits bred today are built on more modest lines.

The heaviest domestic rabbit on record was a five-month-old pure-bred French Lop (Belier Français) doe exhibited at the Reus Fair, NE Spain,

The elephantine 12 kg, 26.6 lb French Lop doe exhibited at the Reus Fair, NE Spain, in 1980.

in April 1980, which tipped the scales at 12.01 kg, 26.67 lb. This Giant Rabbit was bred and raised on a farm in Omellions (Lerida province), and no drugs or additives were used to accelerate her growth. The ideal weight for this breed is said to be 5.5 kg, 12.12 lb.

The heaviest wild rabbit on record (average weight 3½ lb, 1.58 kg) was a buck of 8 lb 4 oz, 3.74 kg killed by Norman Wilkie of Markinch, Fife, Scotland while out ferreting on 20 November 1981.

Smallest

The smallest breeds of domestic rabbit are the Netherland Dwarf and the Polish, both of which have a weight range of 2–2½ lb, 0.9–1.13 kg when fully grown. The Polish, incidentally, is an English breed despite its name, and its ancestry can be traced back to warren rabbits.

In 1960 Jacques Bouloc of Coulommière, central France, set out to produce the world's most diminutive rabbits by breeding downwards from successively smaller generations of Netherland Dwarf and Polish crosses. The programme took longer than he had envisaged but, at the end of 15 years, he had a 'mini-rabbit' which only weighed 14 oz, 396 g when adult and made an ideal pet for flat-dwellers. This furry atom also has another advantage over its larger relatives—it is too small to make a decent rabbit pie!

Oldest

The average life span for all breeds of domestic rabbit is about eight years, but large hybrids and others can live up to 15 years or even longer.

A buck rabbit named 'Blackie' owned by Mrs H Chivers of Brixham, Devon, died on 13 March 1971 aged 16 years 3 months, and a Dutch buck belonging to G H Clement of Offord D'Arcy, Huntingdonshire, celebrated its 16th birthday the following year. In December 1963 a Californian buck named 'Mischief' owned by Miss Elaine Penhaul of Hunstanton, Norfolk, was still alive aged 17 years. He was one of three baby bunnies given to Elaine and her two brothers by a friend of the family. In February 1980 a rabbit named 'Snowy' owned by Sydney Greaves of Morton, near Chesterfield, Derbyshire, was reportedly still alive aged 19 years, and the same year a Dutch buck belonging to a woman living in Desborough, Northants, allegedly entered its 20th year, but neither of these claims has yet been substantiated.

The oldest documented rabbit on record was an 18-year-old English doe which was still alive in 1931. This case was fully investigated by Major Stanley S Flower, famous for his meticulous research into animal longevity.

The average life span of a wild rabbit (*Oryctolagus cuniculus*) is 18 months.

The oldest recorded wild rabbit was a buck named 'Flopsy', who was found as a nestling on 6 August 1964 and was reared and then kept as a family pet by Mrs L B Walker of Longford, Tasmania. He died on 29 June 1983 aged 18 years 10 months 29 days.

Pugnacity

Although rabbits are looked upon as timid creatures, they also have a pugnacious side to their character. A doe, for example, will often fight fiercely to protect her young from a predator, and a buck will respond vigorously if a trespasser comes too near its mate. One such animal was a battle-scarred warrior who lived on a heath in Stoke-on-Trent, Staffordshire. During the early months of the summer this determined guardian of home and family regularly ambushed dogs of all sizes being walked by their owners in his territory, which is why the amused locals nicknamed him 'Thugs Bunny'!

The most famous leporine 'mugger' of them all, however, was the bunny which attacked President Jimmy Carter (1977–81) whilst he was on a fishing trip in his home State of Georgia. According to the official account of the confrontation, which raised many an eyebrow around the world, the President was sitting in a canoe in the middle of a pond when he suddenly spotted the kamikaze rabbit swimming towards him with 'teeth flashing and its nostrils flared'. Luckily there was a paddle readily to hand and America's leader managed to beat the aquatic bunny into submission before it could inflict any damage. How the demented beast managed to evade the Secret Service security net remains something of a mystery, and even to this day no one seems to know what happened to the would-be assassin's body!

Breeding

The normal length of the gestation period in the domestic rabbit is 30–31 days, but pregnancies as short as 28 days and as long as 34 days have been recorded in which the young (known as kittens) survived. The duration is largely governed by the

The 'mini rabbit' specially bred in France for children in small city flats.

size of the doe, the time of year and the size of the litter she is carrying.

On 9 August 1977 Mr Glyn Roberts of Cefn Hengoed, Mid Glamorgan, Wales, mated his New Zealand White doe with a Belgian Hare which, despite its name, is a breed of fancy rabbit, and on 22 August she produced a litter of five kittens. He said the doe had given birth to another litter five weeks earlier, but had not been put with another buck since.

The average litter size is five to six, but the normal range is three to nine. Generally the larger the breed the greater the number of kittens produced in each litter, but hereditary factors and the age of the doe also have to be taken into consideration.

The largest rabbit litter on record was one of 24 produced by a New Zealand White owned by Mr Joseph Filek of Sydney, Cape Breton, Nova Scotia, Canada, in 1978. In April the same year another New Zealand White named 'Lucy' belonging to Ricky Sanchez of Klamath Falls, Oregon, USA, gave birth to a litter of 21 (20 survived). In this case, however, the father was an American Checkered Giant called 'Big Boy'.

The reproductive powers of the rabbit have long been a source of fascination to man, and various writers have tried to estimate the possible number of descendants a pair of rabbits might have if all the off-spring survived for different lengths of time. One 19th century naturalist calculated that a pair of rabbits breeding eight times a year and producing a litter of eight on each occasion would end up with a family of 2 164 800 after four years, but this would never happen in nature because most wild rabbits are killed by predators, starvation or disease before they have reached their second birthdays. Because does can mate within 24 hours of giving birth they could (in theory) produce 11 litters annually, but in reality no rabbit of any type or breed can bear and raise more than six litters a year with any degree of success.

The most prolific breeds of domestic rabbit are the New Zealand White and the Californian, both of which are capable of producing five to six litters of 8–12 kittens a year during their breeding life.

During the period 1972–74 a 14 lb, 6.35 kg New Zealand White buck named 'Mohammed Ali' fathered 6000 bunnies. According to his owner, Mr Eric Russell, who ran a farm at Brompton, Yorkshire, Ali worked only on alternate days—even champions need a rest—and had countless bouts with a choice of 100 does before he went into honourable retirement. Most stud rabbits are worn out by the time they are four years old and have to be killed, but in Ali's case Mr Russell made an exception because he felt the buck had more than earned his place in the sun.

Ali carried out his duties under controlled conditions but, when there are no such restrictions, an amorous rabbit can sometimes become a positive menace. Take the case of a wild-eyed buck named 'Bunger', for instance, whose home patch was in Totterdown, Bristol. No animal was safe when this lusty bunny was in the mood for love, and all the local cats and dogs stampeded for cover—if they were lucky enough to spot him first! One nervous-wreck of a cat steadfastly refused to leave the house after a close encounter of the third kind with this furry Casanova, and when the people next door went on holiday they returned to find their pet doe trying to feed 14 kittens! Things finally came to a head when Bunger (the polite version of his nick-name) took a shine to an innocent terrier trotting past and set off after it in hot pursuit. In its desperate efforts to avoid being seduced the frantic dog became trapped between two walls, and had to be rescued by firemen. It was then that Bunger's owner, Miss Eleanor Walsh, decided that enough was enough and took her outrageous pet to a local vet for 'treatment'. Since then the atmosphere in downtown Totterdown has been a lot more relaxed.

Ears

The longest rabbit ears are found in the Lop family (four varieties). In the English Lop the ears regularly measure 23 in, 58 cm from tip to tip in adults, and a lateral spread of 26 in, 66 cm has been reported for a quality specimen at the age of four months. The greatest length quoted for this type is 28½ in, 72 cm, but measurements up to and exceeding 30 in, 76 cm have been recorded for the slightly heavier French Lop. Because their ears are so exaggerated the Lops, not surprisingly, have long lost the power to move these cumbersome appendages.

Rabbits' ears are also very good conductors of heat, which is why inventor Bill Schulz of Oregon, USA, has recently installed 500 of these lettuce-chomping animals in his 30 000 ft², 2 760 m² greenhouse. He reckons that by radiating heat through their furry coats and transmitting it down their long ears he can make big savings in his fuel bills.

RODENTS

The earliest known rodents were the squirrel-like *Paramyidae*, which appeared in North America about 57 million years ago. From there the ancestral family spread to Europe in the early Eocene (50–54 million years BP).

Largest

The world's largest rodent (nearly 3000 species) is the Capybara (*Hydrochoerus hydrochaeris*), also called the Carpincho or water hog, which is found in tropical South America. Mature specimens have a head and body length of 3½–4½ ft, 1.06–1.37 m, and usually scale 110–121 lb, 50–55 kg, but much heavier weights have been recorded for captive animals including one cage-fat male which tipped the scales at an astonishing 250 lb, 113 kg. A blind farmer in Surinam, who raised one of these animals as a pet after it had been abandoned by its mother, trained it to act as his 'seeing eye'.

Rats

The largest rat in the world (570 species) is the Cane rat (*Thryonomys swinderianus*) of West Africa. Mature specimens measure 420–860 mm, 16.5–34 in in total length (tail 70–250 mm, 2.75–8.43 in), and generally scale 4–7 kg, 8.8–15.4 lb, but weights up to 9 kg, 19.8 lb have been reliably recorded for some individuals. Because this rodent is a vegetarian, African children sometimes keep them as pets, and in Ghana and Cameroon it is now being farmed for use as food.

Only two species of wild rat are found in Britain but because they are classified as vermin by the

Ministry of Agriculture they cannot be kept as pets without an official licence. Phil Drabble, the well-known writer and naturalist, once reared a brown rat from infancy by way of an experiment and discovered that it was a most engaging creature, but wild rats are not really suitable as pets because, apart from the health risk and their strong smell, they tend to panic more easily than fancy rats and can give a very nasty bite when frightened.

A man in Los Angeles, California, USA, was recently charged with violating state health safety laws after the discovery of 50 'pet' Brown rats at his home. A policeman who went to the accused's house said the rats were gnawing the wooden building away!

The largest rat found in Britain is the Brown or Common rat (*Rattus norvegicus*), which was accidentally introduced in 1728 from Russian shipping. The average-sized adult buck (does tend to be smaller) has a head and body length of 8.5 in, 216 mm plus a 7½ in, 190 mm tail and weighs 9–12 oz, 255–339 g, but much larger individuals have been reported. At the end of the 19th century one outsized Brown rat weighing nearly 30 oz, 850 g was caught living under the kennel of a well-fed dog with sloppy eating habits, and on 20 December 1904 the famous naturalist J G Millais killed a very large buck weighing 36 oz, 1.01 kg (total length 19 in, 482 mm) in his garden at Warnham, Sussex.

The largest Brown rat ever recorded in Britain was an aged individual killed at Malton, Yorkshire, in August 1881 which measured 23 in, 584 mm in total length and tipped the scales at 44 oz, 1.24 kg. This weight was matched by another buck taken at Claxton Hall, Yorkshire, in January 1897, but the latter specimen measured 20 in, 508 mm in total length.

Fortunately monsters like these are no longer found in Britain, and today a Brown rat weighing more than 18 oz, 509 g would be considered a giant. In the 1960s Brian Plummer, who has spent most of his life hunting rats, caught an enormous doe (the largest on record) in a maggot factory near Rotherham, Yorkshire. It weighed 28 oz, 792 g and contained 16 foetuses.

The Black rat (*Rattus rattus*), which was first recorded in the British Isles in 1187, is a little smaller and less sturdy than the Brown rat, but it has a longer tail and has been measured up to 500 mm, 19.68 in in total length. Mature animals usually weigh 150–200 g, 5.3–7.06 oz, but one ancient buck taken in Yarmouth, Norfolk, many years ago scaled 280 g, 9.89 oz, which is probably a record weight for this species.

Fancy rats are mutant forms of the Brown rat, and are much friendlier creatures than their wild counterparts because they have been bred from gentle strains. The largest varieties are the albino types, with bucks and does attaining weights of 500 g, 17.66 oz and 350 g, 12.36 oz, respectively.

Breeding

The gestation periods for the Brown and Black rats are 21–24 days and 21–23 days respectively, and fancy rats also come within this pregnancy range.

The size of the litter is closely related to the body weight and age of the doe. In the case of the Brown rat the average litter size is seven to eight young, but 12–16 is not all that uncommon, and one enormous doe bred in a laboratory produced a record 24 young in one litter. The Black rat (average litter size six to seven) has also been credited with litters of more than 12, and in exceptional cases up to 20 young have been observed.

Rats are extremely prolific breeders, and a doe can produce up to eight litters a year under favourable conditions. One writer has calculated that a single pair of rats could end up with 1808 descendants within the space of 12 months if each litter consisted of six young and the sexes were evenly divided, but such a total would only be feasible if there were no fatalities, the mothers did not reject any of their young, and there were no interruptions in their breeding cycles. In other words, it's an impossible figure.

Oldest

Rodents are the shortest-lived animals in the Class Mammalia, and rats are no exception. In the wild they rarely live longer than one to two years, and in captivity the life expectancy of the albino rat is about three years.

The greatest age recorded for a rat is about 5 years 8 months in the case of a laboratory specimen which died at the Wistar Institute in Philadelphia, Pennsylvania, USA, in 1924. This veteran (a white rat) was received as a one-year-old, and spent another 4 years 8 months in captivity. A Hooded rat owned by Dodi Nardini of Waterford, Ohio, USA, was still alive in September 1978 aged 4 years 6 months, but further details are lacking.

Intelligence

Rats have an excellent learning capacity, and a lot of this is due to the fact that these very adaptable animals are extremely curious and love to explore. Laboratory studies have shown that they have good memories and are adept at solving problems such as selecting a letter of the alphabet or picking out an ink blot from a display of several. Many stories have been told of the ingenious methods used by rats to transport stolen fowls' eggs to their nests. In one exercise several eggs were carried from the bottom of a house to the top by two rats devoting themselves to each egg, and alternately passing it up to each other at every step of the staircase. There is also the amusing account of the sea captain trading out of the port of Boston in Lincolnshire who constantly missed eggs from his store room and suspected that he was being robbed by the crew. One night he laid in a fresh stock of eggs and waited to apprehend the thieves. To his great astonishment a number of rats suddenly put in an appearance, quickly formed a line from the egg baskets to their hole and proceeded to hand the eggs from one to another in their forepaws!

One of the most remarkable illustrations of rat sagacity was given by a 19th-century English clergyman who befriended a Brown rat which he found in his house. In the process of time the rat became perfectly tame and seemed to be very attached to his benefactor. One night the man was awoken when he felt a sharp bite on his cheek—and discovered that the curtains surrounding his four-poster bed were on fire! He managed to escape, but the house was burnt to the ground and he never saw the rat again.

Rats can also be extremely crafty at times, and at least one American psychologist would agree with this statement. One day he put a laboratory rat in an exercise wheel while an automatic counter kept track of the revolutions. When the researcher returned to the cage an hour later to see how things were progressing he found the subject of his experiment lying comfortably on its back outside the apparatus while it casually spun the wheel with one of its forepaws!

In 1927 a super-fit laboratory rat set up an endurance record which still stands today when it ran the equivalent of 27 miles, 43.2 km in a single day in an exercise wheel!

Rats also show touching devotion to handicapped members of their own kind. One morning a miner working at Cefn Cribbwr colliery, Glamorgan, S Wales was feeding a rat with left-overs from his lunch when it suddenly picked up a short length of rope and disappeared into the gloom. Soon afterwards it returned with the rope still in its mouth; at the other end, hanging on with a firm grip was a female rat—she was blind. Other observers have also seen old blind rats being helped along in similar fashion by their companions during migration.

Smell

The rat's most important sensory organ is its nose, and this fact has not been overlooked by the US Army, which has trained a number of these rodents to sniff out land mines by associating the smell of TNT with pleasurable brain stimulation. When a mine is located a computer picks up the waves of pleasure sent out by the electrode implanted in the rat's brain, and the information is then relayed to military headquarters. The success rate is reported to be 100 per cent.

On the other side of the globe Hong Kong Police use specially-trained rats to sniff out heroin factories.

Space flights

The most travelled rodents on record were the batch of 30 white rats placed aboard the Soviet biological research satellite 'Cosmos 936' in August 1977. The project was aimed at establishing life support systems to protect astronauts, and all of the animals survived the journey back to Earth in an experimental module.

Toughness

In 1980 scientists working from the small atoll of Enewatak in the Marshall Islands, W. Pacific, discovered a population of rats apparently thriving on the radioactive-contaminated island of Runit. The rats were descendants of an underground rodent population which had survived 43 atomic bomb tests on the isolated mass in the 1940s and 1950s and the ensuing fallout. The island has since been declared unsafe for humans for at least 25 000 years.

It has also been established that British rats are much tougher than their counterparts on the other side of the Atlantic. Recently, when American scientists tried out a 'death ray' machine on laboratory rats, they all died quickly from induced heart attacks; when the black-box device was used on British strains, however, the rays had no effect whatsoever.

Rat kings

No discussion about rats would be complete without mention of the mysterious 'Rat King'. This extremely rare phenomenon occurs only when Black rats (Brown rats are not affected) huddle together for warmth during the coldest parts of the winter, and in so doing get their tails entangled. As they thrash about in an effort to separate themselves they create a complicated knot called a 'king', which condemns the rats to a slow death by starvation. No one quite knows for certain how the king is formed, but one possible explanation is that the rats' tails become soaked in urine, which in turn congeals into a sticky mess that acts like an adhesive and renders the animals inseparable.

Only 57 rat kings have been described since 1564, and 18 of these have not been fully-authenticated. Of the ten reported this century, the last occurrence was in February 1963 when P van Nijnatten, a Dutch farmer, killed a Black rat hiding under a pile of sticks in his barn and found it was part of a king. The seven rats (five females and two males) all looked well-fed and appeared to be of the same age, judging by their size.

The average number of rats forming a 'king' is 12, but larger ones have been found.

The largest 'rat king' on record was one consisting of 32 individuals found dead in a chimney which had been opened up by a miller named Steinbruck at Buchheim, Germany in May 1828. All the bodies were badly scorched and hairless. This superlative example is now preserved in the Altenberg Mauritianum.

Shows

Fancy rats owe their existence to a man named Jack Black, who was official rat-catcher to Queen Victoria in 1850. He noticed that albino and other oddly-coloured Brown rats were occasionally caught in his traps and decided to breed some in captivity. Today there is a small but growing rat fancy in Britain, and shows are put on regularly by the National Fancy Rat Society. So far, however, breeders have not been able to achieve the wide variety of colours that are found in fancy mice, and most of the specimens seen at shows are white. The most handsome variety is the Japanese hooded rat, which comes in several distinct colours (with white) and has black or ruby eyes. Other popular strains include the Siamese rat (which has the colouring of a Siamese cat), the Himalayan rat, the Red rat (which has a curly coat), the Irish Black and the Agouti.

Mice

The most widely-distributed of all mammals is the House mouse (*Mus musculus*), which probably originated in Central Asia. It is found on every continent, including Antarctica, and has been present in Britain since 1200 BC.

More than 130 forms of *Mus musculus* have been described, but there are only about 20 viable strains, and they are all much about the same size. The adult buck usually measures about 160 mm, 6.29 in in total length and scales about 25–30 g, 0.87–1.06 oz, but some individuals measuring up to 250 mm, 9.85 in and weighing over 40 g, 1.41 oz, have been reliably reported. In December 1982 it was announced that 'super-mice' nearly twice the normal size had been bred by American researchers after they had implanted the rat gene for growth

hormone into fertilized mouse eggs. This experiment in genetic engineering—the first successful one involving mammals—indicated that giant mice could be used as a rich source of gene produce for improving breeds of livestock and correcting genetic diseases.

Breeding

The gestation period for the house mouse is 20–21 days. The average litter size is six to seven young, but the normal range is 4–13.

The largest mouse litter on record was one of 34 produced by a doe owned by Marion Ogilvie of Blackpool, Lancashire, on 12 February 1982. One of the offspring was killed by the father, but most of the others survived. Another litter consisting of 32 young was born in a New York laboratory in March 1961.

Mice usually have up to five litters a year in houses, compared to six in cold stores, eight in grain stores and ten in corn ricks. This means some does can produce more than 100 young in a single year, which in turn would make them more prolific than rats.

Oldest

The average life-span of a house mouse in captivity is two to three years. Five cage-bred mice at the Scripps Institute in La Jolla, California, USA, lived for more than four years, the oldest for 5 years 8 months, and a buck named 'Hercules' with 'goo-goo blue eyes' owned by Mrs Roz Hair of Purley, Surrey, died on 26 December 1976 aged 5 years 11 months.

The oldest house mouse on record was a specimen named 'Dixie' who lived for 6 years 6 months. The owner of this veteran, Christopher Newton of Sheffield, Yorkshire, found the mouse wandering in the garden as a baby on 28 October 1974 and housed him in an empty fish tank, where he remained until his death on 25 April 1981.

In 1978 mice embryos which had been frozen in liquid nitrogen and stored at −196°C, −91°F in a Cambridge laboratory five years earlier were thawed out and implanted into a female mouse. Just over a month later, she produced a perfectly healthy litter.

Nests

Mice sometimes make their homes in the strangest places. In the 1960s a 'black-faced' variant of the house mouse was reported to be living at the bottom of at least five coal mines in Yorkshire; even more bizarre are the woolly-coated colonies of mice that

The mouse who managed to get itself trapped in the spout of a disused kettle. It was later rescued and released.

have been found living on frozen meat carcases in refrigerated rooms kept at temperatures ranging from −3°C to −10°C, 26.6°F to 14°F. A team at Glasgow University researched this 'cold-store' phenomenon in the late 1950s and early 1960s and discovered that the mice fed mainly on kidneys which are relatively soft. They nested either in the cork lining of the walls or in the rib section of the carcases themselves, and used the muslin for their nest material. Even more surprising, however, was the fact that they produced on an average six litters a year, and reared them successfully, despite the intense cold.

Racing

In recent years mouse-racing has been growing fast both as a sport and as a fund-raiser for charities in Britain, with meetings being held regularly in pubs and village halls up and down the country. The man who started it all is Brian Turner, a builder and ex-bookmaker of Stockland, Devon, who has been racing thoroughbred white mice at an old coaching inn in Honiton since 1975. The 13 ft, 3.96 m course he uses is an elaborate affair with water jumps and other obstacles. It consists of ten narrow shelves, one for each mouse, which are fixed firmly to a stone wall with a sheet of thick polythene in front to stop them falling off. On either side of the track are blackboards offering punters the latest odds. The only trouble with mice is that they are quite unpredictable and won't run to order. Often they just sit down on the track and clean themselves, and they have also been known to scurry along the track and back again without crossing the finishing line! The record time for the course is a blistering 60 seconds, which is equivalent to 0.34 miles/h, 0.54 km/h. In April 1983 the RSPCA announced that it was planning to investigate mouse-racing in Britain

because it felt that such 'events' were very distressing for the animals concerned and that they appeared to be on the increase. It warned that its uniformed inspectors had been alerted, and that they would 'raid' any meeting they got to hear about.

Mouse racing is also popular in the USA, but there the punters take it much more seriously and sometimes go right over the top when they lose. In May 1983 a county sheriff's deputy in New York State was suspended for eating a live mouse after it had lost a race. The unfortunate mouse had earlier won three races, but the effort had taken its toll and it failed dismally in the fourth—much to the policeman's annoyance, who had a sizeable bet on the animal.

Ferocity

If there were any justice in the world this unfortunate mouse would have got in a few choice bites of its own with its sharp teeth before its life was snuffed out, but sadly this was not to be. Mice can, however, be extremely vicious at times, and snake owners who try to feed their pets with live mice instead of dead ones have had cause to regret it. One such person was Vincent Sazio of Thornton Heath, Surrey. One morning he gave his 4 ft, 1.27 m python 'Monty' a live mouse as a special treat but, when he returned home from work in the evening, he found the snake had been killed and partially eaten by the 6 in, 152 mm white demon. It was later ascertained that the snake had just started to shed its skin when its potential dinner was introduced, and was in a drowsy state when it was attacked.

Another live mouse fed to a Taipan (*Oxyuranus scutellatus*), one of the world's most venomous snakes, at a museum in Darwin, Northern Territory, Australia in February 1982 was quickly killed and eaten by the hungry serpent. But before it died the brave little animal got in one determined bite which later set up an infection that eventually killed the snake—a case of poetic justice!

Singing

In 1846 a 'singing-mouse' with a voice like a canary that could be heard from a distance of 60 ft, 18 m was exhibited in London and proved a major attraction. Since then hundreds of stories have been published about mice with singing ability, and these tiny songsters appear to have completely bewitched those persons fortunate enough to hear their sweet warblings.

One man in this category was W O Hiskey, who wrote of his experience in the *American Naturalist* (1871): 'I was sitting a few evenings since, not far from a half-open closet door, when I was startled by a sound issuing from the closet, of such marvellous beauty that I at once asked my wife how Bobbie Burns (our canary) had found his way into the closet, and what could start him singing such a queer and sweet song in the dark. I procured a light and found it to be a *mouse*! He had filled an over-shoe from a basket of pop-corn which had been popped and placed in the closet in the morning. Whether this rare collection of food inspired him with song I know not, but I had not the heart to disturb his corn, hoping to hear from him again. Last night his song was renewed again. I approached him with a subdued light and with great caution, and had the pleasure of seeing him sitting among his corn and singing his beautiful solo.'

That mice (and certain other rodents) are musical is now a well-attested fact, but normally their melodies are ultrasonic and cannot be heard by human ears. Sadly it is only when their larynx or lungs are diseased that their marvellous songs fall within man's auditory range.

Almost equally as bizarre is the Japanese waltzing mouse, a freak variant of the house mouse, which spends most of its life running around in circles. The gyrations of this animal are caused by an inherited sense of imbalance in the inner ear, and the main problem with such interbreeding is that the fertility of the stock is liable to degenerate over the years.

Space flights

In 1958 two mice named 'Laska' and 'Benjy' reached a height of 1400 miles, 2240 km in a Jupiter rocket fired by the Americans. The nose cone containing the mice was not recovered, but it is believed they survived re-entry.

Shows

Mice have been tamed and kept as pets since early Roman times, but the first fancy breeds were developed in Japan in the 17th century. In Britain the National Mouse Club was founded in 1895, and today shows for exhibition mice are held regularly throughout the year. The most prestigious event in the fancy mice calendar is the Bradford Championship Show, at which rabbits and cavies also compete, and the little town of Shipley, 3 miles, 4.8 km from Bradford, is considered to be the 'mouse capital of the world'.

After nearly 90 years of selective breeding more than 40 different varieties are recognised by the NMC. They are divided into four groups—Selfs, Tans, Marked Varieties and Any Other Varieties (AOV)—and there is a bewildering range of colours and patterns. The two newest breeds are the satin, where the coat is shiny and brilliant in colour, and

the seal-point Siamese which has markings just like its namesake in the cat world. Some creams bred by Tony Jones, Secretary of the North London Long-tails, at his home in Walthamstow reach 11 in, 254 mm in total length, which would make it the world's longest breed of fancy mouse.

Hamsters

The world's most popular small pet is the Golden or Syrian hamster (*Mesocricetus auratus*). It was originally described in 1839, but very little was known about this attractive little creature until April 1930 when an Israeli zoologist, Dr I Aharoni, dug out a live female and a litter of 12 young from a burrow in a field near Aleppo (now Haleb), Syria, and took them back to Hebrew University in Jerusalem. Some of the hamsters later escaped, and another one was killed in a fight, but Dr Aharoni was able to breed from the remaining male and two females, and within one year they had produced 150 offspring. In 1931 two pairs were brought to London for laboratory research. These hamsters also bred in their turn, and some specimens were later sent to the United States Public Health Station at Garville, Louisiana, USA, for further scientific study. A few were also given to London Zoo and, when their numbers started increasing rapidly, some of the surplus stock was passed on to private breeders who had shown an interest in these fascinating rodents. By the mid-1950s the pet-loving public had taken to these furry creatures in a big way, and today the domestic population in homes and research institutions throughout the world can be counted in millions—thanks to the noble endeavours of the trio bred in 1931.

Largest

Most hamsters (13 species) measure about 120–150 mm, 4.72–5.9 in in total length when adult (females are slightly larger than males) and the weight ranges between 140 g, 4.94 oz and 155 g, 5.47 oz.

The largest member of the hamster family (*Cricetidae*) is the Korean grey hamster (*C. triton*). This species normally measures 150–200 mm, 5.9–7.87 in at maturity, but lengths up to 306 mm, 12.04 in (including a 100 mm, 3.93 in tail) have been recorded for wild individuals. Unlike most of its smaller relatives this rodent is not pet material. It is reported to be extremely savage, and London Zoo is one of the few scientific establishments to have bred this animal successfully. The Korean grey hamster is also notorious for its hoarding propensities, and in the run-up to winter it often stockpiles staggering amounts of grain and other foodstuffs in its burrow. (A research worker found 45 kg, 99 lb of seeds and potatoes in one store chamber.) In times of famine these 'granaries' have proved a life-saver to Chinese peasants who would otherwise have starved to death without this food.

Smallest

The smallest species of hamster are the extremely docile Desert hamster (*Phodopus roborovskii*) and the Striped hairy-footed hamster (*P. sungorus*), which have a combined range extending from Siberia through Manchuria and northern China. Of the two, *P. roborovskii* is the more diminutive, with adults measuring only 50–60 mm, 1.96–2.36 in overall.

Breeding

The gestation period of the hamster is the shortest of any known mammal. The average duration is 16 days, but it does vary from animal to animal. Large litters are sometimes born one to two days earlier than normal, while small litters have been known to take 18–19 days.

The average litter size is five to nine, but a large, well-fed female may have as many as 16 or even more on rare occasions. When a large litter does occur, the mother usually kills weaker ones in order that the strong may survive, but most females can rear up to nine young comfortably. On 17 June 1976 a hamster named 'Tony' owned by Michael Vanderhoof of Martinez, Georgia, USA, gave birth to 17 young and subsequently took care of them all until they were weaned, but this female had been given special food additives to keep her milk at full flow. Another hamster belonging to M W Hudson of Cheadle, Cheshire, also produced a litter of 17 on 17 January 1980, but not all of them survived.

The largest hamster litter on record was one of 26 born in Baton Rouge, Louisiana, USA, on 28 February 1974. Owners Loryn and Sheri Miller said the mother killed 18 of them but reared the rest (four males and four females).

Female hamsters usually cease breeding when they are nine months old, by which time they may have produced five litters. Laboratory females, however, have been known to give birth to a sixth litter at the age of 11 months. Theoretically, a single pair of hamsters could end up with 100 000 descendants in a single year, but these rodents have a ruthless enemy which keeps the population under control—namely themselves! To put it in a nutshell, hamsters are anti-social and—apart from the act of mating—will not tolerate others of their own kind in close proximity. During the breeding season the males fight viciously (sometimes to the death) for mates, but the real bloody battles take place one to two days after mating when the fiercely territorial females take a sudden dislike to their spouses and attack them vigorously—usually below the belt! As a result many males are killed or end up sterile.

In 1982 several hundred golden hamsters invaded a council estate at Burnt Oak on the northern outskirts of London and started chewing their way through walls, floors, ceilings and furniture. One hysterical woman found six of the furry beasts scampering around her bedroom early one morning, and another ran screaming from her house when 37 of these unwelcome guests suddenly turned up in her settee. Poisons were laid down with little or no effect, and a local pensioner who despatched 180 of the dumpy intruders with an air rifle during the summer 'season' admitted afterwards that his tally was only the tip of the iceberg. In the end Barnet Council decided to call in a pest control unit but, the very day the men arrived on the scene, the wily rodents disappeared underground. The following spring, however, they were back again in even greater numbers, and today they appear to be a permanent fixture. It is believed that the hamsters, who are said to be bigger than normal with rat-like faces, are the descendants of pets left behind or freed by previous council house tenants. Similar hamster infestations have also been recorded from other parts of the country including Bury St Edmunds, Suffolk, where 70 were captured in 1964.

Hamsters are very excitable creatures, and a sudden shock can kill them. If the village schoolmaster at Cowbridge, South Glamorgan, Wales, had realised this fact beforehand he would not have fired his starting pistol in front of his pupils in order to demonstrate what they should expect on sports day—as it was, the class's unfortunate pet hamster died of a heart attack.

The highest-living species of hamster is the Mouse-like hamster (*Calomyscus bailwardi*), which has been found up to an altitude of 5000 m, 16 404 ft in the mountains of SW Turkestan, Soviet Central Asia. It is not known whether laboratory hamsters have been used in American space flight experiments.

Shows

The original colouring of the hamster was the familiar golden-brown, and 15 years after domestication it was still the only known shade. In December 1945, however, the golden hamster was shown competitively for the first time at the famous

Bradford Championship Show, and today the National Hamster Council recognises 118 different colour mutations. The most valuable strain is reportedly the satinised tortoiseshell and white, which can fetch up to £300 each (cf. £1 for an ordinary golden hamster), but the Angora or Long-haired hamster is also much sought after by enthusiasts. The ultimate in coat mutations is the totally black hamster, but this 'colour' has not yet been achieved by breeders, although there is a new variety of that name.

It should be noted that exhibition hamsters are much larger than those found in pet shops or laboratories. This is because the bigger the body the more it accentuates the best features of the hamster, and this counts a great deal with judges.

Gerbils

The best-known member of the gerbil family (Gerbillinae) is the Mongolian gerbil (Meriones unigiculatus) or Clawed Jird. This friendly little animal was first described in 1811, but domestic breeding did not start until 1935 when a Japanese zoologist collected 20 pairs from the Amur River basin on the Sino-Soviet border. From Japan 11 pairs were sent to the West Foundation in New York, NY, USA, in 1954 for medical research, and ten years later it was launched as a pet on the American market. It was introduced to the British public soon afterwards.

Largest

A fully-grown gerbil (71 species) is bigger than a mouse but smaller than a rat. In the case of the Mongolian gerbil males usually measure about 200 mm, 7.87 in in total length, half of which is taken up by the tail, and range in weight from 90 g, 3.18 oz to 117 g, 4.13 oz. Females are slightly smaller (70–100 g, 2.47–3.53 oz), but both sexes tend to put on excess weight with age, and some 'elders' have been known to reach 141 g, 5 oz.

The heaviest Mongolian gerbil on record was an incredibly obese male named 'Willie' who tipped the scales at 453 g, 16 oz in September 1976. This enormity, owned by Brigette Arenberg of Fairfields, Connecticut, USA, measured 240 mm, 9.5 in in total length and had a maximum girth of 135 m, 5.31 in.

The largest known species of gerbil is the massive Great gerbil (Rhombomys opimus) of Turkestan, China and Mongolia. Males have been measured up to 360 m, 14.17 in overall (tail 160 mm, 6.3 in,) and the weight may exceed 200 g, 7 oz.

Smallest

The smallest gerbil species are the Pygmy gerbil (Gerbillus henleyi) of NW Africa, the South African pygmy gerbil (Gerbillus paeba) and the Tassel-tailed pygmy gerbil (G. vallinus) of Angola, none of which exceeds 30 g, 1.06 oz.

Breeding

Mongolian gerbil litters are born 24–26 days after mating, but the gestation periods of other species may be longer or shorter depending on their size. The average litter is six to seven, but young mothers sometimes produce larger broods. At least two litters of 11 have been born in Britain (1979 and 1980), and on 9 December 1982 a gerbil belonging to Lyndsey Williams of Dundee, Tayside, Scotland, gave birth to 13 young.

The largest litter of gerbils recorded in Britain was one of 14 delivered in March 1983 by 'Honey' owned by Sharon Kirkman of Bulwell, Nottinghamshire.

In the 1960s litters ranging in size from 10 to 15 were regularly produced at the gerbil 'nursery' run by American geneticist George Mears near St Petersburg, Florida, USA. He attributed his success to a special food formula and good selective breeding policies.

Like rats and mice, gerbils are also prolific breeders. A female mated at 10–12 weeks can have 10 to 12 litters during her period of fertility, ie 14–16 months, but the usual maximum is eight pregnancies. In one case a female raised nine litters in 17 months before she became barren, and there is also an extreme record of a gerbil having ten litters and rearing nine of them in an 11-month period. On 24 August 1974 a gerbil named 'Whiskers' belonging to Josephine Lloyd of Sleaford, Lancashire, gave birth to her 11th litter and a total of 49 young. Another specimen owned by Susan Stansfield of Newton Hall, Durham, produced 70 offspring during her breeding life (15 April 1979–13 March 1980), including one litter of ten.

The world's greatest mammalian lover is Shaw's Jird (Meriones shawi) of North Africa, which is frequently used as an experimental laboratory animal. One vigorous 60 g, 2.12 oz male was observed to mate 224 times during one 60-minute period!

Oldest

The average life expectancy for a captive gerbil is three to four years, but much older individuals have been recorded. On 23 September 1977 a male named 'Squirt' belonging to Tom Clouser of Brookfield,

Wisconsin, USA, died aged 7 years 9 months 19 days.

The oldest gerbil on record was probably a female called 'Sahara' owned by Aaron Milstone of Lathrap Village, Michigan, USA, who was still alive in May 1981 aged 8 years 1 month. Another example named 'Tifney' (probably also female) belonging to Debbie and Cynthia Clifford of Dedham, Massachusetts, USA, reportedly passed the eight-year mark in June 1982, but further details are lacking.

Smell

Gerbils have an acute sense of smell, an ability essential for species that hoard food, and the public were made fully aware of this fact in 1982 when the Canadian Government announced that it was planning to train gerbils to sniff out drugs at airports. Officials claimed they had many advantages over dogs: they ate less, needed less space and attention, would take orders from anyone—and didn't bite!

The customs authorities set up an intensive training scheme to make the most of this rodent power. But despite the professional performance of the small creatures, there seemed to be a basic problem in putting the plan into action. Gerbils, it seems, could only be trained to sniff out one odour, which meant that travellers would have to go through a series of checks before they were given full customs clearance. The project was on the point

Aaron Milstone with his ancient pet gerbil 'Sahara'.

of being abandoned when the Federal Correctional Service stepped in. Drug-smuggling, it said, was also a very serious problem at Canadian prisons, and their customers were even more captive than airline passengers. So a University of Toronto zoologist was commissioned to train some of these animals for a pilot project, and he soon had a team of eight ready for action. The furry detectives would hide at the entrance to a prison and push a warning button to alert their superiors the moment they scented drugs passing through the gates. But shortly before the project could be put into operation at a correctional institution near Peterborough, Ontario, the press picked up the story and had a field day with headlines like 'Mounties outmanoeuvred by Gerbils!' appearing over stories deriding the scheme. To add insult to injury the gerbils were accidentally given contaminated water and died before the big day. In February 1984, after several more tests, the FCS announced that it was abandoning the scheme and going back to using security personnel because of technical problems with equipment used to monitor the animals. In other words, admitted a spokesman, the super-sniffing gerbils were too refined for the job.

Mongolian gerbils have an odour gland on the underside of their body and the secretion smells a bit like burnt feathers. Recently a woman living in Johannesburg, South Africa, walked out on her husband because he kept using her expensive perfume to make his pet gerbils more acceptable to visitors!

Shows

The first gerbil show of any size was staged at Alexandra Palace, London, in 1971 under the auspices of the National Mongolian Gerbil Society. The only colour commonly available then was the typical golden brownish-red Agouti, but this was later followed by the Albino, which is really a dark-tailed White, the Dilute (a cross between the Agouti and the Albino) and the White Spot, another mutation from the Agouti. So far breeders have failed to produce the uniform colour varieties that are found, for instance, in fancy mice, but many more mutations will appear in due course. In 1974 a solitary Chinchilla gerbil was purchased from a London pet store. When the buyer later realised the importance of his find he tried desperately to obtain other specimens, but his search ended in failure. Chinchilla has not been recorded since, but this colour will undoubtedly appear again sooner or later. More recently cream and black gerbils have been bred in the USA, but the latter strain has white patches on the chest and feet and cannot be considered a true self (one colour overall).

Cavies

The first rodent to be domesticated by man was the Wild Cavy (*Cavia tschudii*) of the Andes of Peru and Bolivia, which the pre-Inca races were using as a source of meat and occasional sacrifice to the gods as early as 5000 BC. Its descendant, *Cavia porcellus*, was brought to Europe from the Guiana coast of northern South America in 1580, but the 'Guiana Pig', as it was then called, attracted very little interest in Spain and Italy, and it was only in Germany that it became popular as a table delicacy. The domestic cavy eventually reached Britain in 1750, but here it was reared only as a household pet.

Largest

There is very little variation in size and shape between the 20 different varieties of domestic cavy. The White Cavy, however, tends to be the largest strain, with adult boars measuring 250 mm, 9.84 in in length and weighing 1000 g, 2.2 lb; sows are smaller, averaging 200 mm, 7.8 in and 850 g, 30 oz. A few years ago a new breed called the Giant White Cavy was reported to have been developed in the USA, but further details are lacking. Well-fed boars sometimes get terribly obese. In March 1983 a weight of 3 lb 2½ oz, 1.43 kg was recorded for a 3½-year-old cavy named 'George' owned by Julie Wells of Ware, Hertfordshire. This size, however, was dwarfed by an enormous caramel and white short-haired individual named 'Taffy' (born November 1976), who weighed 4 lb, 1.81 kg at the age of 8 months (length 12 in, 304 mm; waist 12 in, 304 mm) and 8 lb 2 oz, 3.67 kg (length 15 in, 381 mm; waist 13 in, 330 mm) when he was 22 months old. According to Taffy's owner, Vickie Spath of Huntingdon, Indiana, USA, her pet had a tremendous appetite and would eat anything except cabbage and potatoes. His favourite 'foods' were said to be soft plastic and rubber, which would seem to suggest that this colossus is no longer with us!

In the wild state this animal, one of 15 species, does not exceed 25 oz, 707 g.

Breeding

Uncharacteristically for a rodent, the cavy has a very long gestation period. The average duration is 67–68 days, but it can range from 58 to 75 days. The litter size is usually two to three, but some sows have been known to produce five, six or even more young in one brood. In September 1975 a litter of eight cavies was found abandoned in a cardboard box near Bury St Edmunds, Suffolk. They were adopted by local school-children.

The largest cavy litter on record was reportedly one consisting of 12 young produced by a laboratory specimen in 1972, but unfortunately further details are lacking.

Once a sow has bred she will remain fertile for six years, and could have up to five litters in any one year, but breeders usually restrict their stock to two litters annually for a period of two years.

Oldest

The average life-span of a cavy in captivity is four to five years, but some pampered examples have lived much longer. One boar owned by George Hindson of Stratton-on-the-Fosse, near Bath, Somerset, was still alive in April 1978 aged 9 years 3 months, whilst its twin brother lived for 8 years 6 months.

The oldest cavy on record was a white sow named 'Snowball' belonging to M A Wall of Bingham, Nottinghamshire. At the time of her death on 14 February 1979 this matriarch was 14 years 10½ months!

According to the findings of an American researcher who watched cavies continuously for long periods these creatures never sleep, although they rest occasionally with half-closed eyes. If this is true then cavies are unique among mammals, but breeders have since pooh-poohed this claim.

There is also another contention that if you pick up a guinea pig (cavy) by its tail, then its eyes will drop out! Fortunately for the animal this statement cannot be put to the test, because the so-called tail is nothing more than a tiny 'root' at the base of the spine which would be impossible to grip.

Luckiest

The luckiest cavy on record was probably the adventurous individual which received an over-warm reception when it sneaked unnoticed into a family home in Oxford and took up residence behind a gas fire. Every time the fire was switched on there was a terrible scratching noise and a smell of burning, and in the end it got so bad that the local Gas Board had to be called in. As an engineer was dismantling the apparatus to investigate, the cavy popped out, a bit scorched but otherwise in good shape. 'Gas Bag', as he was named, was adopted by the daughter of the house and lived to a ripe old age.

BIRDS

The earliest bird was the reptilian-like *Archaeopteryx*, which lived about 165 million years ago. It is known from five skeletons and a single feather impression found in the Upper Jurassic limestone of Germany. Unlike modern birds, this crow-sized glider had well-developed teeth in its jaws and a long jointed bony tail, but the wings bore characteristic feathers. Other avian forms appeared from the Cretaceous onwards, but the group really came into its own during the Tertiary period (65 million years ago) when all the existing major forms appeared.

The earliest bird to be domesticated was the Greylag goose (*Anser anser*) of the Neolithic period (*c* 18 000 BC) of south-eastern Europe, followed by the dove and pigeon (*Columbidae*) which date from 4500 BC in Mesopotamia (modern Iraq).

Largest

The largest living bird, and the ultimate in avian pets, is the ostrich (*Struthio camelus*) of Africa. Adult cock examples of this flightless bird stand about 8 ft, 2.4 m tall on the average and weigh 265–280 lb, 120–127 kg, but heights up to 9 ft, 2.74 m and weights up to 345 lb, 156 kg have been reliably reported for the northern race (*Struthio c. camelus*). In Southern Africa commercially-bred ostriches are rarely kept longer than 15 years for feather production because the quality of the plumage decreases as the birds get older, but sometimes farmers and their families get attached to certain individuals and keep them on as pets. One such person in SW Africa trained his ostrich to herd sheep, and another farmer near Durban, Natal, taught his pet to chase off birds that attacked his crops.

The largest flying bird ever kept as a pet was a female Harpy eagle (*Harpa harpyja*) named 'Jezebel' owned by Stanley Brock, former manager of the vast Dadanawa cattle ranch in Guyana, northern South America. This raptor tipped the scales at 27 lb, 12.2 kg. A female Asian golden eagle or Berkut (*Aquila chrysaetos daphanea*) called 'Atalanta' belonging to Sam Barnes of Pwllheli, North Wales, was also of comparable size. On rabbit-hunting expeditions he flew this eagle—she was killed in a collision with an ice-cream van on 1 May 1984—at a regular 26–27 lb, 11.8–12.2 kg.

Smallest

The smallest living birds are hummingbirds (*Trochilidae*). At one time it was extremely difficult to keep these birds (*c* 300 species) in captivity because, apart from living under varying climatic conditions, they feed mainly on nectar. Over the years, however, commercial pastes have been developed which meet the diet requirements of most hummingbirds. Of the 70 or so species which have been imported into Britain with some degree of success, the smallest is the Reddish Hermit (*Phaethornis ruber*) of the Guianas and the Amazon and Orinoco basins, which has a head and body length of less than 38 mm, 1.5 in and weighs under 3 g, 0.106 oz.

The history of cage-birds stretches back into the mists of antiquity when song-birds were kept as pets in cages of plaited twigs by early Asian civilisations. Aviculture, on the other hand, which is the term applied to the practice of keeping wild birds in aviaries with a view to studying their habits and inducing them to breed successfully, is a much more recent science.

Canaries

The canary (*Serinus canaria*) is a native of the Canaries, the Azores and Madeira. It was introduced into Europe by the Spanish soon after the final conquest of the Canaries in 1495, but some may have been brought to Britain from Madeira before this date. At first traders tried to protect their monopoly by exporting only male canaries, but sexing these birds before they have grown their full adult plumage is not an easy task, and quite a number of hens were sold to foreign buyers by mistake. As a result, the fashion for keeping canaries in cages spread rapidly, and by 1676 they were a common sight in England. Today the canary is the world's second most popular cage-bird after the budgerigar.

Largest

Most canaries measure between 4½ in, 114 mm and 5½ in, 140 mm in length and weigh 15–20 g, 0.53–0.70 oz. The largest strain is the well-built Parisian Frill, which measures 190–220 mm, 7.48–8.66 in, but this size is almost equalled by the Lancashire, Britain's largest native breed, which reaches 190–210 m, 7.48–8.26 in and is probably slightly heavier. Cock birds are larger than hens.

Smallest

The smallest canaries are found in the Miniatures, which are about half the size of ordinary specimens (*c* 112 mm, 4.4 in and 10 g, 0.35 oz). These scaled-down versions are closely associated with Yorkshire and Border types and appear to be the result of a mutation, although they are normal in every other respect.

Breeding

The incubation period for the canary is 14 days. Most clutches average three to five eggs, but some hens have been known to produce seven or even eight eggs occasionally. The breeding life lasts 1–3 years, and two or even three clutches are raised each season.

Oldest

The canary is the longest-lived small cage-bird. The life-span in captivity is normally eight to ten years, but a few cases of birds surviving beyond 20 years have been recorded. On 18 April 1975 a canary named 'Joey' celebrated his 28th birthday in his cage at Mrs Edna Potter's home in St Anns, Nottingham, but died soon afterwards. A canary-goldfinch mule named 'Sweet' owned by John Roberts of Deeside, Clwyd, North Wales was also 28 at the time of his death in August 1981.

The oldest canary on record was a cock bird named 'Joey' belonging to Mrs Kathleen Ross of Hull, Yorkshire. This bird, which was bartered by her late husband David for a packet of cigarettes in Calabar, Nigeria, in 1941, died on 8 April 1974 aged 34 years.

Singing

The only breed of canary developed purely for its song is the Roller canary, which gets its name from its ability to hold and roll a single note of its song. Some cock birds (hens are limited to a few 'tweets') known as 'schoolmasters' can produce every possible song combination embracing eight tours and five rolls. This king of songsters was originally bred by miners in the little German town of St Andreasburgh in the Harz Mountains, where it was tutored by the nightingale, musical instruments such as the flute, and even gramophone records, to give it the clear, sweet rolling tone (both natural and artificial) which has made it world famous. In c 1820 the 'Harz Mountain Roller', as it was called, was imported into Britain and today its descendant, the British Roller, can hold its own with the world's best in singing contests.

During the reign of Louis XIV (1638–1715) a canary fancier named Hervier de Chanteloup attached to the French court used to give 'Canario Concerts' for the ladies and gentlemen of high society. As many as 100 canaries took part in these entertainments and, apart from singing, they would also dance to minuets and gavottes played on a spinet.

Recently the famous all-canary choir of Kharkov in the Ukraine achieved 'a full harmony ensemble' when trainer and conductor Fyodor Fokenko announced that he had at last succeeded in breeding birds which could sing bass. This means the choir, which has been entertaining Russians for more than 30 years with a repertoire of more than 80 classical pieces, including Beethoven's Moonlight Sonata, Strauss waltzes and music by Schubert, Shostakovich and Glinka, will now be able to perform other works which require a bass voice.

In the summer of 1972 Harry P McKeever liberated more than 100 Roller canaries from the two aviaries at his home in Victoria, British Columbia, Canada. Some of the birds had come from Germany, others from local sources, but most of them were youngsters he had bred on the premises. These birds were free to come and go as they pleased, and one returned home two years after he had sold it to a fancier 8 miles, 9.6 km away. All in all the birds were at complete liberty for five years, making them history's first colony of homing canaries.

Gas

Because the canary is 15 times as susceptible to carbon monoxide poisoning as human beings, it has long been employed as an 'early warning system' down coal mines. By law every colliery must keep at the pithead at least two canaries for the use of mine rescue teams. The men take them underground, and at the first whiff of gas they topple over. The birds are then quickly withdrawn and placed in a 'mini oxygen tent' where they soon recover. In August 1983 the National Coal Board announced that it was planning to phase out the 1000 canaries still being used down the mines and replace them with sophisticated electronic devices. Not surprisingly, there was an immediate outcry from the miners, who said they would fight any plans to sack their pit canaries which were quick, certain and 100 per cent reliable. In the end the NCB, back-pedalling fast, had to give an assurance that canaries would be retained in the pits.

In 1982 a coalfield output record was broken when a pair of pit canaries called 'Charlie' and 'Di' produced ten chirping chicks over a period of nine months at Nantgarw colliery near Cardiff, South Wales. The birds raised their broods in a spare facemask in the lamp room, and the miners fed the youngsters on a daily diet of boiled eggs and breadcrumbs. It was the first time pit canaries had bred successfully.

Sadly, however, gas-sniffing canaries have not always been appreciated by man, and during the First World War one unfortunate individual ended up as the sole target for an artillery bombardment at Vimy Ridge in Flanders, Belgium! Apparently British sappers were digging a tunnel beneath the German lines when a canary, carried by the soldiers to give warning of gas, escaped and flew out of the tunnel to perch on the barbed wire of No Man's Land. Fearing that the Germans would put two and two together if they saw the canary, the infantry in the front line at this point tried to destroy the bird with rifle and machine-gun fire, but the little yellow fugitive seemed to bear a charmed life. In the end the exasperated officer in command telephoned through to the nearest artillery post, giving the position of the bird. The big guns opened up, and one shell blew the poor canary to smithereens. After the tragedy work on the tunnel was continued safely, and played a major part in the Canadian assault on the ridge.

Funerals

One of the most bizarre funerals on record was that of a sweet-voiced canary named 'Jimmy' held in Newark, New Jersey, USA, on 3 August 1920. The bird's besotted owner, cobbler Edidio Rusomanno, had always promised he would give his pet a magnificent send-off when the avian equivalent of the grim reaper appeared, and he certainly kept to his word. He hired a 15-piece band, a hearse and two coaches, ordered a fine white casket, engaged an undertaker and invited all his friends and neighbours to the funeral. More than 10 000 people turned up on the day as they would for a circus parade and the band played time and time again 'Nearer my God to Thee'; at the head of the cortege an old Italian friend of Rusomanno's walked behind the flower-bedecked hearse reading extracts from a tattered bible. The canary was buried in a small plot in the local park and, as the mini-coffin was lowered to its final resting place and the band played dirges, the old cobbler wept. After the last spadeful of earth had been thrown into the grave, Rusomanno and the other mourners returned to his shop where a sumptuous dinner was served. One fashionably-dressed woman who had motored from Philadelphia specially to attend the funeral brought a huge wreath for the bird and also contributed towards the funeral expenses.

Mascots

One of the few canaries adopted as a military mascot was a cock bird named 'Jib', who joined the SS *Nea Hellas* of the Anchor Line in November 1944 on the strength of his singing voice. He arrived at Oran, Algeria, on Christmas Day, and received his baptism of fire 24 hours later when the ship came under aerial attack whilst *en route* to Naples, Italy. After service in the Mediterranean and a trip to Bombay, India, via the Suez Canal, Jib returned home in May 1944, but he was soon off again on a voyage to South Africa, where he sang for the troops on deck at open air concerts. From there he went to Crete, where he saw more enemy action, and then Canada. His last, and longest voyage, was to Rangoon in Burma in 1945 where the ship picked up contingents of the 14th Army waiting to be

'Jib', the globe-trotting canary mascot of SS *Nea Hellas*.

repatriated. After his demob Jib was returned to his owner, William 'Lofty' Evans of Caernarvon, north Wales, and settled down happily to a life on shore. The sea, however, was still in his blood, and now and again he would grip the bars of his cage with his beak as if he was rolling on the ocean waves.

Richest

The richest canary on record was a hen named 'Gigi', who was left $250 000 (then £95 000) in the will of her owner, Mrs Andree O Montet. When the 15-year-old bird died in Charlotte, North Carolina, USA, in June 1967 from natural causes (an autopsy was carried out at the request of the estate's attorney because the body was found in suspicious circumstances) the money was jointly inherited by another canary named 'Co-Co' and a cat named 'Tommie', who had earlier been accused of murdering Gigi. In the interests of the surviving canary, however, a permanent close watch was kept on his four-legged companion . . . just in case!

In Brazil canary-fighting is a popular sport in some regions, and champion birds often fetch very high prices.

Budgerigars

The Budgerigar (*Melopsittacus undulatus*) is a native of Australia. The first live birds (about half a dozen) were imported into Britain by the famous English naturalist and artist John Gould in 1840, and the first breeding of budgerigars in captivity was credited to his brother-in-law Charles Coxon, who sold his first pair commercially for £25. The Zebra grass-parrakeet, as it is also known, quickly won favour with bird fanciers not only in this country but Europe as well, and one budgie farm established in Toulouse, France, where the climate is better, had 20 000 breeding birds in 1880 (100 000 in 1913). By the mid-1930s this very colourful bird had ousted the canary as the world's most popular cage-bird. Today it is still the most commonly kept of the caged birds, and there are probably more budgerigars in captivity now than there are in the wild state. Britain's budgie population reached its peak in 1959 when there were 5 250 000, compared to 3 250 000 in 1971 and 1 800 00 in 1983.

Largest

Budgerigars (unlike canaries) vary very little in size and substance, and the ideal length is 216 mm, 8.5 in. The weight of mature birds averages 40–45 g, 1.41–1.59 oz, but some cock birds can reach 60 g, 2.12 oz. During the 1950s a 'long-flight' budgerigar measuring 280 mm, 11 in or more in length appeared on the scene, but when the Budgerigar Society announced a standard length of 216 mm 8.5 in for all show birds, this giant strain virtually disappeared overnight.

Breeding

The incubation period for the budgerigar is 17–18 days. The normal clutch size is three to seven eggs, but ten and even 11 eggs have been recorded. Two broods are usually raised each season and the breeding life is four years. Very few hens lay more than 30 eggs in a cycle (average 12–14). One hen named 'Sparkina' owned by Sharon Johnson of Hove, Sussex, laid 32 eggs in the six-month period July–December 1970. The bird used to be a good talker, but went silent after the first egg was deposited. Hen budgies kept on their own often produce large amounts of infertile eggs, and removing them as they are laid only stimulates further egg-laying. One bird belonging to E M Humphrey of Fulham, London, produced 153 eggs during the period February 1976 to September 1977, and from 30 November 1961 to 18 May 1966 a hen named 'Tina' owned by Edna Lee of Nottingham laid 240 eggs. The smallest 'sport' (an undersized egg emitted from the oviduct before reaching maturity) recorded for a budgerigar was one laid by a Golden Lutino owned by Raymond Hewitt of King's Norton, Birmingham. It measures 7.8 ×

9.4 mm, 0.29 × 0.37 in and originally weighed 206 mg, 0.007 oz. The egg was laid at five weeks (budgies usually start to lay eggs at 11 months). Another example presented to the Natural History Museum at Wallaton, Nottingham, in 1972 measures 10.3 × 8.1 mm, 0.40 × 0.31 in.

Oldest

The average life-span of a budgerigar in captivity is six to eight years, but much older specimens have been recorded. On 13 March 1975 the Gateshead Budgerigar Society in Durham presented a virtually featherless cock bird named 'George', owned by Elsie Ramshaw of Denaby Main, Yorkshire, with a special black and white rosette to mark his 25th birthday. Unfortunately the bird died soon afterwards . . . probably as a result of all the excitement.

The oldest budgerigar on record was a hen bird named 'Charlie' owned by J Disney of Stonebridge, London, who was 29 years 2 months at the time of her death on 20 June 1977.

Shows

The natural colour of the wild budgerigar is light green on a yellow ground, with black throat and wing markings, and it is from this green-and-yellow basic stock that hundreds of colour mutations have been developed since 1840. For many years breeders have been trying to produce a jet black or pink budgie, but so far they have been unsuccessful. Birds fitting this description sometimes get a mention in the popular press, but the majority turn out to be budgies that have been dyed! The rest are either very dark-coloured examples or they have a pale pinkish glow when viewed at certain angles. A prize of £1000 offered by the Budgerigar Information Bureau for the first genuine pink budgie was claimed by breeder Bob Wilson of Bridgwater, Somerset, in April 1983, but when an expert from the Society was despatched to inspect the three 'perfectly pink' chicks he decided that they were not all that they should be. 'In my estimation', he commented, 'they have just turned pink because Mr Wilson has been giving them powdered medicines.' This was vigorously denied by Mr Wilson, who said the secret was careful breeding. 'I started by rearing only white birds', he said, 'to which I introduced a fallow or brown strain to produce pink.' Most breeders consider the pink budgerigar to be a genetic impossibility, although there is reported to be a genuine example in Norwich Museum—albeit stuffed!

The most grotesque budgerigar mutation yet produced is a rare form of throwback called the Feather Duster, which involves the feathers growing over twice the normal length and at all angles from the body. Needless to say these birds cannot fly, and they usually die within a matter of weeks, but one tough individual managed to survive for 17 months. This genetic freak, invariably the offspring of healthy show birds, made its first appearance in Australia in 1960, and two examples bred in Britain were exhibited at the Budgerigar Society's convention in Harrogate, Yorkshire, in 1975.

The ordinary pet budgerigar also comes up with the odd surprise now and again, although in the case of 'Jenny' the problem is more mental than physical. This eccentric hen, owned by June Lowton of Nottingham, refuses to sleep on her perch, but dreams away on her back with her feet in the air at the bottom of the cage. According to experts, the only other budgies that are known to adopt this position are dead ones!

Homing

Liberty budgies get their name from the fact that they spend most of their life at full liberty even though they are domesticated. The first person to keep and breed homing flocks of budgies was the 8th Duke of Bedford, grandfather of the present incumbent, who pioneered the method of getting these birds to stay in the local area after they have been released. During the breeding season (March–October) owners of these winged adventurers allow their pets to come and go as they please, knowing that they will return to the aviary when they wish to feed, nest or roost. One leading enthusiast of the liberty budgerigar is Her Majesty the Queen, who owns a flock which she keeps in an aviary in her private garden at Windsor Castle. During the summer months they sometimes go on 'walkabouts' in the town of Windsor itself.

In 1971 a gentleman living on the island of Tresco in the Scilly Isles released some budgies into the wild in the hope that they would set up a breeding colony and flourish. The birds took up residence in treeholes and soon established a 100-strong community. To qualify as a British bird, however, the budgerigars had to be self-supporting in the wild for ten years and, just as the experiment was reaching a successful conclusion, tragedy struck. The budgerigars' benefactor died, and soon afterwards his wife left the island. As the birds could not survive on their own without winter feeding the population dwindled and finally died out, much to the relief of the British Ornithological Union's records committee, which had never relished the idea of conferring British citizenship on a colonial immigrant!

Mention should also be made of a young budgie named 'Joey' who escaped from his cage in 1978 and survived in the wild for more than five years before returning home on 30 March 1984. His owner, Mrs Phyllis Jones of Pumpsaint, Dyfed, mid-Wales, believes her pet must have taken refuge in the nearby forest where he mastered sufficient skills to keep himself alive. Even more amazing was the fact that Joey was completely white and must have presented an easy target for predators such as hawks or cats.

Talking

The budgerigar is one of the best talkers of all the birds with mimicry ability and, if it is isolated when five-to-six weeks old, it will quickly learn to reproduce the sound it hears. Like all living things, however, individuals vary in their ability, and if there is no success by the age of six months the training is usually abandoned. As a rule young cock birds make the best pupils, and women or young people the best tutors thanks to their clearer and higher-pitched voices.

The first talking budgerigar on record was a specimen tamed by an English convict named Thomas Watling, who was a member of the first white group to settle in Australia in 1788. This interesting character had been found guilty of counterfeiting banknotes in London, and had been transported to the colony of New South Wales, where it was thought his skill with brush and paints might come in useful. His talents were soon recognised, and he was appointed assistant to Dr James White, the colony physician. The animal life of the region fascinated Watling, and it didn't take him long to discover that the little brightly-coloured birds he observed daily could be taught to speak. One day Dr White entered his assistant's hut while he was away, and was astonished to be greeted with the words 'How do you do, Dr White?'. Watling was later given a pardon by Sir Arthur Phillip, the first Governor of New South Wales, but he continued to tame budgies right up to the time of his death.

The most famous talking budgerigar on record was a cock bird named 'Sparkie' who, during his eight-year career of sounding his vowels, mastered 531 words, 383 sentences and eight complete nursery rhymes (cf. 845 words for a basic English vocabulary). Sparkie was purchased as a six-week-old chick by English teacher Mrs Mattie Williams of Newcastle upon Tyne in 1954. She had never owned a bird before, but it took her only three weeks to teach her pet to say 'pretty Sparkie'. From then onwards his elocutionary powers increased daily, and he was soon rattling away without tuition. In 1958 Sparkie was entered by his owner in a budgie-talking contest organised by the BBC. By

'Sparkie Williams', the world's most famous talking budgerigar, at his favourite mirror.

then 'Mr Chatterbox' could speak 300 words and 156 phrases, and he easily outshone the opposition of 2768 entrants. After this outstanding success the avian celebrity was quickly snapped up for a series of TV commercials extolling the merits of a certain bird-seed. This was followed by a record contract, and a 'single' made by Sparkie explaining the methods used to teach birds to talk sold over 20000 copies. During his career as a commercial product Sparkie earned well in excess of £1000 and even opened his own bank account. He was also the first budgerigar to qualify for the dubious distinction of having his own income tax number. On 4 December 1962 Sparkie was found by his owner gasping for breath on the bottom of his cage, and he died soon afterwards in her hands. His last words

were reportedly 'I love Mamma'. Even after his demise this much-loved budgie's immortality was ensured, because he was stuffed and mounted on his favourite perch. He can now be seen at Hancocks Museum in Newcastle where visitors can also hear a recording of his voice.

Parrot-like birds

Man's enthusiasm for parrot-like birds dates back to the earliest civilisations. The Alexandrine parrakeet (*Psittacula eupatria*) of the Indian subcontinent was probably the first psittacine bird to be tamed, and some were kept at the court of Artaxerxes II, King of Persia, in the fifth century BC. The Macedonians under Alexander the Great also met with this species when they advanced into northern India in 327 BC, and some were brought back to Greece as trophies of war. In ancient Rome ring-necked parrakeets from Africa were also highly prized, and by 250 BC these birds and other parrots had become valuable items of trade. When the Portuguese navigator Vasco da Gama (1460–1524) opened up the sea route from western Europe to the East the spice ships started bringing back parrots from Africa, India and the East Indies, and the parrot-like birds of Central and South America began reaching Europe soon after Christopher Columbus had discovered the New World in 1492. During the next 400 years or so parrots and allied species were kept solely as pets, and it was not until after the Second World War that serious breeding really started on a global scale.

Largest

The largest member of the parrot family (excluding the very rare flightless Owl parrot or Kakapo [*Strigops habroptilus*] of New Zealand) is the spectacular Hyacinth macaw (*Anodorhynchus hyacinthinus*) of the Brazilian interior. This bird has been measured up to 40 in, 101 cm in length and can weigh as much as 4 kg, 8.81 lb, which means it is heavier than some species of eagle. Because of its large size and high value this bird is rarely seen in private collections, and the fact that it has an extremely powerful beak and can be quite fierce at times are two other disadvantages.

Smallest

The smallest members of the parrot family are the parrotlets (*Forpus*), and especially Sclater's parrotlet (*F. sclateri*) of northern South America, the Celestial parrotlet (*F. coelestis*) of Ecuador and Peru, and the Spectacled parrotlet (*F. conspicillatus*) of Colombia, all of which measure 120 mm, 4.75 in in length and weigh about 30 g, 1.06 oz.

Breeding

The incubation period ranges from 18 days for the Celestial parrotlet to 35 days for the Palm cockatoo (*Probosciger aterrimus*). Clutch size varies from one in the Red-tailed black cockatoo (*Calyptorhynchus magnificus*) to ten in the parrotlets and lovebirds. Some species also have a very long reproductive life. A pair of Leadbeater's cockatoos (*Cacatua leadbeateri*) obtained by an American breeder in 1903 laid annually from 1922 to 1940, but all the chicks (with one exception) were killed by the cock bird before they could become independent.

Oldest

Although parrot-type birds have long been credited with centenarian status, very few individuals have actually lived longer than 50 years—even under favourable conditions. For the majority of psittacines the average life-span in captivity is about 20 years.

The longest-lived species are the Greater sulphur-crested cockatoo (*Cacatua galerita*) of Australia and the Grey parrot (*Psittacus erythacus*) of West Africa, but even these two birds—particularly the former—have had a number of exaggerated claims made for them.

One Greater sulphur-crested cockatoo named

The famous 'Cocky Bennett' photographed three years before his death in 1916. Notice the overgrown beak.

'Cocky' Bennett owned by Mrs Sarah Bennett, licensee of the 'Sea Breeze' Hotel at Tom Ugly's Point, near Sydney, New South Wales, Australia, was allegedly over 120 years old when he died in 1916, but an investigation revealed that there was no authentic information available regarding the true age of this bird. This cockatoo was in the possession of Mrs Bennett for 26 years, and had previously been owned by Captain George Ellis, skipper of a South Seas sailing ship who said the bird was alive when he was only a nine-year-old ship's apprentice. During the last 25 years of his life Cocky Bennett was practically featherless, and he was often heard to scream 'One more f****** feather and I'll fly!'

On 8 March 1968 the death was reported in the Nottingham Park Aviary of another Greater sulphur-crested cockatoo also named 'Cocky' aged 114 years, but this record is considered unreliable because several cockatoos of this name had been kept in the aviary over the years.

The oldest Greater sulphur-crested cockatoo on record of which there is definite information was probably yet another cock bird named 'Cocky', who was at least 82 years of age when he died in 1982. He was presented to London Zoo in 1925 by a family who had kept him as a pet since the beginning of the century. Cocky greatly enjoyed human company and he would engage everyone he could in conversation. In 1980 he received a medal from the Burlington Arcade Association for his courtesy in helping to make London a friendlier city for tourists, and he was still talking and showing appreciation of company right up to the time he died.

Another example which died at Leith Hall, Aberdeenshire, Scotland, in March 1908 was 51+ years, and three other records of 56 years, 69 years and 80 years are probably also substantially correct, although not so well documented.

'George', a Slender-billed cockatoo (*Cacatua tenuirostris*) was allegedly 85 years old when he died in London Zoo in 1937, but this claim has not been substantiated.

An African grey parrot named 'Pesky' owned by ex-seaman Ronald Dunstan of Bramcote, Nottinghamshire, died in 1968 reputedly aged 99 years, but there are gaps in this bird's history. There is also a French record of a grey parrot which began to lose its memory at 60, moulted irregularly at 65, went blind at 70 and died three years later, but this claim was not accepted by Major S Flower when he investigated maximum longevities in birds in 1938. His oldest specimen was only aged 49 years, but it seems probable that the potential life-span of this species is at least 70 years.

On 5 January 1975 the death was reported of a red and green Amazon parrot (*Amazona sp.*) named 'Jimmy' in Liverpool aged 104 years, but this claim lacks proper documentation. According to the bird's owner, Mrs Bella Ludford, Jimmy had been given to her as a gift by a sailor, Mr Jimmy West, in 1945. He told her he had gone to sea at an early age on board one of the old sailing ships and bought the parrot off a man who said it was born in captivity. West died two weeks after he left Jimmy with Mrs Ludford, but she was convinced the bird's age was genuine because the former sailor had given her a piece of paper which stated that Jimmy was born on 3 December 1870! The fact that the bird was owned by three different people, two of them widely travelled, and Amazon parrots are the commonest large psittacines kept in captivity, would seem to suggest that Jimmy was probably a composite of two or even three parrots all with the same name which had been kept in the original brass cage over the 104-year period.

Shortest-lived

The shortest-lived birds in captivity are hummingbirds (*Trochilidae*) which, due to their high rate of metabolism, live in a continual state of stress, and few species live longer than four to five years in a communal flight. A purple-throated carib (*Eulampis jugularis*) and a green-throated carib (*Sericotes holosericeus*) were kept alive for 10 years 8 months 6 days and 10 years 7 months 1 week respectively in New York Zoological Gardens (Bronx Zoo), NY, USA, but both birds were housed singly.

Most valuable

Following the Australian ban on the export of exotic birds and the securement of international controls on the parrot trade, there is now an acute shortage of species (particularly cockatoos) which can be sold legally under licence, and this has sent prices soaring to record levels. In October 1979 four men were arrested in Sydney charged with illegally exporting 816 Galah cockatoos (*Eolophus roseicapillus*) and 335 Sulphur-crested cockatoos worth £1 million, and two years later 100 Palm cockatoos and 28 Grand eclectus (*Eclectus roratus*) parrots were seized by American Government agents when they swooped on a plane-load of contraband that had just arrived in Florida. The most sought after cockatoo today is probably the Slender-billed cockatoo, and even if one were available you probably wouldn't get much change out of £8000 for it. Leadbeater's cockatoo, the most beautiful of all the birds in this group (see front cover) is another jewel in any collection, and a good example would currently fetch £6000. Other cockatoos much prized by collectors (especially Americans) include the Palm cockatoo of northern

Australia, New Guinea and surrounding islands; the Blue-eyed cockatoo (*Cacatua ophthalmica*) of New Ireland and New Britain (north-east of New Guinea); the Red-tailed black cockatoo (*Calyptorhynchus magnificus*) of northern Australia, the Yellow-tailed black cockatoo (*C. funereus*) of south-eastern Australia and Tasmania, and the Gang-gang cockatoo (*Callocephalon fimbriatus*) of eastern Australia and Tasmania.

Some of the macaws also fetch high prices, and in 1983 the sum of $10 000 (£6500) was paid for a Hyacinthine macaw by an American collector.

The world's most valuable parrot is probably Spix's macaw (*Cyanopsitta spixii*), which was not seen for over a hundred years after its original discovery. According to a recent survey there are only about six breeding pairs in captivity. Two of them are in a bird park in West Germany, and another pair was smuggled into the USA in 1979. There is also a pair in private hands in Britain, and they originally cost £6000. The Glaucous macaw (*Anodorhynchus glaucus*) is another species which has rarely been seen in collections and would command large sums if it were available on the open market.

Since the introduction of the Endangered Species Act in 1976, which tightened up controls on the import and export of exotic birds, prices have also gone through the roof in Britain, which in turn has encouraged 'parrot rustling'. One pair of Golden-shouldered parrakeets (*Psephotus chrysopterygius*) from northern Queensland, where it is strictly protected, was reportedly sold on the black market for £7500 recently, and sums up to £9000 have been paid for other psittacine birds (probably macaws).

Thefts from zoos, wildlife parks and pet shops amount to £50 000 annually, and the Parrot Society offers rewards of up to £1000 to anyone supplying information leading to the conviction of those responsible for stealing rare birds.

Not all parrots brought in from the wild, however, are tamable. Those that do not conform are called 'growlers' by the breeding fraternity, and some of these birds more than live up to their reputation for ferocity. One particularly nasty Green-winged macaw (*Ara chloroptera*) owned by a 19th century English writer caused so many problems in the house that in the end it was banished to the stables, where it had a belligerent bull terrier for company. One day the two animals decided to settle their differences once and for all, and a bloody battle ensued. It left the dog dead (the beak of this macaw can exert a pressure of 300 lb per in^2, 2 068 428 Pa) and the bird virtually featherless with both wings broken. The macaw was later restored to health, but it showed no gratitude whatsoever for the kind help and attention it had received and remained just as unapproachable as before.

The African grey parrot 'Prudle', the world's most talkative bird.

In 1963 a man died from his injuries after he was attacked by a flock of 200 African grey parrots at Iguoriakhi, Nigeria.

Talking

A number of birds are renowned for their talking ability (ie the reproduction of words), but the African grey parrot reigns supreme in this depart-ment. Not only can it reproduce a human voice right down to the smallest detail of intonation, but it also has the largest vocabulary of any talking bird, although individuals vary considerably in their ability.

The most famous talking African grey parrot is a cock bird named 'Prudle' owned by Mrs Lyn Logue of Seaford, Sussex. He won the 'Best talking parrot-like bird' title at the National Cage and

Aviary Bird Show held in London in December 1965 and successfully defended the title for 12 consecutive years before he retired in 1977. Prudle was taken from a nest in a tree about to be felled at Jinja, Uganda in 1958. Today he has a vocabulary of more than 800 words, and his owner claims that he actually reasons and makes up his own coherent sentences. Prudle's most impressive rendering (from My Fair Lady) is: 'The rains in Spain stay mostly on the plain, they say, but in Hertford, Hereford and Hampshire hurricanes hardly ever happen.'

Another grey parrot which speaks Russian won a prize in Moscow in 1979 for its vocabulary of 100 words, but it wasn't exactly overjoyed with its success. It told admirers: 'All birds sit on branches, but I live in a cage.'

For a long time it was widely believed that talking birds do not actually understand what they say, and that they are incapable of communicating their thoughts by way of words. Recently, however, a study in the USA has revealed that parrots are much brighter creatures than had hitherto been realised. Dr Irene Pepperberg, an ethologist in the Department of Biological Sciences at Purdue University, Indiana, used for her experiments an African grey parrot named 'Alex' who had been acquired at the age of just over one year. The bird proved a brilliant pupil, and during the course of the next 30 months he built up a very impressive vocabulary, including the names of more than 40 different items.

He could also distinguish between a square, a triangle, an oval and a pentagon, and even tell the difference between such colours as rose, green, blue, grey and yellow. One day he caught sight of himself in a mirror and asked a graduate student what colour he was. When she told him 'grey' he repeated the answer over and over again until he had taught himself the word. Another talent he quickly acquired was the use of a nail-file to trim his beak. Most astonishing of all, however, was Alex's ability to compose sentences and carry on conversations with his tutors. He would make demands for food or toys even if they were not visible, and would also refuse to do certain things or accept something he didn't want. Dr Pepperberg believes that Alex, who is still only six years old, may one day be able to demonstrate that a bird, like a chimpanzee, can acquire the rudiments of language-like behaviour.

Amazon parrots are also accomplished talkers, but cockatoos and macaws and most other parrots generally have a much more limited vocabulary of no more than 20 words, and many speak in a rather thin voice. Some cockatoos also have the disadvantage of possessing an ear-splitting screech that doesn't exactly recommend them to people of a nervous disposition.

Parrots also have a reputation for being noisy at times, particularly when alarmed, which leads us to the sad story of 'Fred'. As thieves were ransacking a house in Bargoed, Mid Glamorgan, Wales, the resident green parakeet, who had been watching the proceedings with some interest, suddenly panicked and started kicking up the very devil of a row. Fred was immediately yanked out of his cage by one of the callous intruders and shoved into a convenient freezer, where he was found frozen solid when his owner returned home.

Another parrot, however, got its own back on thieves who broke into a pet shop in Tiberius, Israel. As the men chatted together it listened intently, and later recited their names to police. As a result, the culprits were quickly apprehended.

The finest mimic in the avian world is the Hill mynah (*Gracula religiosa*), which is basically a large starling. Its vocabulary is nowhere near as large as that of some parrots, but it has a clearer and more

'Raffles', the world's most famous mynah, who reportedly sold over $1 million's worth of World War II Savings Bonds.

distinct voice and a capacity for mimicry or the imitation of sounds other than words that is unsurpassed.

The most famous Hill mynah on record was a cock bird named 'Raffles' owned by American explorer Carveth Wells, who took him from the nest in Malaya in 1938. This feathered extrovert displayed an amazing talent for mimicry at a very early age, and his ability to sing and whistle 'The Star Spangled Banner' quickly attracted the attention of radio and film producers alike when the Second World War broke out. In one year alone Raffles earned $15 000 in appearance money, and Walt Disney even gave a luncheon in the bird's honour. In 1943 Raffles was presented with the 'Lavender Heart' for entertaining war casualties in hospitals across the USA, and he was also responsible for selling over $1 million worth of war savings bonds. Sadly Raffles died prematurely in 1946, aged only eight years, and his stuffed body is now on display in the American Museum of Natural History in New York.

It is also interesting to note that the only talking bird able to repeat the word 'antidisestablishmentarianism' is an Indian Hill mynah named 'Rajah' owned by Colin Kerry of Toronto, Canada. This 'speechmaster' was acquired in 1964, and is the only mynah bird insured by Lloyd's of London.

Other birds noted for their ability to mimic speech and other sounds such as the trilling of a telephone include the starling, which is the best of all wild-bird mimics, and the members of the crow family (raven, rook, jackdaw, magpie and jay).

According to a recent Soviet news report a talking raven near Minsk regularly inspects anglers' catches and then tells them what kind of fish they have caught!

Finally, some people claim that the budgerigar is an even better talker than the African grey parrot, but in a hypothetical contest between Sparkie (see page 139) and Prudle the latter bird would have been an easy winner.

In the early 1970s a number of people who had bought Ringneck parrakeets (*Psittacula krameri*) as pets rapidly became disenchanted with their sullen behaviour and surreptitiously released them into the wild. The first sightings of this bright green bird were in the London area, but they later moved into the Home Counties as their numbers increased and colonies have recently been seen as far north as Cheshire where they are said to be flourishing. This is bad news for farmers, because in the USA the Ringneck parrakeet has been declared a pest in 26 States because of the damage it causes to crops and orchards.

A number of other exotic bird escapees have also managed to survive in the British climate. One Sulphur-crested cockatoo set up home on Wimbledon Common, south London, with three rooks, and an African grey parrot lived quite happily in a rookery in the same area for several years. There are also many records of budgerigars joining flocks of sparrows.

Pigeons and doves

Pigeons and rock doves (*Columba livia*) have been associated with man since ancient times. The earliest record of domestication dates back to c 4500 BC in Mesopotamia (Iraq), where they were held sacred, and by 3000 BC doves were being raised in Egypt as table birds. There are also frequent references to doves in the Bible, where it became the symbol of the Holy Ghost. The Romans kept pigeons in enormous numbers, and built towers called Columbria where the birds were specially fattened to supply food in the form of plump nestlings (squabs). They were introduced into Europe by returning Crusaders in the 12th century, and in medieval England only royalty, the nobility and the clergy were allowed to keep pigeons. They were bred mainly for culinary purposes or as an ornamental garden bird until the late 18th century when the first show types were developed. (For the purpose of this book, all show, racing and tumbler types with short tails are classified as pigeons, and all decorative types with long tails as doves.)

Domesticated pigeons (excluding utility birds bred for the table) can be divided into three basic groups: Homing (racing) pigeons, which are kept for their ability to return home when released at a distance; Flyers, which are renowned for their aerial somersaults; and Fancy pigeons, which are bred solely for their colour and appearance.

Homing

The first people to take advantage of the pigeon's ability to find its way home over strange territory and at varying distances were probably the Chinese who, as early as 650 BC, were using these birds to carry messages between dovecotes set up in towns where top government officials were in residence. Their potential was also realised in the early days of the Persian Empire, and the Greeks learned about them when they defeated the Persian fleet in 492 BC. They, in turn, used them to carry results from the ancient Olympic Games to the outlying towns and villages. The next homing pigeon enthusiasts were the Egyptians and the Romans, and Julius Caesar used these birds to carry military intelligence during his conquest of Gaul. In 1150 the Sultan of Baghdad set up the first pigeon post system, and during the Crusades the Saracens' exploitation of pigeons for military purposes caused a lot of problems for Richard the Lionheart. At the siege of Leyden in 1574 the Dutch used pigeons to carry messages to the beleaguered inhabitants telling them that help was on its way, and they were also gainfully employed in the siege of Vienna in 1849.

The greatest use of pigeon messengers occurred during the great Siege of Paris in 1870–71. The city had been cut off completely from the outside world by the Prussian army, and no news or military orders could get through to the 2½ million people living in the French capital. To get round the problem a group of hot-air balloonists and pigeon-fanciers got together and organised regular balloon flights over the enemy positions carrying men, messages and pigeons. When the balloonists reached Tours, 120 miles, 192 km from Paris, and other unoccupied parts of France, dispatches for the capital were fastened to the birds, which then flew back to their home lofts.

During the five-month siege, which ended in January 1871 when the city was relieved, the pigeons carried no less than 1 150 000 different airmail messages and 15 000 government telegrams into Paris using the microdot technique, which meant each message was photographed and then drastically reduced in size.

After the siege of Paris the governments of the major powers were quick to recognise the importance of pigeons in the military sphere and, during both World Wars, their message-carrying missions saved countless human lives on both sides when telephone lines were down and they were the only means of communication with the home base.

The most famous homing pigeon of the First World War was a cock bird named 'Cher Ami' (Dear Friend), one of the 500 000 pigeons brought to Europe by the American Expeditionary Force. He served with a unit of infantry known as the 'Lost Battalion', and delivered 12 messages during his tour of duty on the battle front. On the day of his last—and most important—mission from the Argonne Forest, NE France, the Lost Battalion was being pounded by German shells, and the brave little pigeon was sent aloft with an urgent message asking for assistance. Sharp-eyed German troops surrounding the Americans, however, saw the bird as it took off on 4 October 1918 and started firing at him. As watching Americans groaned in despair, an enemy bullet struck the flapping pigeon and he plummeted to the ground. Then someone shouted 'Cher Ami, go home'—and the plucky avian messenger responded to the call. Painfully he took to the air again, but within seconds a rifle slug pierced his breastbone. As he struggled to gain height another

The gallant US Army carrier pigeon 'Cher Ami' shown mounted in the Smithsonian Institution, Washington, DC, where he is described as 'the feathered hero of World War I'.

one tore off his right leg, and a third shot out one of his eyes.

Yet despite these appalling injuries the valiant pigeon refused to give up the fight and struggled on his way. Twenty-five minutes after taking off from the battalion's position—which was also being shelled in error by American artillery—the bloody and exhausted bird collapsed on the roof of division headquarters. He had flown an incredible 24 miles, 38.4 km. The message found hanging from the ligaments of Cher Ami's torn-off leg informed headquarters of the trapped battalion's map location and desperately pointed out that 'our own artillery is dropping a barrage directly on us . . . for heaven's sake, stop it'. Cher Ami had saved the Lost Battalion. At the end of the war the soldier pigeon was presented with the Croix de Guerre, one of France's highest military honours. He was taken back to the USA in April 1919, but he only lived for a short while, and died at Fort Monmouth, New Jersey, on 13 June of that year. His body was later mounted, and today Cher Ami can be seen on display in the Smithsonian Institution in Washington, DC, under the heading 'The feathered hero of World War I'.

During the Second World War pigeons were used even more extensively, and 31 of these birds were awarded the Dickin Medal for their heroism.

One of the bravest recipients of the medal was a hen named 'Mary', who served with the National Pigeon Service from 1940 to the end of the war and ended up with a total of 22 stitches in her little body. On one occasion she went missing for four days, and came back with her neck and right breast ripped open. She had been attacked by a hawk, but had still managed to retain the message. Two months later she disappeared for three weeks before returning with part of her wing shot away and three pellets in her body. During the German air raids on Exeter a 1000 lb, 453 kg bomb exploded just outside her loft, killing most of the inhabitants, but Mary miraculously survived. Two nights later another bomb fell outside the garage in which she had been temporarily housed, and again she escaped alive from her basket. After a short rest Mary returned to active duty but, within ten days, she was picked up in a field more dead than alive. This time she had an ugly gash down the side of her head and neck, and her body had sustained other injuries. Once again, however, the plucky little pigeon refused to give in, and after more stitches were put in, her owner nursed her back to health.

The only American homing pigeon to win the Dickin Medal was a cock bird named 'G I Joe', who served with the US Army Signal Corps in Italy. On 18 October 1943 the Allied XII Air Support Command received orders to bomb the heavily fortified German position at Covi Vecchia some 20 miles, 32 km to the north but, just as the planes were about to take off, the pigeon arrived with a message to say that the town had been captured by the 169th Infantry Brigade. If the bird had arrived just a few minutes later at least a hundred American soldiers would have been killed by their own men. G I Joe received his decoration at an investiture held at the Tower of London in October 1946, and the ribbon was slipped over his head by Major General Sir Charles Keightley, who commanded the 5th Corps in Italy and knew all about the bird's exploits personally.

On 13 April 1983 a Dickin Medal awarded to a pigeon named 'Mercury' (1937–46) for the 'most outstanding single performance of any one pigeon on special service' was sold at Christie's in London for £5000. On 30 July 1942 the five-year-old blue hen, bred by Ipswich pigeon fancier Mr Jim Catchpole, flew 480 miles, 768 km non-stop over the North Sea with a message for British Intelligence from a Danish resistance group. The medal was bought by millionaire Mr Louis Massarella of Chorley, Lancashire, a keen pigeon fancier, who later presented it to the Royal Pigeon Racing Association.

The longest recorded homing flight by a pigeon was made by a cock bird owned by Mr Peter Robertson of Northumberland. The pigeon was released at Beauvais, northern France, on 16 June 1972, and turned up exhausted in Durban, Natal, South Africa, two months later after having flown an airline route of 6000 miles, 9600 km, but an actual distance of possibly 7600 miles, 12 160 km, to avoid the Sahara Desert. It was just skin and bone, said Mr Hendrick Strydom, who found the pigeon in his loft. The previous record had been set by a pigeon belonging to the 1st Duke of Wellington (1769–1852). Released from a sailing ship off the Ichabo Islands, South West Africa, on 8 April 1845, it dropped dead a mile, 1.6 km from its loft at Nine Elms, Wandsworth, London, 55 days later, having flown an airline route of possibly 7000 miles, 11 250 km.

Homing pigeon fancier Claude Frison of Cartignies, Flanders, Belgium, whose champion bird 'Fleurette' failed to return after a local racing event at Easter 1973, received a letter three months later from a fisherman in Martinique, in the West Indies, saying he had found the pigeon drinking on the river

'G I Joe' proudly showing off the Dickin Medal which was awarded to him for saving the lives of at least a hundred American soldiers.

bank. Although birds have been blown across the Atlantic from west to east, the reverse cannot happen because of the prevailing westerly winds, and the only way this bird could have possibly made this trip would have been by hitching a ride on a ship. A similar case occurred in 1983 when a racing pigeon named 'Percy' was entered in a 300 mile, 480 km race from Penzance to Manchester by owner Jack Roberts of Marple, Cheshire, and struck a fog bank. Sixteen days later the bird was found half-dead 6000 miles 9600 km away at Thunder Bay on the shores of Lake Superior, Ontario, Canada, by Mr Bob Balina, who nursed the pigeon back to health. It was later claimed that Percy, who was given a free flight home by Air Canada, had hitched a lift across the Atlantic aboard the royal yacht *Britannia*, but the Navy said Percy had made his flight after the ship had sailed. It is interesting to note, however, that the crew of *Britannia* did pick up a pigeon during the voyage and kept it happy on a diet of biscuits and beer until the ship docked in Nova Scotia.

Racing

Pigeon racing developed from the use of homing pigeons. The sport originated in Belgium from commercial services, and the earliest long-distance race was from London to Antwerp in 1819. By 1880 pigeon racing was well established in Britain, and the following year the United Counties Club was formed.

The earliest recorded occasion on which 500 miles, 800 km was flown in a day was by 'Motor' (owned by G P Pointer of Alexandra Palace Racing Pigeon Club), which was released from Thurso, Scotland, on 30 June 1896 and covered 501 miles, 802 km at an average speed of 1454 yd, 1329 m per minute (49.5 miles/h, 79.6 km/h).

It has been calculated that a man weighing 140 lb, 63.5 kg would have to run 10 000 miles, 16 000 km in a single day to use the equivalent energy spent by a pigeon in a 500 mile, 800 km race.

The official British duration record (into the United Kingdom) is 1173 miles, 1887 km in 15 days by 'C S O' (owned by 'Rosie' and 'Bruce' of Wick) in the 1976 Palamos race. In the 1975 Palamos race 'the Conqueror', owned by Alan Raeside, homed to Irvine, Strathclyde, Scotland, a distance of 1010 miles, 1625 km in 43 h 56 min.

The greatest number of flights over 1000 miles, 1600 km flown by one pigeon is that of 'Dunning Independence' owned by D Smith, which annually flew from Palamos to Dunning, Perthshire, Scotland (1039 miles, 1662 km) between 1978 and 1981.

Even injuries sustained in flight will not deter this greyhound of the sky from reaching its destination, and there is one record of a pigeon stranded with a broken wing *walking* the final 6 miles, 9.6 km back to its coop in Klagenfurt, Austria.

In level flight in windless conditions it is very doubtful if any pigeon can exceed 60 miles/h, 96 km/h.

The highest race speed recorded is one of 3229 yd, 2952 m per min (110.07 miles/h, 177.14 km/h) in the East Anglian Federation race from East Croydon on 8 May 1965 when the 1428 birds were backed by a powerful SSW wind. The winner was owned by A Vidgeon & Son of Wickford, Essex.

The slowest racing pigeon on record was a one-year-old cock bird named 'Blue Chip' owned by Harold Hart of Leigh, Greater Manchester. He was released at Rennes, northern France, with 2000 other pigeons for a cross-Channel race in June 1967 and arrived back in his loft on 29 September 1974! He had covered the distance of 370 miles, 595 km at an average speed of 0.00589 miles/h, 0.00948 km/h, which is slower than the world's fastest snail!

Racing pigeons sometimes disappear down chimneys in the mistaken belief that they are lofts, and as a result end up trapped. They can normally survive one to two weeks in such a situation without food and water, but even if they are rescued in time they don't usually fly again. On 18 February 1979 a pigeon named 'Calendar' belonging to Andrew Jermakowicz of Newark, Nottinghamshire, dived down the chimney in his kitchen after a race and remained there. Three attempts were made to get the hen out over the next three weeks, but in the end she was given up as dead. On 22 March, however, Calendar came out of the chimney of her own accord after being incarcerated for a record 32 days, and within a week she had made a full recovery. A month later she took part in a 62 mile, 89.2 km race, from Newark, and she later went on to race from France.

The highest recorded price paid for a racing pigeon is approximately £25 000 by a Japanese fancier in October 1978 for a bird named 'De Wittslager' bred by George Desender of Belgium.

Today pigeon power is still a force to be reckoned with, despite modern technology.

The giant Lockheed Corporation in California, USA, uses pigeons to carry micro filmed data between their two plants because the birds can cover the 25 mile, 40 km journey in half the time it takes a motor cyclist. In other countries these winged messengers are employed as carriers of blood samples from hospitals to laboratories, and the latest brainwave is the training of pigeons for sea rescues. Apart from having very keen sight, pigeons also have extremely good colour vision and they are much better suited than humans for the job of spotting distant objects floating in the water. They also have a long attention span, which means they can stare out over the ocean surface for long periods of time without suffering the eye fatigue that afflicts helicopter-crews looking for survivors at sea. In trials carried out by the Naval Oceans Systems Centre in Honolulu, Hawaii, scientists discovered that pigeons strapped to the underside of helicopters could spot survivors 90 per cent of the time compared to 38 per cent for human observers.

In laboratory tests carried out in Britain keen-eyed pigeons have also been trained to work as quality inspectors on mock-up car component production-lines for rewards of grain. They rejected any plastic nuts that were not perfect and were remarkably quick at spotting defects. Similar production line experiments with pigeons have also been carried out by a Soviet scientist, although this time he used ball bearings. He found they could classify between 3000 and 4000 in an hour.

Largest

The largest of the 200 or so breeds of pigeon recognised by the Fancy is the utility Valencian Giant Tenat (*Tenat Gigante Valenciana*) of Valencia province, Spain. The average weight of adult cocks is 3 lb 9 oz, 1.61 kg, but before the Second World War much larger birds were recorded. One famous old cock tipped the scales at 5 lb, 2.26 kg and had a wing-span of 3 ft 8 in, 111.7 cm! The only other breeds approaching anything like this size are the Giant Mallorquina Runt and the American Giant Runt, both of which have been credited with weights up to 3½ lb, 1.58 kg.

By way of comparison, the average weight of an adult racing pigeon is 14–17 oz, 396–481 g.

Smallest

The smallest breed of pigeon is the Prague Short-Faced tumbler, which weighs only 4–5 oz, 113–141 g.

Breeding

Pigeons lay one to two eggs, and the incubation period is *c* 18 days. The breeding life is normally five to six years, but some hens have produced a clutch as late as their ninth year. Pigeons, incidentally, are the only birds that suckle their young, the milk forming in the crop of both parents during the hatching period.

Oldest

The pigeon has an average life-span of *c* 12 years, but much greater ages have been recorded. One famous racing pigeon died at the age of 24 years, and Major Stanley Flower mentions a domestic pigeon which lived for 30 years. A dove purchased by Manuel C Rose, Sr, of San Pablo, California, at a festival for Portuguese descendants in 1933, was still alive in April 1974, aged 41+ years. There is also a reliable record of a Barbary dove (*Streptopelia risoria*) at the Tiergarten Schönbrunn, Vienna, Austria, which was 40 years old at the time of its demise, and a pair of Blue crowned pigeons (*Goura cristata*) in the same menagerie lived for 49 years (cock) and 53 years (hen) respectively.

Tumblers

Tumblers make up one of the oldest and largest families of domestic pigeons. Some types have been bred for show purposes, but others like the Tipplers and Rollers have been developed for their flying ability and performance. The most important attribute of the tippler, which originated in England in *c* 1840, is its capacity to spend long hours in the air. In contests a kit or group consisting of three to five tipplers has to stay on the wing and within sight of the loft (except for the first hour) for as long as possible. They are not allowed to drop until clearance is given, and this is indicated by the switching on of lights on top of the loft or the fluttering of lure birds. Good specimens that have been rigidly trained have been known to stay aloft for anything up to 20 hours, which would go a long way to explaining why contest kits have a short competitive life!

The roller's performance is entirely different: it has been trained to fly to a reasonable altitude and then tumble down to a lower level in a spectacular series of aerial somersaults.

The finest performing pigeon in the world is the famous Birmingham Roller, which is a cultivated tumbler. Its rolling ability is so highly advanced that it can spin over backwards with tremendous rapidity (ie four to five revolutions per second) over a considerable distance. An average achievement is ten spins over a fall of 12 ft, 3.65 m, but some rollers have been known to spin 25 times to a depth of 25 ft, 7.62 m and still pull out of the dive safely. Contestants are judged on their rolling ability, the revolutions of which should be clean and concentric, and their general standards of flight. Rollers are usually flown in large kits consisting of anything from 20 to 50 birds because they make a wonderful display. As soon as one of the birds starts to go into its routine it generally triggers off the rest of its companions and the whole kit suddenly explodes into action!

Another very interesting variety is the Parlor tumbler, which performs somersaults, or a series thereof, *on the ground*! In 1939 a yellow hen, bred and owned by Ray E Gilbert, established a world record distance when it rolled 75 ft, 22.8 m, and another 40 years elapsed before this feat was surpassed. On 12 December 1979, however, a tiger black hen bred and owned by Charles H Johnson of St Paul, Minnesota, USA, eclipsed this distance with a roll of 91 ft 4 in, 27.8 m at the Minnesota State Pigeon Association's winter show held at the University of Minnesota.

Shows

The first pigeon society in England was founded in 1720 for the exhibition of the Carrier (originally a homer), the Pouter and the Almond Tumbler. Today the Olympiad of the pigeon world is the Federation Colombophile Internationale (International Pigeon Federation), which is staged every other year and attracts competitors from 26 different countries. At this prestigious event there are show standards for more than 175 different varieties of pigeon, and it would require another book just to discuss each bird individually before even venturing into the superlative aspects of the subject!

Table 9. Maximum Recorded Longevities of Cage and Aviary Birds (excluding raptors)

Species	Years	Species	Years
Greater sulphur-crested cockatoo (*Cacatua galerita*)	82[a] [b]	Goldfinch (*Carduelis carduelis*)	24
African grey parrot (*Psittacus erythacus*)	72[b]	House sparrow (*Passer domesticus*)	23
Scarlet macaw (*Ara macao*)	64	Common mynah (*Acridotheres tristis*)	22
Moluccan cockatoo (*Cacatua moluccensis*)	59[c]	Carrion crow (*Corvus corone*)	20[b] [c]
Vasa parrot (*Coracopsis vasa*)	54	Starling (*Sturnus vulgaris*)	20
Blue-crown pigeon (*Goura cristata*)	53	Blackbird (*Turdus merula*)	20
Golden-naped parrot (*Amazona auropalliata*)	49	Red-bellied woodpecker (*Centaurus carolinus*)	20
Blue and Gold macaw (*Ara ararauna*)	43	African cordon-bleu finch (*Uraeginthus angolensis*)	19[c]
Domestic dove (*Columba livia domesticus*)	42	Jackdaw (*Corvus monedula*)	18[b] [c]
Leadbeater's cockatoo (*Cacatua leadbeateri*)	42	Zebra finch (*Taenopygia castonotis*)	18[c]
Western slender-billed cockatoo (*Licmetis pastinator*)	40	Fieldfare (*Turdus pilaris*)	18
Banksian cockatoo (*Calyptorhynchus banksii*)	40	Mourning dove (*Zenaida macroura*)	17
		Wood pigeon (*Columba palumbus*)	16
Bare-eyed cockatoo (*Cacatua sanguinea*)	40	African village weaver (*Ploceus cucullatus*)	15[c]
Barbary dove (*Streptopelia risoria*)	40	Steller's Jay (*Cyanocitta stelleri*)	15[c]
Raven (*Corvus corax*)	40[b]	Great tit (*Parus major*)	15
Canary (*Serinus canaria*)	34	Blue Jay (*Cyanocitta cristata*)	15
Magpie (*Pica pica*)	33	Blue-winged parrakeet (*Psittacula columboides*)	14
Rook (*Corvus frugilegus*)	30[c]	Robin (*Erithacus rubecula*)	14
Orange-winged parrot (*Amazona amazonica*)	30	Cuckoo (*Cuculus canorus*)	13
Roseate cockatoo (*Cacatua roseicapilla*)	30	Song Thrush (*Turdus ericetorum*)	13[c]
Skylark (*Alauda arvensis*)	30	Turtle dove (*Streptopelia turtur*)	13[c]
Vermilion cardinal (*Cardinalis phoeniceus*)	30	Waxwing (*Bombycilla garrulus*)	12
Budgerigar (*Melopsittacus undulatus*)	29	Greenfinch (*Chloris chloris*)	12
Chaffinch (*Fringilla coelebs*)	29	Masked weaver (*Ploceus velatus*)	11[c]
Linnet (*Carduelis cannabina*)	28	Hawfinch (*Coccothraustes coccothraustes*)	10
South African finch (*Fringilla sp.*)	26[c]	Green-throated carib (*Sericotes holosericeus*)	10[d]
Orange weaver (*Ploceus aurantius*)	25	Hedge sparrow (*Prunella modularis*)	9
Principe weaver (*Ploeceus princeps*)	25[c]	Mistle thrush (*Turdus viscivorus*)	9
Garden warbler (*Sylvia borin*)	24	Blue tit (*Parus caeruleus*)	8

[a] Spent 55 years in London Zoo (1925–82) [c] Still alive
[b] Credited with centenarian status [d] The longest-lived member of the hummingbird family (Trochilidae)

MISCELLANY

The first ever balloonists to take to the air were a sheep, a cockerel, and a duck. They achieved 'lift-off' at Versailles, 16 km, 10 miles west of Paris, France, in September 1783, and landed eight minutes later. Both the sheep and duck were found to be in good health after their ordeal, but the cockerel was said to be 'unwell'. At first it was believed the fowl had been affected by the rarefied atmosphere, but closer inspection revealed that it had been trodden on by the sheep!

The world's largest birdhouse is a 120 ft, 36.5 m tall steel tower in Lake Charles, Louisiana, USA, which is dedicated to the memory of the 1500 servicemen from Louisiana who were killed in Vietnam. The 16-storey structure, erected in 1968, has 48 aluminium bird houses with 1116 nesting compartments that can accommodate over 5280 of the purple martins *(Progne subis)* that arrive in the area during the summer months. The birds continue to return each year and occupy the same house in which they were born.

The largest known butterfly is the rare Queen Alexandra birdwing *(Ornithoptera alexandrae)*, which is restricted to the lowland forests of Papua New Guinea. Females (the more colourful males are smaller) sometimes measure more than 11 in, 280 mm across the wings, and native children often keep them as pets. Lengths of fibre are tied to specimens and their young owners fly them like small kites!

The largest chicken ever recorded was a murderous 22 lb, 10 kg rooster named 'Weirdo', who more than lived up to his name. In 1966 ten-year-old Grant Sullens of West Point, California, USA, decided to go into the chicken breeding business when his father won a lorry load of the birds in a dice game. Young Grant started selling eggs, and all was going well until the first snows of the winter began to fall on the Sierras and he lost more than 100 hens and roosters. It was then that somebody told him that Rhode Island Reds could tolerate low temperatures. By crossing and re-crossing the largest members of this breed with other varieties he produced hens that grew rapidly, could survive the cold nights of the Sierra Mountains and 'laid eggs like hell'. The only problem was that the super-roosters were unusually aggressive, particularly Weirdo, who was so big and rough that he killed two cats, crippled a dog and ripped through a wire fence to attack and kill one of his own progeny, an

18 lb, 8.16 kg rooster. For a long while afterwards Grant was besieged with offers from foreign governments, companies, chicken breeders and cockfight organisers, but it is not known if he is still in business.

The largest chicken ever recorded in Britain was a 17 lb 3 oz, 7.78 kg Cobb capon bred by Mr Henry Ransom of Brancaster Staithe, Dorset, and sold at the Annual Christmas Poultry Show and Sale held at Wimborne in December 1982. A White Ross rooster weighing 16 lb 8 oz, 7.48 kg bred by Mr Ralph Churchill of Yetminster, Devon, was also sold at the same show.

The longest feathers grown by any bird are those of the Onagadori or Long-tailed fowl (a strain of *Gallus gallus*), which has been bred in south-western Japan since the mid-17th century. Only the roosters grow the long tails, which may exceed 30 ft, 9.14 m and take ten years to achieve. In 1973 a tail covert measuring 34 ft 9.5 in, 10.6 m was

The Onagadori or long-tailed fowl of SW Japan which sometimes grows tail coverts measuring in excess of 30 ft, 9.14 m.

reported for a specimen bred by Masasha Kubota of Kochi, Shikoku.

In June 1983 a sack of dead chickens was thrown into a freezer by shop-owner Mr Bob Alcott of Frome, Somerset. When it was taken out two weeks later he found to his astonishment that one of the hens was breathing faintly. He called in Mrs Irene McCulloch, an animal lover who keeps chickens and geese on her smallholding, and she nursed the bird back to health. It was believed that 'Esmerelda', as she was named, owed her survival to the fact that she was in the middle of the sack of chickens and their feathers kept her just warm enough to stay alive.

There have been many records of sex changes in chickens resulting from a hormone imbalance. The most usual change is from cockerel into hen (known as 'cock hens'), but sometimes hens manage to change into cocks and end up with a well-endowed comb. In such situations, however, the hen usually ceases to lay eggs, although there have been a few cases in which the birds later reverted to their normal plumage and resumed laying. It is extremely rare for a cockerel to lay eggs, and some poultry experts believe such a feat is impossible, but it has been known to happen. In 1977 a cockerel owned by Mrs Swarna Kulasiri, a housewife in Gampoula, Sri Lanka, started laying one egg a day regularly. Because she wanted to see the process with her own eyes, Mrs Kulasiri isolated the 10 lb, 4.5 kg bird, the only cock in her 100-strong poultry run, and watched it lay a large brown egg. The cock had a

The world's largest bird house at Lake Charles, Louisiana, USA. It can accommodate over 5000 purple martins.

large comb and glossy feathers, and a resonant cock-a-doodle-do and reportedly had no effeminate traits!

A black Minorca hen came out unscathed after being buried for a record 21 days in a hay shed in Portland, Oregon, USA, in May 1940. A load of hay had been accidentally dumped on the bird as she sat on her nest. After the ordeal she went on to lay a further 448 eggs before being pensioned off.

A hen named 'Muriel' owned by Mrs J Osborne of Cottingham, north Humberside, scorned the traditional chicken coop—at night she used to roost 50 ft, 15 m up in the top branches of an old elm tree at the bottom of the garden.

In July 1976 cooks working in a restaurant in Dnepropetrovsk in the Ukraine, USSR, noticed that one of the cockerels due to be cooked was unduly heavy. When it was opened up they discovered to their amazement that the bird had nine hearts and three livers! The hearts were arranged like grapes on a single stem, and all were well developed and functional.

The champion fighting cock of Majorca, the largest island in the Balearics, was stolen in June 1981. When the thieves were eventually caught the remains of the £2000 bird were found in the kitchen—they had made soup with it!

The largest reptiles in private hands are two male Estuarine crocodiles (*Crocodylus porosus*) belonging to George Craig, who operates 'Marineland Melanesia' on Green Island off Queensland, Australia. 'Oscar' measures 17 ft 10 in, 5.43 m in length and weighs about 1800 lb, 816 kg, and 'Gomik' is 17 ft 4 in, 5.28 m. Both these giant 'pets' were caught in the Fly River, southern New Guinea.

Frank C Bostock, the English animal trainer, had a pet Nile crocodile (*Crocodylus niloticus*) which accompanied him on all his foreign travels. Crocodilians are excellent swimmers and, when Bostock was visiting the Niagara Falls with his show in 1901, he decided to earn himself a bit of publicity by putting the 7 ft, 2.13 m long saurian in the river above the falls to see what would happen. Up until then no creature of comparable size had ever survived a trip over the mighty cataract and Bostock was hoping his protégé would be the first

to come through the terrifying ordeal with flying colours. Below the falls a dozen men were placed waiting in position on both banks of the river so that they could spot the crocodile if and when it swam into the calmer waters. Twelve minutes after being towed out into the fast current the unsuspecting crocodile was swept over the top and plunged into the abyss. For 90 minutes there was no sign of life but, just as the observers were about to give up their vigil, the beast was spotted further up river making for the bank, apparently none the worse for its experience. After recapture it ate a hearty meal of fish!

The oldest ducks (*Anas platyrhynchos domesticus*, etc.) on record were a pair owned by Miss Gladys Blackbeard of Grahamstown, Cape Province, South Africa, which celebrated their 49th birthday in June 1966. The ducks, by then both nearly blind but otherwise in good health, were given to Miss Blackbeard in 1917 by a young soldier who was going on active service. Mention should also be made of a white Aylesbury duck owned by Mr Edmond Walsh of Gormanstown, Co Kildare, Ireland, which died on 3 December 1978, aged 28 years 6 months and laid eggs every year right up to her 25th birthday.

The oldest duck ever recorded in the UK was a veteran belonging to Mrs Jean Gosling of Ottery St Mary, Devon, which was still alive (albeit very feeble) in January 1977 aged 23 years. The same age was also reported for a Khaki Campbell duck named 'Bibbler' (1942–65) owned by Mr M J Cutten of Barnham, Sussex, and currently on display in Bognor Museum.

In 1976 a Muscovy duck (*Cairina moschata*) owned by Mrs C Evans of Llanfyllin, Montgomeryshire, Wales, laid a clutch of 28 eggs and hatched them all out. On 30 June 1977 another Muscovy, belonging to Mrs Emily Enderby of Wrangle, Lincolnshire, surpassed this feat with a clutch of 31 eggs, but she was only able to hatch out 25. The Mallard may lay 80–100 eggs, and there is a record of one duck producing an incredible 146 eggs in an effort to achieve a nest complement.

A number of ducks have served as mascots with the armed forces, particularly during the Second World War. One of the most famous was a happy-go-lucky individual named 'Donald', who spent 18 months as a POW in Siam (Thailand) when a company of the 2nd Gordon Highlanders was captured by the Japanese. The enemy ordered all pets to be destroyed, but the duck's master and 'pal', Cpl William Gray, told the guards that Donald (who was in fact a female) could not be killed or harmed

'Bran', the most pampered ferret in Britain, drinking milk from a crystal goblet.

because she was a sacred bird. He said the company worshipped Donald every morning, and it was customary for the Scots to venerate ducks. The Japanese were suitably impressed and Cpl Gray was allowed to keep the duck. In return she laid 163 eggs during her internment, and these were divided up amongst the sick prisoners. Donald was brought 'home' to Scotland by Cpl Gray in October 1945, and spent the rest of her life in peaceful retirement in Forgue, Aberdeenshire.

One of the world's greatest animal opportunists must be the ferret that set up home alongside 50 show rabbits in breeder Pat Pearce's garden at Chariton Common, Bristol, in December 1982

The most pampered ferret in Britain is undoubtedly a ten-year-old hob named 'Bran' owned by the Lady Louise, daughter of the Duke and Duchess of Argyll. This impeccably mannered furry aristocrat (imported from Woking, Surrey) regularly sits at the dinner table at Inverary Castle on the shores of Loch Fyne, and is waited on hand and paw by the family butler. He eats only from the best silver plates (his favourite food is raw mince and egg yolk) and drinks milk from a crystal goblet, and all

that is asked in return is that he catches a rabbit now and again—just to stop him getting too fat and lazy!

The largest marine aquarium fish is the inoffensive Nurse shark (*Ginglymostoma cirratum*) of the tropical Atlantic. This species (juvenile size 12 in, 30 cm) spends much of its time on the bottom where it respires by pumping water over its gills. It can reach a length of 14 ft, 4.26 m.

The largest freshwater fish kept in a privately-owned lake in Britain was a 60 lb, 27.2 kg Wels or European catfish (*Silurus glanis*) netted at Woburn Abbey, Bedfordshire, in 1947. Another report claimed this fish measured more than 6 ft, 1.83 m in length and weighed 78 lb, 35.3 kg.

The most common aquarium fish is the Guppy (*Poecilia reticulata*) of north-eastern South America (Venezuela, Brazil, Guyana), Trinidad and Barbados.

The largest Piranha (*Serrasalminae*) ever kept in Britain was probably an outsized specimen named 'Percy' who measured 13.25 in, 337 mm in length and weighed 3 lb 6 oz, 1.53 kg. He died on 10 April 1980 when he inadvertently bit through the heating cable in his tank at Marineland in Morecambe, Lancashire, and electrocuted himself.

Another food-crazy piranha, also named 'Percy', bit off more than he could chew when he gobbled down a 1 in, 25 mm rubber sucker in his aquarium at Aberdeen University, Scotland. The fish had to be given a life-saving operation on his stomach.

In September 1966 the death was reported of a Brook trout (*Salmo trutta fario*) aged 34 years at Fisnes, northern Norway. It had been caught in 1936, when aged four years and was placed in a 5 ft, 1.5 m deep farmer's well where it spent the rest of its life. The fish was never fed but existed on natural food found in the water. During the winter the well was covered with ice and snow. Shortly afterwards another farmer living at Egge reported that he had kept a trout in a well for 39 years (1904–44), and a longevity of 42 years was claimed for a specimen kept in a well at Nordekvaal.

The world's most valuable domesticated fish is the Japanese Koi, a form of fancy carp, and some amazing prices have been offered for grand champions (Kohaku). Dr Takayaki Hosogi, the owner of a seven-year-old 35 in, 89 cm long individual called 'Fujitavo', who won the All-Japan Koi Championship on 1 March 1982, has since refused an offer of £69 400 for this fish. The finest examples have deep red colouring and a pattern that is both sharp and distinct.

Another fancy fish that commands very high prices is the Lionhead (Shishigashira), also a Japanese breed, which has a grotesque head that resembles an unripe raspberry. One international winner named 'Benihana' owned by a leading fish farm concern in Santa Rosa, California, USA, was valued at more than $10 000 (£4540) in 1980.

The Red fox (*Vulpes vulpes*) seldom lives longer than 12 years in captivity. There is one record (1949) of a vixen living for 15 years, and in 1981 a fox aged 16 years was reported, but these life spans were exceptional. The oldest Red fox on record was a vixen named 'Vicky' owned by Mr M V Rowlinson of Thurnby Lodge, Leicester. She was found abandoned when only a few days old, and died in February 1978 aged 19 years 11 months.

The finest jumpers among amphibians are frogs, the abilities of which are largely dependent on body-weight, hind-leg length and the surface from which they take off. The jumper *par excellence* is the South African sharp-nosed frog (*Rana oxyrhyncha*), and on 21 May 1977 a female named 'Santjie' covered a record distance of 10.3 m, 33 ft 9¼ in in three consecutive leaps at a Frog Derby held at Larula Natal spa, Paulpietersburg. At the annual Calaveras Jumping Jubilee held at Angels Camp, California, USA, in May 1976 a male of this species named 'Davey Croakett' owned by Dennis Matasci made a *single* leap of 20 ft 3 in, 6.32 m.

The unluckiest goat on record was 'General Bill E Goat', mascot of the US Marines' peacekeeping force in the Lebanon. This much-loved animal received a lot of publicity in the American press and in July 1983 he was scrubbed, decorated and given a VIP flight back to the USA, where he was to be adopted by an 11-year-old girl. Unfortunately, when the goat arrived at Kennedy Airport, New York, he met up with some Agriculture Department officials who didn't read newspapers and they decided, in their infinite wisdom, that General Bill E Goat was an illegal immigrant and ordered him to be destroyed!

In 1969 two women in Louisville, Kentucky, USA, inherited an estate worth $115 000 from a goat! Their benefactor, 'Sugah', had been the pet of an old lady who left her entire estate to her pride and joy. When the goat died at the age of 17 the property was handed over to the testator's two nieces.

In 1981 a one-year-old goat named 'Lancelot' with a solitary 10 in, 254 mm horn sprouting from the middle of his forehead was a popular attraction at Marine World, an amusement park near San Francisco, California, USA. According to owners, husband and wife naturalists Otter Gazelle and Morning Glory [sic] of Mendocino Co, California, they bred the unigoat from a pair of Angora goats, both of which had horns, and used an ancient secret formula they had discovered for producing unicorns. However, a professor of animal sciences at the University of California, who examined the weird beastie, was not over-impressed and said it was a rare 'congenital abnormality'.

The size of the Common goldfish (*Carassius auratus*) is controlled almost entirely by environmental factors. One goldfish, kept in a 6 gal, 22.7 litre aquarium for 25 years, measured only 4 in, 101 mm when it died: in a large aquarium, however, it should reach a length of 7–8 in, 177–203 mm within five years, and may eventually reach a length of 10 in, 254 mm or more if the conditions are good. A Common goldfish owned by Mr B Jerman of Welshpool, Montgomeryshire, Wales, measured 13 in, 330 mm in length, 13 in, 330 mm round the middle and tipped the scales at 2 lb, 907 g in October 1977 when it was 12 years old. In South Africa, where the Common goldfish is now found in many lakes and rivers, specimens measuring up to 15 in, 381 mm in length have been caught, and in South America goldfish kept in ponds for breeding have been known to reach a length of 2 ft, 609 mm!

Common goldfish kept under good conditions can live 25 years or even longer. One specimen in an aquarium at Woolwich, London, survived for 29 years 10 months 21 days (20 May 1853 to 11 April 1883), and a female named 'Goldie' owned by Mr H S Tyler of Sleaford, Lincolnshire, died on 26 February 1978 aged 36 years. **The oldest goldfish on record** was a female named 'Freda' who died in Worthing, Sussex, on 1 August 1980 aged 41 years. She was acquired early in 1939 by Mr A R Wilson, who said his pet survived numerous attacks by cats and seagulls. On one occasion every fish in the pond was taken except

Freda! After her death she was preserved and mounted in a glass bottle.

Goldfish have also been known to live for over 40 years in China, its country of origin.

Fancy goldfish have much shorter life-spans because they are less hardy. The shubunkin usually lives about 14 years on the average, but the maximum lifespan for the fantail is reported to be only 13 years.

The most travelled goldfish on record was a male named 'Fish', who was purchased on 5 November 1977 in Nagoya, Japan. During the next three years he logged 270 206 nautical miles 432 329 km aboard the MV *Maersk Cadet*, consisting of ten round trips from Japan to Nigeria and one Caribbean cruise.

The most famous goldfish on record was probably a Black Moor named 'Miss Liberty' owned by Otto Gbeiding of New Jersey, USA. During the First World War this red, white and blue patriot toured the USA promoting the sale of Liberty Bonds, and his owner valued him at $5000.

Goldfish can live for a surprisingly long time out of their natural element, thanks to their thick and close-fitting gill covers which prevent evaporation.

In March 1981 Miss Christine Richardson of Wisewood, Sheffield, Yorkshire, claimed a survival record for her pet Common goldfish 'Miracle' after he had lived an amazing 14 hours out of water. The fish was being transported by car when the vehicle was involved in a crash and the bowl was smashed. Miracle was found lying on the floor of the car the following morning and, after artificial resuscitation, made a full recovery. It was believed that the carpet on the floor was slightly moist and this stopped the goldfish's gills from drying up.

Dr Francis Buckland, the eccentric Victorian naturalist, was once given a dozen goldfish, which he took home wrapped in wet moss and cloth. After 18 hours six of the fish were dead, but the others were still alive and they soon recovered from the effects of their experience when they were placed in an aquarium.

During the Vietnam war (1961–73) six geese were used by a squad of American riflemen to guard a strategic bridge in Saigon. The birds honked when anyone came near their cages at each end of the bridge, thus alerting the Americans to any possible North Vietnam saboteurs. These sentry geese had their feathers died purple to distinguish them from the civilian white geese—and to ensure that they were kept out of Vietnamese cooking pots!

Although hyenas have an unsavoury reputation, and are supposed to be untameable, there are at least two authentic records of this animal being hand-reared

Geoffrey Morton with his pet striped hyena.

and kept as a pet. One of them was a female striped hyena (*Hyaena hyaena*) named 'Ebby', who was adopted by an American woman, Rose Butler, at the turn of this century and remained in her household for at least 13 years. The other hyena, a male example of the same species, was befriended by Englishman Geoffrey J Morton in 1933 while he was serving as a policeman in Palestine. He found the tiny cub, apparently abandoned by its mother and near to death, during a patrol in the Jordan Valley, and took it back to his quarters in Nazareth where, with the aid of a baby's bottle and scraps of meat, he eventually restored the animal to full health. Mr Morton kept the hyena in the police stables for about a year, and used to take it out each evening for a stroll through the narrow streets of the town. He was later posted to Haifa, and donated his unusual pet to Tel Aviv Zoo before he left.

Because of their unpredictable and destructive nature monkeys cannot really be recommended as pets, but this still doesn't seem to deter people from buying them!

The oldest monkey ever recorded is a male White-throated capuchin (*Cebus capucinus*) called 'Bobo', who celebrated his 49th birthday in 1984. He was donated to the Mesker Park Zoo in Evansville, Indiana, USA, in 1935, and was given to Dr Raymond T Bartus, Director of CNS Research at the American Cyanamid Co. in Pearl River, NY, in 1980. Bobo is the 'granddad' of the geriatric primate colony currently being studied by Dr Bartus.

In *c* 1928 monkey jockeys were introduced at the greyhound race meetings held at White City, Victoria, Australia—much to the delight of spectators. They were attached to the dogs by straps and appeared to enjoy their rides over the hurdles.

The oldest stuffed parrot in the world is believed to be an African grey parrot which died of grief after its owner, the Duchess of Richmond and Lennox, and mistress of King Charles II, died in 1702. It is perched next to her wax effigy in Westminster Abbey.

A monkey jockey astride his 'mount' at a greyhound race meeting held at White City, Victoria, Australia.

The 'mini maialino', the smallest breed of pig in the world.

Nine out of ten parrots are left-footed, although the reason for this is not known.

———————

A Chinese silver pheasant (*Gennaeus nycthemerus*) owned by Mr J V Bodenheimer of Kernersville, North Carolina, USA, celebrated its 20th birthday in September 1978.

———————

When the German battle cruiser *Dresden* was sunk by the Allied forces during the First World War the sole survivor was the ship's mascot, a little pig. It was later exhibited in Britain and raised more than £1700 for charity, and today the stuffed head of this war veteran can be seen in the Imperial War Museum, London.

The smallest breed of pig in the world is the 'mini maialino' developed by Stefano Morini of St Golo d'Enza near Bologna, northern Italy, after ten years of experiments mainly using Vietnam pigs. The piglets weigh 400 g, 14 oz at birth and 9 kg, 20 lb at maturity and are easily house-trained.

———————

In 1814 the financier Nathan Rothschild made a 'killing' on the London Stock Exchange when homing pigeons brought him news of the outcome of the Battle of Waterloo a full day before the general public knew that Napoleon had been defeated.

———————

The oldest pet sea-bird on record was a Herring gull (*Larus argentatus*) called 'Tommy', owned by Miss Olive Watson of Macduff, Banffshire, Scotland. He was found in a street in 1943 with a damaged wing, and remained a member of the family until his death on 1 January 1984, aged 41 years.

———————

A lost sheep found alive in March 1984 after being buried under snow for a record 45 days at Leochel-Cushnie, Aberdeenshire, Scotland, only survived because it had been kept as a pet and was very overweight.

———————

The largest snake ever owned by a private individual was a female Reticulated python (*Python reticulatus*) called 'Cassius', who measured 25 ft 6 in, 7.77 m at the time of her death on 3 April 1980. She was collected in Malaysia in 1972 and was purchased by Adrian Nyoka, owner of Knaresborough Zoo, Yorkshire. This 240 lb, 109 kg snake yielded a 29 ft, 8.8 m skin.

Adrian Nyoka with his enormous reticulated python 'Cassius'.

The ancient herring gull 'Tommy' with his owner Miss Olive Watson.

The most suitable species for pets of the large tarantulas (ie 'bird-eating' spiders) are *Avicularia avicularia*—which the Indian children of Brazil tie cords around and lead about like dogs—and the Mexican red knee (*Brachypelma smithii*), both of which are docile animals and don't mind being handled by humans.

The largest spider ever kept as a pet was a female *Pamphobeteus antinous* imported into Britain from Peru by Mr Ian Wallace of Halesowen, West Midlands. Two months before her death in December 1982 she was assessed by the author and recorded a weight of 78.4 g, 2.77 oz (leg span 241 mm, 9.5 in).

The largest toad in the world is the Marine toad (*Bufo marinus*) of South America which—thanks to man—is now the most widely distributed amphibian living today. In Queensland, Australia, where this species was introduced in 1935, giant toad races are staged regularly, and it was in a beer garden in Proserpine, near the Great Barrier Reef, in 1975 that champion 'Gerty', primed up as usual on the local beverage, staggered off the track in an alcoholic haze and ended up squashed under the metal chair of an excited onlooker. A plaster replica of this sorely-missed female, who reportedly weighed nearly 6 lb, 2.72 kg, is now on display in the Brisbane Museum.

The Mediterranean spur-thighed tortoise (*Testudo graeca*) makes up the bulk of the pet shop tortoises sold in Britain today, and most of them come from Morocco. In the majority of cases they die within the year because our climate is too cold and damp, but specimens kept in large gardens in southern England have been known to survive for many years.

The oldest Mediterranean spur-thighed tortoise on record was a specimen belonging to Archbishop Laud which lived in the grounds of Lambeth Palace, London, from 1633 to 1753; even

'Felix', the only tortoise to be commemorated in a church's stained glass window, and (inset) with his present owner Mrs Olive Hunwick.

then its death was attributed to the neglect of the gardener rather than to old age. In 1957 another ancient individual named 'Panchard' died in Paignton Zoo, Devon, aged 116+ years. This tortoise was purchased at a fair in 1851, by which time he was already fully grown.

Britain's oldest living tortoise is a Mediterranean spur-thighed male named 'Joey' owned by Mrs Rosamund Aldis of Catford, south London, who found him on her allotment in 1933. In 1949 he was examined by a leading herpetologist who said he was at least 50 years old, and today his age is believed to be somewhere between 85 and 100 years. He measures 15 in, 381 mm in length (cf. 10–12 in, 254–305 mm for a good-sized specimen) and weighs over 5 kg, 11 lb.

On 19 October 1983 a Mediterranean spur-thighed female named 'Kizzi' belonging to Miss Christine Halls of the Isle of Sheppey, Kent, dropped a record clutch of 14 eggs, all of which hatched out, including one which contained twins. Tortoises rarely breed in captivity in Britain, and when they do the average clutch size is two to three.

The only tortoise known to be commemorated in a church's stained glass window is a spur-thighed male called 'Felix', who celebrated his 74th birthday in 1984. He was purchased by animal-lover Miss Ada Lance in 1910, who stipulated in her will (1938) that the tortoise should be immortalised in a stained glass window donated by her to the parish church at Kelvedon, Essex. Felix now resides with Miss Olive Hunwick, who is the third generation of owners.

When Miss Eileen Armfield of Brockham, Surrey, died in 1982 aged 86 she left a £1000 legacy in her will to Chessington Zoo to ensure that her 50-year-old pet tortoise 'Bob' would be well looked after when she had gone. Today Bob shares an enclosure with some other tortoises and terrapins in the children's section.

In 1904 a flock of turkeys numbering 10 000 strong was shepherded through the market town of Cuero in Texas, USA, by a team of drovers who had travelled 160 miles, 256 km in 20 days. The men used long whips tipped with flannel streamers to keep their less than bright charges under control during their daily dawn to dusk walk and, as can be imagined, the operation required an awful lot of nimble footwork.

In 1906 a turkey in Leicestershire laid 49 eggs in 56 days.

Rosendo Ribeiro, the first doctor in Nairobi, Kenya, bought a zebra in 1907, and was a familiar sight as he rode the animal around the straggling township visiting patients. Years later he sold it to Bombay Zoo for 800 Rupees. In 1914 Dr Ribeiro became the Portuguese Vice-Consul, a post he held until 1922, but he carried on his practice until a year before his death in 1951 aged 80 years.

Dr Rosendo Ribeiro astride the pet zebra which he used on his medical rounds in Nairobi, Kenya.

INDEX